MY FIFTY YEARS IN THE NAVY

CLASSICS OF NAVAL LITERATURE
JACK SWEETMAN, SERIES EDITOR

The purpose of this series is to make available attractive new editions of classic works of naval history, biography, and fiction. In addition to the complete original text, each volume will feature an introduction and, when appropriate, notes by an expert in the field. The series will include the following texts:

My Fifty Years
in the Navy

By Charles E. Clark, Rear Admiral, USN
With an introduction and notes by Jack Sweetman

NAVAL INSTITUTE PRESS
Annapolis, Maryland

This book was originally published in
1917 by Little, Brown, and Company,
Boston, Massachusetts.

Copyright © 1984 on the introduction and notes
by the U.S. Naval Institute
Annapolis, Maryland

Third printing, 1988

Unless otherwise noted the photographs are printed
courtesy of the Naval History Division. The illustrations
are identical to those in the first edition with the
exception of the pictures of Admiral Farragut, the *Ossipee,*
and the *Ranger,* which are slightly different views of the
original subjects. All captions are original.

Library of Congress Cataloging in Publication Data

Clark, Charles E. (Charles Edgar), 1843–1922.
  My fifty years in the navy.

  (Classics of naval literature)
  Reprint. Originally published: Boston, Mass. : Little,
Brown, 1917.
  Includes bibliographical references and index.
  1. Clark, Charles E. (Charles Edgar), 1843–1922.
2. Admirals—United States—Biography. 3. United States.
Navy—Biography. I. Title. II. Title: My 50 years in
the navy. III. Series.
  V63.C43A35 1984   359'.0092'4 [B]   83-63449
  ISBN 0-87021-401-2

Printed in the United States of America

CONTENTS

ILLUSTRATIONS

ACKNOWLEDGMENTS

For their assistance in the preparation of the introduction and notes to Admiral Clark's story, it is a pleasure to thank my ever-resourceful friends of the reference section of the Naval Academy's Nimitz Library; Mrs. Alice Creighton, head of Special Collections at Nimitz Library, and the members of her staff; and my colleagues, Professor Emeritus Neville T. Kirk, Professor Wilson L. Heflin, Professor Paolo E. Coletta (retired), and Associate Professors Kenneth J. Hagan and Robert W. Love, Jr., of the Division of English and History, U.S. Naval Academy. I am also grateful to Dr. Clark G. Reynolds, director of Patriot's Point Naval and Maritime Museum, Charleston, South Carolina; Mrs. Agnes Hoover of the Naval Historical Center; Mrs. Patty M. Maddocks, director of the Library and Photographic Service at the U.S. Naval Institute; Ms. Connie Buchanan, my excellent editor at the Institute; The State Historical Society of Missouri; my parents, for their unfailing interest; and, as always, Gisela, nature's most nearly perfect wife.

Rear Admiral Clark.

INTRODUCTION

Charles Edgar Clark is known to naval history as the man who commanded the battleship *Oregon* when she made her dramatic race from San Francisco to the Caribbean via Cape Horn in time for the Battle of Santiago on 3 July 1898. By then-current standards, the voyage of the ship that became known as the "bulldog of the fleet"—14,700 miles in sixty-seven days, at an average speed of almost 12 knots—was a tremendous technical achievement, in the words of a contemporary, "nothing approaching it being known in the history of battleships."[1] Breathlessly reported in the press, it captured the imagination of the American people and, coupled with the distinction he won at Santiago, made Clark one of the heroes of the Spanish-American War. His experiences in that conflict form the climax of his book, as they did of his life. In a real sense his thirty-eight years in uniform had been spent preparing for those fateful four months in 1898. It is not merely as a background to his command of the *Oregon* that Admiral Clark's autobiography is of interest, however. His career spanned one of the most eventful periods in the history of the U.S. Navy.

When in the autumn of 1860 seventeen-year-old Charles Clark left his native Vermont to enter the U.S. Naval Academy, the fleet that defended America's seaways consisted of ninety vessels, all wooden hulled, of which less than half were in active commission. One recent historian has estimated that the number of truly serviceable warships was

[1]John R. Spears, *The History of Our Navy*, vol. 5 (New York, 1899), p. 315.

twenty-four.[2] The strength of the navy's personnel was correspondingly modest: 1,173 officers, including surgeons, paymasters, and chaplains, and 7,600 men. The Academy itself had been established only 15 years before, when Secretary of the Navy George Bancroft circumvented long-standing congressional opposition to such an institution by a feat of bureaucratic legerdemain. At the beginning of the academic year, in October 1860, its student body totaled 281, which included the 114 members of Clark's incoming class.

The size of America's naval force reflected a view of its purpose that, though sometimes challenged, had prevailed in Congress since the foundation of the navy in 1794. According to this consensus, the United States had no need of a powerful navy: of the outside world the young republic asked nothing more than the right to conduct peaceful trade; overseas she had no political interests to uphold, no colonies to defend. The Monroe Doctrine, prohibiting the expansion of European power in the Western Hemisphere (and thereby safeguarding Britain's Latin American markets), was conveniently enforced by the Royal Navy. The task of the U.S. Navy in time of peace was to promote American commerce and protect American lives and property abroad. In time of war it was to complement the army's coastal fortifications by shielding the country from invasion; offensively it was to practice the strategy of *guerre de course*—cruiser warfare against merchant shipping—as it had done in the Revolution and the War of 1812. There was no thought that it should contend with an enemy battle fleet for command of the sea.

But if the little navy of 1860 seemed to Congress sufficient to perform its traditional duties, it was obviously unequal to the demands of the great Civil War which began in April 1861. Sea power played a vital part in Union strategy, aptly named the Anaconda Plan. While the army pushed across the rebel land frontier, the navy would seal the agrarian Confederacy off from the industrial resources of Britain and France with a blockade of its 3,500-mile shoreline; seize control of the Mississippi, cutting the South in two and restoring the Midwest's outlet to the sea; and, wherever possible, support the army's operations by making use of coastal and inland waterways. The fulfillment of these missions required an enormous increase in the naval establishment. In the course of the conflict the service underwent an expansion of more than sevenfold. By April 1865 the Union navy had 671 ships in commission, including 71 ironclads, and its personnel numbered 7,000 officers and 51,500 men.

[2]Dana M. Wegner, "The Union Navy," in Kenneth J. Hagan, ed., *In Peace and War: Interpretations of American Naval History, 1775–1978* (Westport, Ct., 1978), p. 109.

Among the officers was Charles Clark, whose Academy class of 1864 had been graduated early—one section in May 1863 and a second in September of that year—to help satisfy the burgeoning fleet's demand for officers. Since 1860, the 114 young men who had formed the class of 1864 had been reduced to 50. (At least 22 of its nongraduates resigned to fight for the Confederacy.) Remarkably, all of the 50 graduates would survive the war. Four besides Clark would figure prominently in the history of the war with Spain: Charles D. Sigsbee, who commanded the battleship *Maine* when she blew up in Havana harbor; Charles V. Gridley, to whom at the Battle of Manila Bay Dewey said, "You may fire when you are ready"; Clark's roommate, Francis A. Cook, Commodore Schley's flag captain at Santiago; and Robley D. "Fighting Bob" Evans, captain of the *Iowa* at Santiago and later first commander of the Great White Fleet.

At the end of the Civil War, the U.S. Navy was in many respects the strongest in the world. It was largely a coastal and riverine navy, having been built in response to the particular challenge posed by the Confederacy, and therefore lacked the global reach of the Royal Navy, but for the first time in history it was clearly capable of defending America's shores against all comers. Furthermore, its strength was not merely a matter of numbers. The technology of the Union ironclad fleet was unsurpassed. It has been reckoned that Ericsson's original *Monitor* alone contained no less than forty patentable inventions. American naval ordnance was equally advanced, thanks primarily to the work of Admiral John A. Dahlgren, and in Engineer-in-Chief Benjamin F. Isherwood the navy possessed the most brilliant engine builder of the era. In 1868 the trial speed achieved by his masterpiece, the cruiser *Wampanoag*—a record-breaking 17.8 knots—made her the fastest ship afloat.

The navy did not retain either its strength or its technological lead for long. Dramatic expansion was swiftly followed by drastic decline. The war over, the nation turned its attention to continental concerns. Congress wanted a distinctly "American navy" to do the things it had always done—show the flag in foreign parts and, should war come, conduct *guerre de course*. For these functions a few dozen wooden cruisers would suffice.[3] Most of the monitors went into reserve, from which they could be recalled if invasion were imminent. In the interests of economy and independence of foreign bases, it was decided the navy should continue to rely on sails; the *Wampanoag* herself was adjudged unfit for service

[3]For a provocative discussion of this period, see Lance C. Buhl, "Maintaining an 'American Navy,' 1865–1889," in *In Peace and War*, pp. 145–73.

because she carried too few of them. The "acting" officers of 1861–65 were honorably discharged, leaving a corps of approximately 2,000 regulars. Enlisted strength was cut by 80 percent. The size of the fleet was similarly reduced. By 1870 it had shrunk to 238 ships, of which only 52 were in full commission—exactly 10 more than at the onset of the Civil War. Five years later the total number of U.S. naval vessels, active and reserve, had fallen to 147. Technology stagnated as bare-bones budgets and conservative senior officers combined to block innovation. Alfred T. Mahan never forgot the mortification he felt one day in the 1880s when a French admiral, visiting his ship, gazed nostalgically at her obsolete muzzle-loaders and exclaimed, "*Ah! Capitaine, les vieux canons!*"[4]

The turning point can be seen to have come with the appropriation for the ABCDs in 1883. Even though they were rigged for sail, these steam-powered, steel-hulled vessels—the protected cruisers *Atlanta*, *Boston*, and *Chicago* and the dispatch boat *Dolphin*—were the first really modern ships built for the navy since the Civil War. The cruisers were "protected" by an armored deck shielding their engine spaces; all the ABCDs included such state-of-the-art features as electric power and underwater compartmentation. Two other significant steps forward had been taken a year earlier, with the creation of the Office of Naval Intelligence, the primary purpose of which was to keep abreast of technical developments in foreign navies, and the appointment of Lieutenant Commander French E. Chadwick to the London Embassy as the first U.S. naval attaché.

As is often the case with historical turning points, the importance of these events is more apparent in retrospect than it was to contemporary observers. In 1882 the personnel strength of the navy had dwindled to the point where there was one of the navy's 1,100 officers for every four enlisted men. In a drastic measure to remedy the situation, Congress passed a zero-sum personnel act stipulating that the number of officers commissioned annually would be limited to the number of vacancies that had occurred the preceding year. Made retroactive to the graduates of the Naval Academy class of 1877, who were then performing probationary tours of sea duty as cadet-midshipmen, the personnel act of 1882 put an end to many careers; of the fifty-four graduates of the class of

---

[4]A. T. Mahan, *From Sail to Steam: Recollections of Naval Life* (New York, 1907), p. 197. For a detailed discussion of the *Wampanoag* controversy, see Lance C. Buhl, "Mariners and Machines: Resistance to Technological Change in the American Navy, 1865–69" in *Journal of American History* (Dec 1974), pp. 703–27.

1883, for example, only thirteen were accepted into the navy. But while the act checked the influx of new officers, it did nothing to accelerate the promotion of those already in service. Officers who became lieutenants in 1872 remained lieutenants in 1892. Clark himself experienced mid-career stasis; after a quick climb to lieutenant commander between 1863 and 1868, it took him another twenty-eight years to make captain. The buildup of the fleet also proceeded at what must have seemed a glacial pace. As late as 1889, Secretary of the Navy Benjamin F. Tracy could assert that, among the world's navies, that of the United States ranked twelfth.

By that date, however, it was unmistakably evident that a new day was dawning. In 1884 Stephen B. Luce had succeeded in his long struggle to establish the Naval War College, which, after a precarious infancy, emerged as a center of naval professionalism. The following year Congress approved the construction of two more protected cruisers and two gunboats. In August 1886 it authorized the building of the first two American battleships, the *Maine*, originally designated an armored cruiser, and the *Texas*, which was an "armored battleship" from the start. Prompted by Brazil's purchase of the British-built armored cruiser *Riachuelo*, which the chairman of the House Naval Affairs Committee declared could meet and defeat the entire U.S. fleet, this appropriation marked the beginning of the battle line that was to be the standard of American naval power until World War II. Nine more cruisers, including the navy's first armored cruiser, the 8,100-ton *New York*, larger though less heavily armed than the two battleships, were approved in 1887 and 1888. The latter year also witnessed the repeal of the personnel act of 1882. In 1889, by which time the construction of the *Maine* and the *Texas* was just getting under way, Secretary Tracy went to Congress with a request for funds to build eight battleships, two armored cruisers, and two torpedo boats. This was more than the legislators were ready to accept, but in 1890 they did authorize the three battleships of the *Indiana* class and the armored cruiser *Brooklyn*. The *Iowa*, the last battleship completed in time to take part in the war with Spain, was funded in 1892. She was followed by the two battleships of the *Kearsarge* class in 1895, the year the *Maine* and the *Texas* entered service; and by the three ships of the *Illinois* class in 1896. Thus, at the beginning of 1898, the United States had six battleships and two powerful armored cruisers in commission, as well as five battleships building.

Along with its new ships, the navy acquired a new strategy—command of the sea. No longer would its wartime role be limited to commerce raiding and coastal defense. From now on its mission would be to seek out and destroy the enemy's battle fleet. The most important single agent in this revolution in American naval policy—for such it was—was Alfred Thayer Mahan's study, *The Influence of Sea Power upon History, 1660–1783*, which appeared in 1890. The book was an outgrowth of Mahan's assignment as an instructor at the Naval War College. Upon being ordered there, he analyzed the prolonged maritime struggle between England and France to see whether any general principles of naval warfare could be deduced from its course. He decided that such principles were indeed evident, and that they revealed commerce raiding to be a strategy of failure. The French, who used their naval forces to conduct *guerre de course* or to gain local and temporary control of the sea in pursuit of specific objectives, never won; and the English, whose policy was always and simply to attack the French fleet, never lost. History's lesson, concluded Mahan, was that the most effective use of a navy was to win command of the sea through the elimination of the opposing fleet. Once that had been achieved, the accomplishment of every other objective of naval warfare—destruction of the enemy's commerce, isolation and conquest of his overseas territories, amphibious invasion of his homeland—was assured.

As modern historians have been at pains to point out, Mahan's ideas were not exactly new. The Royal Navy, after all, had been putting them into practice since the Restoration, and over the centuries many writers had touched on the points he developed. Yet *The Influence of Sea Power* was not simply a statement of what had been "often thought but ne'er so well expressed." No one before Mahan had articulated the philosophy of sea power with such compelling consistency, and no one had yet attempted such a wide-ranging analysis of maritime strategy. The fact that acclaim for his book first arose in England before traveling across the Atlantic is sufficient testament to its originality.

The enthusiastic if slightly belated welcome the Mahanian synthesis met in the United States was both a consequence of and a contribution to the temper of the times. Public attitudes were changing. After a quarter century's immersion in internal affairs, the nation was turning its attention to the outside world. The wave of New Imperialism that arose in Europe in the 1870s proved infectious. While many Americans remained as adamantly anti-imperialist as ever, others were attracted to the romance of assuming the "white man's burden," a burden the doctrines of social Darwinism held were not only their duty but their due. Naturally, the profits expected to be reaped from imperial expansion were not overlooked. Probably more widespread, however, was the concern over the possible effects of European encroachment on American business abroad. What if one or another of the maritime powers should attempt to exclude the United States from foreign markets? At the very least the country must be able to defend its economic place in the world. Mahan himself advocated the acquisition of colonies for use as naval bases, without which a coal-burning navy could not maintain an independent overseas presence, without which it could not adequately protect the nation's commerce. Perhaps most important was the emergence of an uncomplicated conviction that a great nation should have better than a twelfth-ranked navy. The American naval renaissance was already under way when Mahan found a publisher for his book. What he did was to give to the renaissance fresh impetus, intellectual justification, and a strategic rationale.

In a technological sense the beneficiary of that rationale was the battleship, the only vessel capable of defeating others of her kind to win command of the sea. Congress was still of two minds regarding that function when the *Indiana* class, to which the *Oregon* belonged, was authorized on 30 June 1890. Congress's ambiguity, its reluctance to break completely with the tradition of coastal defense, was apparent in the original designation of the *Indiana*s as "seagoing coast-line battleships." It was no less apparent in their specified displacement of 10,000 tons, which, by limiting the quantity of coal they could carry, confined their cruising radius to 8,000 miles and thus reduced their potential for offshore operations. Since the navy gave them the heaviest guns and armor they could handle, it also held their design speed to a moderate 15 knots. In every other respect, however, they were fully comparable to contemporary foreign battleships, which was not the case with the *Maine* and the *Texas*.[5]

There were three *Indiana*s: the *Indiana* herself [BB1], the *Massachusetts* [BB2], and the *Oregon* [BB3].[6] A third again as large as their two predecessors, which displaced 6,300 tons, they carried bigger guns and their main battery was disposed differently, in what became the

---

[5]Technical data on the *Indiana*s in general and the *Oregon* in particular has been drawn from John C. Reilly, Jr., and Robert L. Scheina, *American Battleships, 1886–1923* (Annapolis, 1980); Sanford Sternlicht, *McKinley's Bulldog: The Battleship Oregon* (Chicago, 1977); and the Naval History Division, Department of the Navy, *Dictionary of American Naval Fighting Ships* (Washington, D. C., 1959–81).

[6]In 1920 the navy instituted the practice of giving ships hull numbers. The first battleships to receive numbers were the *Indiana*s.

conventional arrangement of centerline turrets fore and aft (the heavy turrets of the *Maine* and the *Texas* were positioned diagonally on the edge of the deck, one on the starboard bow and one on the port quarter). Like those ships, the *Indiana*s had low freeboards, an inheritance from the monitors, and were very wet in rough weather. They also gained a reputation for heavy rolling, a tendency aggravated by the fact that their main turrets' axis of rotation was 4 feet behind their center of gravity. When both turrets were trained broadside, the ships heeled over to such a degree that the armored belt was lifted out of the water on the opposite side, exposing the unprotected hull below. Yet, with all their faults, the *Indiana*s were by no means unsatisfactory. Considering American inexperience in the design of battleships and congressional limitation of their tonnage, they were probably as successful as could have been expected. Their wartime performance in 1898 proved them capable of hard and sustained service.

The *Oregon*, last of the *Indiana*s, was the first battleship built on the West Coast. Her contract was awarded to Union Iron Works of San Francisco on 19 November 1890, and her keel was laid exactly a year later, on 19 November 1891. She was launched on 26 October 1893 and commissioned on 25 July 1896. The cost of construction was $6,575,032. Designed to carry a crew of 32 officers and 441 men, the *Oregon* measured 351 feet 2 inches in length, 69 feet 3 inches abeam, and had a draft of 27 feet 1.75 inches. Her main battery consisted of four 13-inch guns mounted in pillbox-type double turrets armored with 15 inches of steel. Her secondary armament included eight 8-inch guns mounted in four double turrets with 6-inch armor at the corners of her superstructure, twenty shielded 6-pounders distributed more or less equitably from stem to stern, six one-pounders, and six Whitehead torpedo tubes. In contrast to her sister ships, whose turrets traversed on steam power, the *Oregon*'s were turned by hydraulics. Her interior was protected by an armored deck and, at the waterline, by an armored belt with a maximum thickness of 18 inches, which ran two-thirds the length of her hull. At both ends the belts were joined by latitudinal armored bulkheads, and amidships they extended up and over, rather like the cab of an automobile, to enclose the superstructure in a central citadel. All of this armor was Harveyized—carbon-hardened—steel specially produced for the *Indiana*s by Carnegie Steel Corporation. Power for the *Oregon*'s twin screws was provided by a pair of vertical, triple-expansion, reciprocating steam engines that had four double-ended boilers each. There were also two auxiliary boilers. On her trials this machinery drove the ship at a speed of 16.8 knots, earning her builders a handsome bonus in increments of $25,000 for every quarter knot by which she exceeded her design speed of 15 knots.

That the *Oregon* entered the Spanish-American War under the command of Charles E. Clark was a matter of luck: good for him, bad for Captain Alexander H. McCormick. When the *Maine* exploded in Havana harbor on a February evening in 1898, Clark, a junior captain, was commanding the monitor *Monterey* at San Diego, California. McCormick had the *Oregon*, which was based at San Francisco. As the clamor for war neared a crescendo, McCormick was ordered to take the *Oregon* to a Peruvian port and there to await further instructions. Upon the commencement of hostilities, the *Oregon* could be directed to proceed to either the Philippines or the West Indies. Her sailing date was set for 18 March. On 16 March Captain McCormick suddenly fell ill. Immediately after receipt of this news, the Navy Department ordered Clark to assume command of the *Oregon*. He reached San Francisco on 17 March. The *Oregon* sailed two days later.

It was typical of Clark, "a man of most lovable character,"[7] that in the chapter of his autobiography devoted to the cruise of the *Oregon* he would include a roster of her officers. He remarks that, even though most of them were unknown to him, he felt no uneasiness as to their ability, for the quality of the average American naval officer precluded apprehension. How well justified his confidence was to prove he could not possibly have foreseen. Excluding himself, there were eighteen line officers on the *Oregon*. Of this number, no less than four were destined for positions of great responsibility. Lieutenant Junior Grade E. W. Eberle, USNA 1885, captain of the forward 13-inch turret, became the third chief of naval operations in 1923. Assistant Engineer Joseph M. ("Bull") Reeves, USNA 1894, pioneered the development of carrier tactics between the world wars and was commander in chief of the U.S. Fleet from 1934 until his retirement in 1936. He was recalled to active duty in World War II to serve as the navy's lend-lease liaison officer and in other administrative assignments, during which he was promoted to full admiral on the retired list. Naval Cadet Harry E. Yarnell, USNA 1897, another aviation pioneer, commanded the Asiatic Fleet from 1937 to 1939 and, like Reeves, was recalled to duty during World War II. Most distinguished of all was Yarnell's classmate, Cadet Engineer and future

---

[7] *New York Times*, 3 October 1922, Obituaries section.

Fleet Admiral William D. Leahy, who would go on to become chief of naval operations in 1937 and chairman of the Joint Chiefs of Staff in 1942. (Leahy's diary provides a junior officer's perspective of the cruise of the *Oregon*.)

Reference has already been made to the excitement engendered by the *Oregon*'s voyage. This is evident in the following contemporary account:

> The splendid battleship *Oregon* had set sail from San Francisco nearly simultaneously with the leap into war. Her voyage was the longest attempted by a modern warship. . . . At a thousand points from Cape Horn to the Bermudas, a brace of Spanish battleships might have waylaid the cherished ship. . . .
>
> Our own seamen, knowing well what they would have done, were such a chance offered to their enterprise, made little doubt that the *Oregon*, if ever she reached her consorts, would have to run a thrilling gauntlet, but much more likely she would be sent to the bottom—for the men of our navy knew the traditions too well, to fear that her captain would give the Spaniards the satisfaction of capture, unless the major forces of disaster joined in commanding surrender. Day after day, week after week passed, and even among the thrilling actualities reported, the conjectural possibilities of this lonely voyager ploughing the somber seas, took chief hold on the imagination of men. When she was reported at the extreme end of South America, the public heart thrilled as over the preliminary details of a substantial victory. When she was reported at Bahia . . . it was reckoned as joyful an event as the conquest of a Cuban town. But as the vessel finally cast off from the friendly safeguards of neutral ports and waters, the public excitement rose. It is hardly a figure of speech to say that from the Cabinet of the President to the cabin of the logger, hearts beat more swiftly. The [Spanish] Cape Verde fleet was just where the ship ought to pass in ending her immense voyage. Would she be waylaid, turning into some haven and find herself beset by overwhelming odds . . . ? The heart of the country swelled with an emotion easy to understand, when the welcome telegram announced the pilgrim in safety, lying tranquilly in the waters of the Florida coast.[8]

The presumably purple waters in which the pilgrim lay were off Jupiter Inlet, where the *Oregon* anchored on May 24. The strategic situation that developed in the Caribbean over the following days was somewhat confused. At the beginning of the war the Spanish government had ordered a squadron of four armored cruisers and two destroyers

---

[8] Henry F. Keenan, *The Conflict with Spain* (Philadelphia, 1898), pp. 162–63.

under Rear Admiral Pascual Cervera y Topete to proceed to Cuba. Correctly surmising that there would be American forces waiting for him off Puerto Rico and Havana, Cervera coaled at Dutch Curaçao and slipped safely into Santiago, on the southeastern coast of Cuba, where his ships were discovered by Commodore W. S. Schley's Flying Squadron on 28 May. Rear Admiral W. T. Sampson, commander of the North Atlantic Squadron, immediately ordered a close blockade of the port. The result was a stalemate. Cervera could not get out—at least, not without encountering a greatly superior force—but Sampson could not get in, because the narrow, twisting channel into Santiago harbor was sown with minefields backed by formidable shore fortifications. An attempt to bottle the Spanish up in port by sinking a ship across the channel on the evening of 3–4 June was a gallant failure.

Sampson thereupon requested the dispatch of an army expeditionary force to capture the Spanish batteries so that he could sweep the mines. The Fifth Corps, 16,000 men under Major General W. S. Shafter, sailed from Tampa, Florida, in mid-June. The two commanders reached what each assumed was an understanding in a conference on 20 June and the army landed unopposed east of Santiago between 22 and 25 June. Pushing forward over difficult terrain in the heart of a tropical summer, Shafter's men ran into entrenched Spanish outposts at San Juan and El Caney on 1 July and carried them by storm—at the cost of casualties amounting to ten percent of the entire expedition. Staggered by these returns, the next day Shafter wrote Sampson, urging him "to make effort immediately to force the entrance [to the harbor] to avoid future losses among my men."[9] His request in turn staggered Sampson. The army that had been sent to help the navy by capturing the batteries was asking the navy to help it capture the city. On the morning of 3 July Sampson set out in his flagship, the armored cruiser *New York*, to confer with Shafter down the coast near Siboney. Less than an hour after the *New York* left the blockade line, the Spanish squadron unexpectedly solved the American problem by making a desperate bid to break out.

The *Oregon* played a leading role in the action that followed, engaging each of the Spanish cruisers as they emerged from the channel and overhauling the *Cristóbal Colón*, supposedly a much swifter ship. "This performance," wrote Sampson in his report of the action, "adds to the already brilliant record of this fine battleship and speaks highly of the

[9]E. B. Potter and Chester W. Nimitz, eds., *Sea Power: A Naval History* (Englewood Cliffs, N.J., 1960), p. 374.

skill and care with which her admirable efficiency has been maintained during a service unprecedented in the history of vessels of her class."[10]

For all practical purposes, the victory at Santiago brought the Spanish-American War to an end. The forces defending the city capitulated to Shafter's army on 15 July, and Spain requested an armistice, which was signed on 12 August. By then, the epithet Clark of the *Oregon* had become nationally known.

Captain Clark's rewards were by no means commensurate with his renown. At this time promotion was by seniority, precedence being determined by the place each officer held in the list of officers in his grade. However, exceptional service could be recognized by advancing an officer so many numbers "in grade," which would move him closer to the top of the list and, thereby, to promotion. At the beginning of 1898, Clark was number thirty-five on the navy's list of forty-five captains. On 10 July Admiral Sampson recommended that his flag captain, French Chadwick, and the captains of his five battleships—Henry C. Taylor of the *Indiana*, Robley D. Evans of the *Iowa*, F. J. Higginson of the *Massachusetts*, Clark of the *Oregon*, and John W. Philips of the *Texas*—be advanced five numbers in grade. In the event, Clark was awarded six numbers; Higginson, whose ship was coaling at Guantanamo during the battle of Santiago, three numbers; and the others, five. Despite the praise heaped on the *Oregon*'s "unprecedented" services, Clark's reward was to be advanced only one number more than the Santiago captains whose ships had served in the Caribbean throughout the war.

Worse was to follow. In 1899 and 1900 the officers Clark had jumped were restored to their original positions, and four others—two of whom had commanded cruisers under Dewey at Manila Bay—were advanced over him. So although between 1898 and 1901 Clark moved up to number twenty on the captains' list, in relative terms he lost four places.

Understandably, even as modest a man as Charles Clark resented this treatment; but it was characteristic that he made no attempt to publicize his grievance.[11] In this book he dismisses the promotion issue with a passing reference to the prejudicial effect of the Sampson-Schley controversy, in which the two senior officers present at Santiago contested the credit for the victory, an unseemly quarrel that did much to tarnish the laurels the navy had won in the war.

[10]*The Conflict with Spain*, p. 512.
[11]Gardner W. Allen, ed., *Papers of John Davis Long, 1897–1904* (Norwood, Mass., 1939), pp. 428–30.

Clark's friends and admirers did not share his reticence. On 14 April 1900 the *New York Times* printed a letter, signed Sailor, which expressed the dissatisfaction many felt over the lack of recognition accorded to Clark. After reviewing the *Oregon*'s war record, the author asked:

> Did we not think well of . . . "Charlie" Clark then? Everybody felt that he would get some special reward. It was such a matter of course that no one made it his business to attend to it.
>
> How has it worked out? His sole reward was a leave of absence on reduced pay, given that he might restore his health, ruined by exertions and exposure. . . . But if he got no reward, he got some punishment. As a result of the promotions made after Manila and of the Personnel bill, he now stands relatively lower on the list than before the war. . . . It is a damnable shame.
>
> "Charlie" Clark will never go begging and whining to Congress to do him justice; he is too modest and too proud. He will continue to be the same simple, sweet-hearted man, always jolly and always beloved, and he will quietly go on doing his duty without complaint until he dies.

The injustice the author of this letter and others perceived was finally redressed in June 1902, when Clark was advanced an additional seven numbers and promoted to wear the two stars of a rear admiral. He spent his three years as a flag officer in assignments ashore. Retiring at the statutory age of sixty-two on 4 August 1905, he died of heart failure at his home in Long Beach, California, on 2 October 1922. He was seventy-nine.

One of Admiral Clark's obituaries asserted that his services were "never sufficiently rewarded."[12] In terms of preferment this statement is certainly arguable, and in a larger sense it is clearly untrue. This book makes it obvious that Clark viewed his fifty years in the navy as their own reward. It must have been satisfying to him, too, to reflect that he had played a prominent part in the events that set the seal on the American naval renaissance. After 1898 there could be no going back. The war with Spain made the United States a world power, possessed of distant territories that could be defended only by a battle fleet dedicated to the Mahanian principle of command of the sea. While Clark was still on active duty, President Theodore Roosevelt set out to build a fleet second only to that of Great Britain, traditional ruler of the waves; during his retirement, President Woodrow Wilson announced his intention to

[12]*New York Times*, 3 October 1922, Obituaries section.

have a navy second to none; and shortly before his death, that aim was achieved at the Washington Naval Conference, where Britain accepted parity in capital ships with the United States. The voyage of the *Oregon* had in itself contributed to the development of American sea power through its dramatic illustration of the advantages to be gained by constructing an interoceanic canal across Central America. To a man who could recall the naval nadir of the 1870s, it all must have seemed like a great dream come true.

The *Oregon* outlived Admiral Clark by many years. In August 1898 she was among the ships of Sampson's squadron that steamed into New York harbor to launch a rousing victory celebration, after which she entered the Brooklyn Navy Yard for a much-needed refit. Upon its completion, she was sent to reinforce Dewey in the Philippines, entering Manila Bay on 19 March 1899. That summer she supported the army in landing operations against Filipino insurgents along Lingayen Gulf and put ashore a party of her own to occupy the town of Vigan. At the outbreak of the Boxer Rebellion in June 1900, she was employed to rush troops from the Philippines to northern China. It was during this voyage that she suffered the only damage of her career: a rock in the Gulf of Pechili tore a 19-foot gash in her side. Repairs were made at the Japanese naval base at Kure, and in June 1901 the *Oregon* returned to San Francisco. After a refitting at the Puget Sound Navy Yard, she was ordered back to the Far East, where she served from 1903 until 1906. In April of the latter year she was decommissioned at Puget Sound.

The *Oregon* went back to sea, operating along the West Coast in August 1911. By then, the advent of the dreadnought had made her obsolete, but she was still the most famous battleship in the navy. In 1914 it was proposed that she lead the parade of ships at the opening of the Panama Canal. The idea was not adopted, but she was on hand to participate in the opening of the Panama-Pacific Exposition in San Francisco in 1915. Her captain on that occasion was the same J. M. Reeves who had sailed in her as an assistant engineer in 1898.

Following American intervention in World War I, the *Oregon* was initially employed as a training vessel in coastal waters. Her routine was interrupted in June 1918, when she was assigned to escort the transports of the Siberian expedition to Vladivostok. This was her final war cruise as a fighting ship. In the autumn of 1919 President Wilson stood on her deck to review the Pacific Fleet at Seattle, and on 4 October 1919 she was decommissioned for the last time.

With the return of peace, the navy decided that the remaining Spanish-American War battleships could perform a final service if they were used for target practice. When this plan became known, the United Spanish War Veterans and other groups appealed to the government to spare the *Oregon*. Their efforts were successful. Though the *Indiana*, the *Massachusetts*, and the *Iowa* went to watery graves, in 1920 Assistant Secretary of the Navy Franklin D. Roosevelt directed that the *Oregon* be retained. A new threat was posed in February 1922 by the conclusion of the Washington Naval Treaty, which bound the United States to scrap almost a million tons of ships. The *Oregon*, no longer of any military value, was among the vessels slated for destruction. That choice was challenged by the movement that had now grown up to convert America's oldest battleship into a permanent memorial, and once again she was saved. In January 1924 enough of her machinery was removed to make her "incapable of further warlike service," satisfying the terms of the Washington Treaty, and on 3 July 1925—Santiago Day—she was put on indefinite loan to the State of Oregon. For the next sixteen years the *Oregon* led a new life as a floating monument and museum in a berth near the Broadway Bridge in Portland.

Ironically, the veteran of Santiago fell victim to the demands made upon American resources during World War II. In the wake of the attack on Pearl Harbor, Oregon Governor Charles A. Sprague offered to return the ship to the navy for "coastal or other defense use."[13] His offer was declined, but soon rumors arose that the *Oregon* was to be scrapped for her steel. In September 1942 the Navy Department responded to the ensuing protests and petitions with the announcement that there were no plans to disturb the ship. Simultaneously, however, Undersecretary of the Navy James V. Forrestal advised Governor Sprague that, owing to the "great necessity for scrap metal and the pressure exerted upon us to make every possible contribution towards the building up of an adequate stockpile, this decision will probably have to be reconsidered." It was, and quickly. The matter went all the way to President Roosevelt, who had once approved the ship's salvation. On 26 October 1942 he informed Secretary of the Navy Frank Knox that "with great reluctance . . . I authorize the Navy Department to turn the USS *Oregon* over to the War Production Board for reduction to scrap metal." In reply to a letter from the Battleship *Oregon* Naval Post of the Veterans of Foreign Wars, Secretary Knox declared that through this metamorphosis the *Oregon*

[13]*McKinley's Bulldog*, p. 115.

would "again join in battle, a choice I am sure the good ship would make, were it within her power to do so."[14]

Accordingly, on 7 December 1942 the *Oregon* was sold to two Portland businessmen, Edwin M. Ricker and William O. McKay, for $35,000. Prior to her removal from the city, her foremast was detached and placed near the sea wall, where it still stands. In September 1943, by which time she had been gutted, the navy decided that it had a need for her sturdy old hull. All that was left of the *Oregon* was requisitioned for use as an ammunition hulk. During the summer of 1944 she was loaded with 1,400 tons of high explosives and towed across the Pacific to Port Merizo on the island of Guam. Once her cargo was unloaded no further employment was found for her, and at Guam she remained, under the jurisdiction of the Apra Naval Base. When Hurricane Agnes struck the island in mid-November 1948, the *Oregon* disappeared out to sea. Although it seemed probable that she had sunk, an aerial search was made on the chance that she might be afloat somewhere, a menace to navigation. On 8 December she was discovered 500 miles to the southwest, apparently en route to the Philippines, and towed back to Guam.

The publicity attracted by this incident reminded people that at least the core of the *Oregon* still existed, and voices were raised urging that the ship be brought home and rebuilt. The cost of so doing was deemed prohibitive, and eventually Congress authorized her disposal. On 3 March 1956 the *Oregon* was sold to the Massey Supply Company for $208,000. A Japanese firm, the Iwai Sanggo Company, bought her from Massey, and she was taken to Kawasaki and scrapped. Today a length of her anchor chain is displayed inside the main gate of the Japanese Maritime Self-Defense Force base at Yokosuka. A tablet bears the inscription, in English and Japanese;

IN MEMORY OF A GALLANT SHIP
U.S.S. OREGON
1896–1919

This section of anchor chain from the historic U. S. S. *Oregon* was presented to the U.S. Naval Base at Yokosuka, Japan, through the generosity of Ryozo Hiranuma, the Mayor of Yokohama, in cooperation with Lionel M. Summers U.S. Consulate General, Yokohama. Presented 26 February 1957.[15]

In retirement Admiral Clark was responsible for the publication of two books, of which this is the second. The first, published in 1915, was

---

[14]Ibid., pp. 115–17.
[15]Ibid., pp. 121–22.

a slender volume entitled *Prince and Boatswain*, for which the sep-
tuagenarian admiral had the unsuspecting distinction of collaborating
with a young man who would become a noted American novelist, John
P. Marquand. As a senior at Harvard Marquand began making notes of
his conversations with Clark, to whom he was distantly related.[16] His
interest encouraged Clark to write to his friend James Morris Morgan, an
academy classmate who had "gone South" in 1861 and had recently
published several sketches of his adventurous career. After com-
plimenting Morgan on his articles, Clark continued:

> You may allow that I have had some experiences as well as yourself.
> One of my auditors of long ago was little Margaret Fuller, not the
> gifted Margaret, Marchioness d'Ossoli, but her niece and namesake.
> Now her son, John P. Marquand, has been taking down some of my
> yarns and I hope taking off some of the rough edges at the same time.
> Now it seems to me that you and he could collaborate and get out an
> interesting volume. . . . Shall I write to Marquand and have you get
> together?[17]

The result was a collection of reminiscences, three by Clark as told to
Marquand and two by Morgan. In the year of its publication, Marquand
was twenty-two and a reporter for the Boston *Evening Transcript*. It was
his first book, one by which he was slightly embarrassed in later life. Of
Clark's role in its production he wrote, "He thought this way I might
make some money. He was a better Admiral than a critic."[18] That
disclaimer notwithstanding, *Prince and Boatswain* is not a bad book. The
boatswain of the title was P. J. Miller, one of the old navy's best-known
characters; the prince was Queen Victoria's sailor son, Alfred Ernest,
with whom Miller claimed to enjoy an intimate acquaintance. If the
book does not reach the literary standards Marquand demanded of his
mature novels, it does at least contain passages which foreshadow some
of the features characteristic of them.[19]

My Fifty Years in the Navy appeared in 1917. It is very much a sailor's
autobiography. Admiral Clark's hobby was the study of history, but he
did not write as an historian.[20] He tells us nothing of the reform
movements of the post–Civil War era, when the navy's "Young Turks"
rallied around the cause of a Naval War College, won acceptance for an

---

[16]Millicent Bell, *Marquand: An American Life* (Boston, 1979), p. 81.

[17]Charles E. Clark, James Morris Morgan, and John Phil[l]ip Marquand, *Prince and
Boatswain* (Greenfield, Mass., 1915), p. 4.

[18]*Marquand: An American Life*, p. 81.

[19]Ibid.

[20]*The National Cyclopedia of American Biography*, vol. 25 (New York, 1936), p. 117.

Office of Naval Intelligence, unsuccessfully agitated for the creation of a naval general staff, championed new technologies, urged the application of modern managerial methods to naval administration, pondered ways to improve the quality of the enlisted force, wrote articles for the *Proceedings* of the newly established Naval Institute, and conducted an informal public relations campaign to convince their countrymen of the importance of a strong navy to the national well-being. The reason, quite simply, is that Clark took no part in these activities. The aims a naval officer could pursue behind a desk, praisewothy as those might be, did not appeal to him. He was, first and last, a seaman. At the beginning of chapter 9 he wrote, "A naval officer's periods of shore duty are like the country without a history, the happier for having little to recall." Some of his assignments ashore he mentions in passing; others, such as his attendance at the new torpedo school in Newport in 1885, are omitted altogether. When Charles Clark looked back over his long career, he did not think of institutional change or the evolution of policy. He thought of the ships aboard which he had served and the people he had known. What he tells us, modestly and with great good humor, is the way it was to be a midshipman at Annapolis when the secession crisis broke; to fight in the Battle of Mobile Bay; to carry a dispatch to Farragut, receive an unauthorized shore liberty from Alfred T. Mahan, serve under John Rodgers—of whom Clark's portrait is almost Dickensian—and chat with Joe Fyffe; to be shipwrecked in the proximity of an Indian tribe of uncertain intent; to survey the coast of Central America; and, of course, to command the *Oregon*. And in so doing he conveys, as only a participant could, the texture of naval life in his era. The entry on Admiral Clark in *The National Cyclopedia of American Biography* states that "he was noted throughout the navy as a raconteur."[21] Readers of this book will see why.

JACK SWEETMAN

---

[21]Ibid.

FOREWORD

Doctor S. Weir Mitchell, scientist, author, and physician, who instructed, delighted, and cared for me, made me promise that sometime this record should be published. It is now gratefully inscribed to those who so devotedly and capably served on board the *Oregon* and to all who so tensely watched and waited while,

"Through tropic heat,
Through snow and sleet
She hastened onward still."

Chapter 1

FIRST DAYS AT ANNAPOLIS

Bradford, Orange County, the Vermont village where I was born, on August 10, 1843, is situated upon the left bank of the Waits River, nearly a mile above its junction with the Connecticut. From the elevated ground on which it stands, one looks across the intervening meadows to the New Hampshire hills and the mountains beyond them: Moosilauke, forty-six hundred feet high, Sugar Loaf, or Black Hill, Owl's Head, Cube, and Dorchester, while the more distant blue peak of Mount Lafayette of the Franconia Range rises to its height of fifty-two hundred feet, between two perfect saddles formed by the nearer mountains.

From my earliest childhood I never wearied of watching every changing aspect of the different mountains, and I felt the general devotion to them all not uncommon perhaps to boys brought up among the hills; but Mount Lafayette was the special object of my admiration, and one of my first extravagances was the purchase of a small telescope to bring this wonderful mountain nearer.

My parents were James Dayton Clark,[1] also born in Bradford, and Mary Sexton Clark, a native of Brookfield, Vermont. The first of our family to live in Vermont were Thomas and Lois Williams Clark, my great grandparents, who came to Bradford from Roxbury, Massachusetts, at the beginning of the last century. My great grandfather

---

[1] Rear Admiral James Dayton, U.S.N., and James Dayton Clark were first cousins, but the former was junior to me in rank. [Author's note]

was a member of the General Court towards the close of the Revolutionary War, in which his health had never permitted him to take an active
part. The records show, nevertheless, that when a battle was imminent,
he had joined the provincial army. My mother's father, Major Hiram
Sexton, had served during the War of 1812, and her grandfather,
Captain Williams of Wilmington, Vermont, was an officer in the
Revolutionary army. Several relatives had also served with credit in the
colonial, or earlier wars, so there was enough of the military spirit on
both sides to account for a longing on my part to enter the army. As my
father, however, left an orphan at two years of age, had neither means nor
political influence, I generally pictured myself as carrying a musket in
the ranks.

I was very young indeed when I established a military post on the roof
of our house. I was working out some ideas in fortification, when my foot
slipped, and I began a rapid slide towards the eaves. I must have gone
headfirst, for I still have a picture in my mind of a neighbor, who, with
her arms upraised in horror at my performance, seemed to me to be
walking on her hands. A lucky grab at the waterspout, which held long
enough to partially right me, was responsible for my landing on the
ground, rather less damaged than might have been expected.

I did not come off quite as well in my first and only experiment in
aviation. I had been reading of the possibilities of the parachute, and it
occurred to me, as it did to Mr. Richard Swiveller, that an umbrella
might have its uses, outside its regular sphere. I spread the news among
my comrades, one Saturday afternoon, that at a certain hour I was
prepared to jump from the second-story window of our house. My
appearance at the window was greeted by quite a number of spectators
who were very free in their expressions of opinion, some derisively
calling out that I "wouldn't dare!" and others that I'd "better not!"
Affecting a composure that I was far from feeling at that exciting
moment, I climbed the sill, spread my umbrella, and launched myself
into space. All went well for one brief second. Then the umbrella
collapsed, and when I recovered consciousness, my faith in parachutes
had collapsed likewise.

I only recollect one other experience in the military line that occurred
during my early boyhood. My brother and I owned a little cannon,
which made a very desirable racket when it was fired, but which we felt
might be made to do even better. So we tried ramming down the charge
with wooden plugs, and this not giving entire satisfaction, we finally
drove in the iron rammer, and shoved its outer end against a rock. When

the explosion came, something resisted, but it was the rock and not the cannon. We got a very fine notion of how it feels to be in the path of a projectile. This one, fortunately, cleared our heads, flying past us into the woodshed where, after splintering a beam, it came to rest in a much agitated pile of chips in a corner. We were quite unaware at the time that we were actually demonstrating the principle of the Congreve rocket.[2]

My favorite companion in Bradford was William Rogers, a boy about a year older than myself. He had a fine mind and was an omnivorous reader. We were almost inseparable, and from him I was for some time content to take a great deal of my reading at second-hand. I was an imaginative youngster, and while not lacking in courage to meet the ordinary give and take of my boyish world, my head was pretty well stuffed with a tissue of fanciful dangers. Preëminent among these was a fearful trio—Abductors, Barn-burners, and Ghosts. I had once seen in an illustrated paper a picture of the abduction of some fair lady by armor-clad knights, and her terrified expression haunted me. I felt that my mother, the most attractive woman in the world, according to my notion, would naturally be the next to be carried off. I often used to make some excuse to run home from school at recess, to assure myself that she was really there, and I soon found it was quite useless to try to spend the night at a playmate's house. My apprehensions were certain to urge me out of bed about midnight, to travel home through a darkness peopled with ghosts and burglars, just to make sure that nothing had happened in my absence. I used to plead homesickness as my excuse, for I did not wish to have my mother alarmed about the dreadful dangers to which she was exposed.

There was a little more reality mixed with the barn-burner terror. Just why the village of Bradford should have been harried as it was a few years previously by one or more incendiaries, it would be hard to say, but it was a fact that during this period the number of barns that had gone up in flames furnished the village chronicles with matter for some time to come. I used to sit in Pritchard's store in the evening, my ears wide open, while the old patrols recalled their experiences and disputed as to who was first to arrive on the scene, on that memorable night, when Jake Flanders, having fired at one barn-burner, was slashed by the knife of another. Then some cynic would suggest that Flanders himself might have cut that slash in his clothing, just to make a good story, and I, for

[2] In the nineteenth century the military rocket was commonly named after the person who pioneered its development, the English artillerist Major General Sir William Congreve (1772–1828).

one, would feel that this was a cruel doubt. Generally speaking, the patrols seemed to have traveled conveniently in pairs, so that one was able to tell how the other had been shaken with fear, while he had supplied the courage for the occasion.

My ideas about ghosts were largely derived from some of Washington Irving's tales, which Will Rogers and I read and discussed together. I must confess that Ichabod Crane's "headless Hessian" and Dolph Heyliger's specter, with its dreadful habit of walking right through locked doors into any house, gave me some very bad hours. Will, who was more sceptical than I, assured me that these were only old Dutch legends, but I retorted with the story of Cæsar's ghost that appeared to Brutus at Philippi, and the spirit that pursued Xerxes' brother in so vigorous a fashion, and this argument seemed to us both unanswerable, for of course history could not lie, and therefore ghosts must exist.

I began my education at the district school in Bradford, and after that was a pupil for several terms at the Bradford Academy. Its principal, Roswell H. Farnham, was afterwards an officer of Vermont troops in the Civil War, and later became governor of the State. He had an inspiring personality which ought to have brought out the best in his scholars, but I fear I cannot claim that I was a special credit to him at that time. Another principal of the Academy, to whom I was strongly attached, was George A. Low, a tall graduate of Dartmouth; my liking was based not so much perhaps on his scholarly qualities as on the interest he showed in our sports, notably football, which we often played in front of his house.

During my vacations I was expected to make myself more or less useful in my father's bookbindery, but as he remarked, when there was any real work to do, I suddenly became a great reader. There was no lack of opportunity, with so many books lying about. I was particularly fond of military history and read everything I could lay my hands on concerning Hannibal, Napoleon, Marlborough, and other great generals. Fed on this reading, my desire for a soldier's career became very strong, and I often used to talk to my father about it. It was during one of these talks that I suggested that he write to the Honorable Justin S. Morrill, with whom he was acquainted, for an appointment to the Military Academy for me. My father finally agreed to do so, telling me at the same time not to set my heart on it too much, as about all he could say for me was that I had reached the required age—sixteen years.

Mr. Morrill did not leave us long in doubt. Within a few days a letter arrived with his frank on the envelope. That letter meant so much to me that I have never forgotten its exact words, which ran thus: "There is no vacancy from this district at West Point, as I have just appointed Doctor Rockwell's son, of Brattleboro. But there is one at the Naval Academy, Annapolis, which I have offered to Judge Hibbard's son, of Chelsea. He is hesitating about accepting it. Should he decline, I shall be glad to let your son have it. Would he like to be a sailor boy?''

While I did not consider a commission in the navy, with its prospect of captain, the highest rank then attainable, as equal to one in the army, with its more high-sounding titles, yet I was excited and anxious enough about that appointment to harbor very sinister thoughts about the Hibbard boy. These vanished when Judge Hibbard told my father that he did not care to have a son of his go into the navy, and I realized that the coveted position was actually to be mine. The appointment came in the spring of 1860, one year before the breaking out of the Civil War. Soon after its arrival, finding that I could not endure the sight of my mother's unhappiness over our impending separation, I decided to return it to Mr. Morrill. That fine statesman, whose continuous service in Congress for forty-four years exceeded that of any other American, giving him the title of Vermont's Life Senator, and who had declined Cabinet positions, took the trouble to write to us, letting us know just what we were setting aside, explaining the advantages of an education at government expense and something of what it meant to be a graduate of Annapolis. With this better understanding my mother insisted that I should not sacrifice my opportunity, and the appointment was returned to me. So I might say that I owe it twice over to Mr. Morrill.

Sleeping-cars were probably not in existence at the time I made my journey to Annapolis. At least, I had never heard of them. Traveling by day was thought to be a sufficiently risky business. Many, if not all roads, ran their trains by a time schedule. When a train reached a station, its conductor waited for a certain length of time, after which he acquired the right of way and ran full speed for the next. When watches did not happen to agree, collisions were in order.

On my journey to Annapolis I slept one night on the boat from Troy to Albany, and the next in Philadelphia, where I saw "The American Cousin" played at the Arch Street Theatre. The rôle of Lord Dundreary, made so famous afterwards by Sothern, was then only a secondary one.[3] When I boarded the train at Baltimore, I had my first sight of a

---

[3] *Our American Cousin*, a comedy of manners by Tom Taylor, probably the most popular English playwright of his day, opened in New York in May 1858. Among its characters was an eccentric English nobleman, Lord Dundreary, played by Edward A. Sothern, who rose to stardom in this role. The first London production, in 1861, ran almost five hundred nights.

midshipman's uniform. The boy who wore it was engaged in conversation, the greater part of the trip, by a father and son who were evidently getting information from him about Annapolis, in which I would have gladly shared.

Annapolis, of course, was full of boys arriving for the examinations, and as I was walking along one of its quaint streets, I overheard one little group making inquiries as to whether a certain Stirling, from Baltimore, had received a passing mark. Strange to say, Thomas Williams, the boy in uniform on the train, the first midshipman I ever saw, and Yates Stirling, the first whose name I heard, were my roommates during my first year ashore at the Academy. The combination lasted no longer, the commandant being heard to remark that it was a good one to break up. Williams was found deficient and dropped. Stirling, who became a rear admiral and commanded a fleet on the Asiatic Station, now lives in Baltimore.[4] The boy whom I had noticed on the train, talking to Williams, and whose name was Carmody, had one of the lengthiest careers at the Academy. He "bilged", to use the Academy term, that next February. Reappointed to the next class, he was turned back for another year, and then he was suspended for a year. So he was accustomed to speak quite contemptuously of some of the officers who returned to Annapolis as instructors, saying that they came into the service long after his time.

Not long after I entered the Naval Academy, my parents left Bradford and moved to Montpelier, the capital of the State, which became their permanent home and mine, as far as a naval officer can be said to have one. My leaves of absence were always spent there, and I was still young enough when the change was made to have many of my youthful memories connected with the town.

Montpelier, as is well known, was the birthplace of the late Admiral Dewey, and I could feel that I was certainly regarded as her adopted son when I heard of the speech made by a local orator, who after referring to the battles of Manila and Santiago, spoke with true native humor of the Spanish American War, as "the war between the village of Montpelier and the kingdom of Spain."[5]

----

[4] Between 1902 and 1905 Admiral Stirling successively commanded the Philippine Squadron, the Cruiser Squadron of the Asiatic Fleet, and the Asiatic Fleet itself. He died in 1929. His son, Rear Admiral Yates Stirling, Jr., USNA 1892, commanded the Yangtze Patrol (1927–29), and was the author of numerous books on naval subjects, including *Sea Duty: The Memoirs of a Fighting Admiral.*

[5] At one time in Montpelier much was said about the astonishing escape of Dewey and Clark, but this referred to the Admiral's nephew William and my brother Lloyd. The

The superintendent of the Naval Academy, at whose little office near the south gate I reported, September 29, 1860, was Captain George S. Blake. Because of his judicious management of affairs, he was kept in command with the title of "commodore" several years beyond the usual term of superintendents. He was a portly old gentleman, who had a habit of placing his hand upon his stomach and remarking impressively: "I can lay my hand upon my heart, and say I never wronged a midshipman!"[6]

His colored office attendant, Jim Holliday, also had the welfare of the midshipmen at heart, and remarks overheard at the conferences of the Academic Board were often used by him as a basis for a word of friendly advice or warning, to such of the boys as consulted him about their standing,—and they were not a few. A tip from Holliday was not to be despised. "Yo' mus' sutinly pay mo' attention to yo' mechanics, suh," he would gravely admonish some young questioner, "or I'm ve'y much afraid yo' are going to 'bilge.'"

One of my classmates, returning from leave, brought back a message of remembrance from an officer he had met, which greatly pleased Holliday, but at the concluding words—"And he told me to ask you, Holliday, how the 'Epidemic Board' was getting on?" Holliday's face fell. "Did he say that? 'Deed, suh, I'm ve'y sorry that eveh got out in the service."

The historic frigate *Constitution*—"Old Ironsides"—had just been fitted out as the schoolship, and also with quarters for the fourth class, so I at once went on board.[7] Her commander was Lieutenant George W. Rodgers, a nephew of the hero of Lake Erie. He was soon afterwards

---

Rialto Building that spanned the Branch collapsed during the great fire, falling on the ice in the river bed below. Dewey remained under it and Clark in it, until the crash came. [Author's note]

[6] Captain Blake, who had spent much of his career in the Coast Survey, served as superintendent of the Naval Academy from 15 September 1857 until 9 September 1865, by far the longest tour of any occupant of that post. Whether he was retained because of his "judicious management of affairs" or because more dynamic officers were wanted at the front to fight the Civil War is open to question. For an account of the trying times of his superintendency, see Jack Sweetman, *The U.S. Naval Academy: An Illustrated History* (Annapolis, 1979), pp. 58–75.

[7] The sloop *Plymouth* was attached to the Academy in October 1859 to relieve overcrowding in the midshipmen's quarters. She served as a dormitory and classroom for the fourth (freshman) class. The following year she was replaced by the *Constitution*, whose glorious history was expected to "exercise a salutary influence on the minds of the pupils" (Edward Chauncey Marshall, *History of the Naval Academy* [New York, 1862], p. 39).

killed, fighting bravely for the Union.[8] Next in rank was Lieutenant John H. Upshur, a true scion of the Old Dominion, who loved it much, but the country more. At this day, active in body, as well as in mind, his many friends hopefully and affectionately see him approaching the century mark.[9]

Mrs. Upshur, whose father fell at Monterey, and whose unusual beauty was enhanced in the eyes of our Southern comrades by her ancestry, captured all hearts. She not only was lovely to look upon, but had an unrivalled faculty for detecting the homesick, shy, and despondent among the boys and drawing them into the charmed circle about her. It was the knowledge of this quality that prompted her husband one evening, after a reception, to offer William K. Pipkin, painfully awkward and homely, and just arrived from the backwoods of Missouri, the privilege of escorting her home. Instead of accepting with eagerness the honor that had fallen to him, the embarrassed youth, blushing hotly, managed to stammer out, "Excuse me, sir, but the last thing Dad and Ma said to me when I left home, was: 'Bill Pip, you beware of the women!'"

"Bill Pip" had entered the class next ahead, but had failed in some branch and had fallen back into ours. Rumor says he became the colonel of a Confederate regiment when only twenty-three, and ended his life as a millionaire.[10] However that may be, he passed many bad hours at the Academy and would doubtless have "bilged" at the first semi-annual examination but for Mrs. Upshur's tactful encouragement and sympathy. Later, when promoted to the rank of rear admiral, I had sincere pleasure in asking the Navy Department to order an officer to the

[8] Commander Rodgers was killed while in command of the monitor *Catskill* during an engagement with Battery Wagner at Charleston, South Carolina, on 17 August 1863.

[9] John H. Upshur received his warrant as a midshipman in 1841 and retired in the rank of rear admiral in 1885. He died in May 1917.

[10] Alas, the rumor was unfounded. Upon his return home William Moss Pipkin enlisted as a private in Company E, Second Missouri Cavalry. Later he transferred to the Confederate navy, in which he must have also served as an enlisted man, as his name does not appear in the list of commissioned and warrant officers in the Confederate navy registers for 1 January or 1 June 1864. After the war he practiced law in Missouri until around 1880, when he deserted his wife and two children to become a miner in Idaho, where he is believed to have died about 1919. A sketch of him also appears in James Morris Morgan's *Recollections of a Rebel Reefer* (Boston, 1917). For details, see Colonel William P. Pipkin, ed., *Pipkin Family Association Newsletter*, May 1978, The State Historical Society of Missouri, pp. 16–17.

Constitution. "Old Ironsides." The frigate's advance over the ancient galley hardly exceeded that of the modern battleship over the frigate.

Academy, knowing that his wife, the only daughter of our battle scarred President,[11] was like Mrs. Upshur in loveliness of character.

Belonging to the academic staff on shore were a number of officers, who afterwards attained high rank, or gained distinction in the Union or Confederate navies. C. R. P. Rodgers, then commandant of midshipmen,[12] Edward Simpson,[13] and Stephen B. Luce, afterwards first president of the Naval War College,[14] became rear admirals. Lieutenant Flusser, a Southerner, was killed fighting bravely for the Union.[15] Lieutenants John Taylor Wood, Hunter Davidson, and William H. Parker joined the Secessionists.[16]

[11] The lady in question was Rutherford B. Hayes' daughter, Fanny, who married Harry Eaton Smith, USNA 1891, in September 1897. Smith retired as a captain in 1920.

[12] Often called the Chesterfield of the Navy, Lieutenant Christopher Raymond Perry Rodgers impressed the midshipmen as the very ideal of a naval officer. During the Civil War he saw combat as captain of the *Wabash* and the *New Ironsides* and was promoted to captain in July 1866. Flag captain on the European station (1869–70), he subsequently served as chief of the Bureau of Yards and Docks (1871–74), superintendent of the Naval Academy (1874–78 and again in 1880), and commander of the Pacific Squadron (1878–80), retiring in the rank of commodore in 1881. He also served as president of the U.S. Naval Institute (1875–78 and 1882–83).

[13] Edward Simpson was appointed a midshipman in 1840. Soon specializing in ordnance, he spent several years at the Academy as an instructor of gunnery (1853–54 and 1858–62) and as commandant of midshipmen (1862–63). Just before retiring as a rear admiral in 1886, he served as president of the Board of Inspection and Survey. He was president of the Naval Institute from the date of his retirement until his death in 1888.

[14] Tireless reformer, founder of the Naval War College, and patron of Alfred Thayer Mahan, Stephen B. Luce was the most important naval progressive of the post–Civil War era. He was also a superb shiphandler whose *Seamanship*, repeatedly revised, was the Naval Academy textbook for almost forty years. He retired as a rear admiral following three years in command of the North Atlantic Squadron in 1889 but remained active in naval affairs, as president of the Naval Institute (1887–98) and on numerous boards and special assignments until shortly before his death at the age of ninety in 1917. See Rear Admiral Albert Gleaves, *Life and Letters of Rear Admiral Stephen B. Luce* (New York, 1925).

[15] Lieutenant Commander Charles W. Flusser, USNA 1853, was actually a native of Maryland. He was killed while commanding the USS *Miami* in action with the Confederate ironclad ram *Albemarle* in Plymouth Sound, North Carolina, on 20 April 1864.

[16] A grandson of President Zachary Taylor and a nephew by marriage of Confederate President Jefferson Davis, John Taylor Wood had an eventful career in Confederate service, at the war's end distinguished by the twin commissions of commander, CSN, and colonel, CSA. On Sunday, 2 April 1865, it fell to him to inform Davis that Lee could no longer defend Richmond. See Royce Gordon Shingleton, *John Taylor Wood: Sea Ghost*

Lieutenant Parker was the first naval officer I ever saw, but as he was in citizen's clothes at the time, I was not deeply impressed. He was the author of nautical sketches, sailing directions, and artillery tactics. He became superintendent of the Confederate States Naval Academy, and the last I heard of him, before his death, he was president of an agricultural college.[17] The way his resignation came about was rather curious. Despite his Southern birth—he was a Virginian—William Parker was strongly disinclined to leave the service in which he had been reared. His brother, Foxhall Parker, a commander in the navy, was of the opinion that his duty lay with the South. The brothers happening to meet just before the outbreak of hostilities, each urged his side of the question upon the other, Foxhall pleading their birth, connections, and traditions, and William loyalty to the flag, and to the service in which they had been educated. After separating, each reflected upon the other's arguments to such purpose that William ended by sending in his resignation, while Foxhall decided to withhold his.

Years later, in Washington, William Parker pointed out his brother to a friend, saying: "There goes Foxhall, the disloyal Unionist, on full pay, and here stands William, the loyal Secessionist, down on his uppers."[18]

To return to the *Constitution*. Having been hauled in as near the Academy sea wall as possible, she had been moored head and stern, and a narrow footbridge connecting her with the shore had been constructed. Under the poop deck, and in a small deckhouse amidships, were four recitation rooms. The three study rooms were on the gun deck, bulk-

---

of the Confederacy. Hunter Davidson became a leader in the Confederacy's highly innovative practice of mine warfare. By chance, both he and Wood were aboard the CSS *Virginia* (ex-*Merrimack*) in her action with the *Monitor*, the first battle between ironclads, on 9 March 1862.

[17] When Clark entered the Academy, William Harwar Parker was head of the Department of Seamanship and Gunnery. "Going South," Parker served as captain of the armed tug *Beaufort* in the battles of Roanoke Island, Elizabeth City, and Hampton Roads, and as executive officer of the ironclad ram *Palmetto State* at Charleston. He was appointed superintendent of the Confederate States Naval Academy in March 1863. After the war he was a captain in the merchant marine, president of Maryland Agricultural College (now the University of Maryland), and U.S. consul in Bahia, Brazil. At his death he left behind a delightful memoir, *Recollections of a Naval Officer, 1841–1865*.

[18] One of the foremost students of naval tactics of his generation, Commodore Foxhall A. Parker, Jr., died on active duty as superintendent of the Naval Academy in June 1879. In addition to several professional treatises, he wrote two works of naval history, *Fleets of the World: The Gallery Period* and *The Battle of Mobile Bay*.

heads having been run along parallel with the sides, and the gun ports serving as windows. Our lockers, one for each midshipman, were fitted against the sides on the berth deck. Forward was the wash room, the number of basins averaging about one to five of the washers, who scrambled for the first chance, and then put in claims—which were always respected—for second and third places. Inspection came before breakfast, so delays were inveighed against, and much attention to the ears or neck reprobated. In the interval between supper and evening study hours, one of the six gun crews would be marched over to the bathhouse on shore. I think I may say that the majority of us considered it a great hardship that one of our short periods of recreation should be taken for such a purpose.

The only guns remaining on board the *Constitution* were eight or ten of the thirty-two pounders of the quarter-deck battery, and with these we were exercised after four o'clock, when the afternoon studies and recitations were over. At the end of the first month, it was found that in one of the crews were six of the ten men first in class standing, but as the second crew, to which I belonged, could run the guns in and out, and shift trucks and breechings in the shortest time, and also pull our cutter the fastest, we were the fellows that were envied and looked up to by the others.

I remember very well the first time Lieutenant Rodgers attempted to teach us something about sails. He had the mizzen topsail broken out, and stretched along the deck. "Now," said he, "Mr. Clark, you and Mr. Glidden lay aloft and overhaul down the buntlines."

"The buntlines?" I repeated, staring at him.

"Yes, sir! the b-u-n-t-l-i-n-e-s!" he roared, spelling it out, and without waiting for any further explanation, I hurried aloft, determined to overhaul down any rope that offered.

We were quite fearless by this time about running up the rigging, and those of us who had imagination enjoyed looking down from the royal jack upon the deck, which "once had felt the victor's tread" and where "knelt the vanquished foe." I had read the poem beginning,—

"Old Ironsides at anchor lay
In the harbor of Mahon"

with its account of how the captain's little son had climbed to the main truck, and stood swaying there, until his father by threatening him with a rifle, had made him jump into the sea. I was inclined to think that there was more poetry than truth in this alleged occurrence, yet I have seen

Rear Admiral Harry Taylor, who was one of the little fellows in my class, sitting on the main truck of "Old Ironsides" amusing himself by rolling up the pennant and letting it flow again. His only rival was "Brick Top" English, who once got on his feet on the truck, aided a little by the lightning conductor, which projected about a foot above it.[19] Finally the superintendent got wind of these proceedings, and ordered that no midshipman should climb above the eyes of the royal rigging.

The colored servants who waited on us at mess were slaves, hired from their masters, in or near Annapolis. Except Dorsey, the steward, I recall the name of but one, and that only because of a couple of accidents in which he figured. He came sliding down the ladder at dinner hour, one day, holding up an inverted soup tureen, and pouring its hot contents over himself, *en route*. Very soon after this he again engaged public attention by falling overboard. One of the crew, promptly seizing a boat hook, succeeded in shoving it under the waistband, but although his rescue seemed thus to be assured, another negro from his place in a gun port continued making a great outcry.

"Oh! shut up!" cried a sailor impatiently. "They'll save him! Can't you see they've hooked on to him all right?"

"'Taint all right, nuther! Dat's my brudder, Caleb Watkins, an' he done got on my bes' Sunday breeches!"

Another name I recollect among the colored personnel was that of Moses Lake, the Academy barber. He had been the servant of Commodore Buchanan during a European cruise, and the walls of his shop were decorated with pictures and inscriptions, such as the following: "Windsor Castle, visited by Mr. Moses Lake, September, 1858." "Mount Vesuvius, first seen by Mr. Moses Lake, October, 1858."

[19] Gustavus English was a nongraduating member of the class of 1864.

Chapter 2

RUMORS OF WAR

E ver since my class entered the Academy in September, the growing unrest and trouble of the country had been disturbing the equilibrium of our little world. There were much wrangling and many arguments among the boys, but no real quarreling. In the general sense of upheaval, no one—this was especially true of the Northerners—felt certain enough of the ground under his feet to take an assured position. In fact, the youngsters at the Academy were in about as bad a muddle as the country at large. After the secession of South Carolina in December, however, our classmates from the South began to talk with more conviction. They insisted, for one thing, that as in a division of the country the North would have West Point, the Naval Academy should go to them. They declared that New York City sympathized with their cause, and if a war should come, the Seventh Regiment, the finest in the country, would be sure to fight on their side. As for Baltimore, they knew she would never allow Abolitionists and John Brown sympathizers to pass through her streets, nor even Northern troops to march through to the support of Washington, if it were attacked.

These opinions were being hotly voiced by the Southern element in a little group of midshipmen, one day, when a first-class man who was walking by overheard a sentence that brought him to an abrupt halt. He was the late Rear Admiral Sampson,[1] then at the head of the first class.

---

[1] William T. Sampson, the first-ranking graduate of the class of 1861, enjoyed a distinguished career culminating in the command of American naval forces in the Caribbean during the Spanish-American War.

He was the ranking cadet officer, as adjutant wore the most gold lace, and, being strikingly handsome moreover, was probably a greater man in the eyes of the junior classmen than any of their officers or instructors.

"You say," he slowly and deliberately repeated the words of the last speaker, "if the capital of the nation is attacked, Northern troops will not be permitted to march through Baltimore to protect it? Well, then," his voice, usually so quiet, rang out like a call to arms, "the North will march *over* Baltimore—or the place where it stood!"

He said nothing further and went his way, leaving a silent group behind him, and with the Northern boys an indescribable sense of comfort. Those few words, so clear and decisive, seemed like a flag around which we could rally. We realized for the first time what it would mean to us if war really came, and the safety of the Republic were at stake. At the same time, I believe there were very few of us that had any misconception of the herculean task the North would have to face. Even six months' association with our Southern comrades had taught us that they came from a military class. Every one of them was an unerring marksman, and we heard that they could ride as well as they could shoot. We were not prepared, however, to swallow their assumption that one Southerner was equal to four Northerners, nor did subsequent history bear out this boast.[2] Yet it must be conceded that until inured to war, or thoroughly trained, no *equal* number of men in the world could have stood against the quarter million of slave-holders, who practically formed in the South a military caste, like the Samurai in Japan, or the Spartans in Lacedæmon.

It has always been easy to persuade the unread soldier who fought in the Southern ranks that he was never defeated except when overpowered. This cherished idea was probably never so completely refuted as by the publication of Henderson's *Life of Stonewall Jackson*.[3] The admiration felt by this accomplished English officer for the Southern hero makes it impossible to question his carefully prepared statements, and he shows

[2] The rifle-carrying poor white who shot squirrels in the head only, was as yet thoroughly dominated. So the South was prepared or organized for war. But this homogeneity and even the social fabric could not last. Only on the great plantations was slave labor really profitable, so there was a natural limit to the number of slaveholders. And while the planter's son was taught that virtue was more than the courage which must never be questioned he was exposed to a great temptation, and this was deplored by thoughtful men and the notably loyal women of the South. There were many who felt keenly the condemnation of slavery that was increasing in the civilized world. [Author's note]

[3] Colonel G. F. R. Henderson's classic biography, *Stonewall Jackson and the American Civil War*, met with immediate and enduring acclaim upon its publication in 1898.

that except at Chancellorsville, where the Union army, overpowering in strength, was defeated through wretched handling, the victory generally went to "the strong battalions"; that the claim of triumphs won by inferior numbers, without the advantage of position, was unfounded.

The first of my classmates to resign was Bryan of South Carolina, who soon wrote back that he was a *real* midshipman, on board the *Excel* in Charleston harbor. Then the Gulf State fellows began to fall out rapidly, among them William Earle Yancey, son of the noted Alabama secessionist. In March came the inauguration of Lincoln, followed by Anderson's retirement to Sumter. This fort, with its walls rising perpendicularly from the water, we had fondly imagined to be impregnable, and its fall was a shock, but at least it opened our eyes to the fact that the North was united.

After this, reports came rapidly of the seizure of one fort after another, culminating in that of the arsenal at Harper's Ferry. The capture of this arsenal gave us the uneasy feeling of being cut off from our base, as it was situated farther north than Annapolis. Next, there were rumors that Maryland, being a slave State, intended to secede, and in that case, one of her first steps would be an attempt to capture our frigate and the guns and munitions of war at the Academy. Our authorities at once began to make preparations for defense. Old Fort Severn, which stood in the Academy grounds, had been used as an exercising battery for the midshipmen, but as it was actually valueless for defensive purposes, and its guns, if they fell into the enemy's hands, could have been turned against the *Constitution*, they were hastily dismounted, taken aboard, and added to our battery. When it was reported that troops had appeared north of the Severn, ammunition was served out, and the midshipmen, both afloat and ashore, were stationed to repel an attack. There were no marines at the Academy at this time, and not more than twenty-five seamen on board the *Constitution*. Her gun-deck ports were closed at night, and Number 1 gun's crew told off to guard that deck. The rest of us were to fall in on the spar deck, in case of an alarm. One of the crews was kept on duty at night, and from it the sentries were detailed. I remember my first watch was from midnight to two A.M., on the bowsprit, where I could see anything approaching from up the river.

One of the sentries on shore one night (Midshipman Benjamin Porter, who was afterwards killed at Fort Fisher) discovered a number of men on the wharf, just outside the north wall of the Academy, making preparations to remove the ferryboat which was moored there. Having had his instructions as a sentry, he ordered them to desist, and when they refused to obey, he fired, and called for the guard. When the guard arrived, it was in charge of Lieutenant Hunter Davidson, and the offenders, who by that time had judged it best to submit, expressed their satisfaction in having a Secessionist to deal with. Davidson, however, promptly warned them to expect nothing from him, for although he had resigned, he still wore the United States uniform.

When the Union troops were fired upon while passing through Baltimore, and the city seemed to be completely in the hands of the Secessionists, it was evident that we were cut off by land from the North and from Washington as well, if the report were true about the large force assembled at Annapolis Junction. Concern for our own position almost disappeared in the greater anxiety that was felt for the safety of the Capital.

Early one Sunday morning in April, we heard that a large steamer filled with troops was on her way up from the bay, and we soon learned that she was the *Maryland*, diverted from her usual employment of taking trains across the mouth of the Susquehanna at Havre de Grace. She had on board the 8th Massachusetts Regiment, with General Butler in command. At the request of Governor Hicks, it was decided not to land the troops at once. The Governor, himself a Union man, feared that an exhibition of armed force just then might cause the State to secede. No one realized at that time how strong the Union sentiment actually was in Maryland.

The Academy authorities took advantage of the presence of the steamer to change the unfavorable position of the *Constitution*. It fortunately happened that the Massachusetts soldiers were from the eastern part of their State, and consequently many of them were seamen. With their help, the anchors were soon raised, and our frigate, with the *Maryland* alongside, moved slowly out into the bay. Ten of the class were kept on board, and they were naturally proud of this selection, but the rest of us could feel, at least, that in joining the three classes on shore, we were going to what was supposed to be the post of danger. I have often thought since what an anxious time that must have been for our superintendent and his officers. If they had known the real depth of loyalty among the people surrounding us, they would have had little occasion to feel uneasy, but the Secessionists were the ones in evidence, and according to their noisy talk, Baltimore was backing them. What had we to oppose to a determined attack? We numbered less than two hundred in all, and the average age of the midshipmen in the four classes was eighteen years—the age of admission being then fourteen to seventeen inclusive. The low brick wall around the Academy grounds was not intended for defensive purposes, and had no projections from which an attacking party could be swept by a fire along its face.

A couple of days passed slowly, while we were in this state of tension, and the sense of relief was great, when late in the afternoon of the second or third day, a steamer was sighted coming from the Roads. She hauled in at the wharf, and the famous 7th New York marched ashore. More troops followed, and it was decided to open the road to Washington. The only locomotive at the station had been disabled, but the 8th Massachusetts men were mechanics, as well as sailors, and it was soon put in working order.

Other regiments arrived; among them the 71st New York, the 69th Irish, a German regiment talking their own language, but cheering for the flag, and the 1st Rhode Island, under Colonel—afterwards General—Burnside. The soldiers of the last named wore blouses belted at the waist, and had such a businesslike air that the Southern boys admitted they did not like their looks. Neither had they greatly relished the sight of the much-talked-of 7th, which they had formerly claimed as their own.

Of course there could be no school at such a time, and we imagined it was done with forever, and rejoiced accordingly. We flung our textbooks from the windows, causing much vexation of spirit to the officers of the German regiment, which was drilling below, for their men would persist in leaving the ranks to pick up the books, and then try to drill, holding them under their arms. The efforts of one stout private to manage his musket and retain his hold on two corpulent dictionaries were especially conspicuous.

It was on one of these idle days that a rumor ran the rounds that a steamer which had hauled in to the wharf had a passed midshipman on board. A number of us hurried to the waterfront to verify this report, and there, sure enough, he sat upon the rail, a bit of gold lace upon his shoulder, apparently quite oblivious to the gazing crowd below. He knew he was a rare bird, and expected us to stare at him. The grade was soon after abolished, so he was the only one of his kind I ever saw.

Finally came the change which we had all been expecting. One morning at roll call, we were ordered to be ready to go on board the steamer *Josephine*, which would take us out to the *Constitution*. Part of the first class had already been detached and gone with the troops to Washington, and there were twenty Southerners who had resigned and would be left behind when we embarked. They took their usual places in the ranks, when we formed to march down to the wharf, and the soldiers closed in, front and rear. The wharf was crowded, and there was some confusion, the Southern boys falling out of ranks, and saying good-by to their classmates, but when the commandant of midshipmen, C. R. P. Rodgers, came down the long line, and paused opposite its center, all were hushed, for it had been said he meant to give us a farewell address. Looking at the rows of boyish faces turned expectantly towards him, and at the flag floating above their heads, he raised his arm, and pointing to it, began, "Be true to the flag", and then broke down completely. I am sure many others were in tears; I know I was. But what affected us the most, and amused us as well, was the behavior of the soldiers, who broke into the ranks, embracing the midshipmen and crying out: "Never mind! You'll soon be coming back, boys! We'll see that you get your school again!" To this day I remember how thankful I felt that the big soldier who was hugging me had not seen me throwing my books out of the window.

As the *Josephine* shoved off, some one shouted to run up a bigger flag than the one she was carrying. So a large ensign was hoisted, but just as it reached the staff, the knot at the lower corner gave way, and the flag became nothing but a streamer. In trying to lower it, the wind carried it so far astern that it could not be reached, and we were well down the river before it was finally hoisted. If our late classmates felt that this was a good omen for their cause, they did not show any signs of exultation. In fact, the last we saw of them, they were a sorrowful looking lot.

We found changes on board the *Constitution*. The study rooms had gone, and the guns had been shifted from the spar deck. Never did a man-of-war sail with such a motley crew! There were midshipmen from all four classes, about twenty-five sailors, and two companies of the 8th Massachusetts from Marblehead and Salem—if I remember rightly—the one in blue uniforms, and the other in zouave costumes. I suppose these companies were selected because there were so many seafaring men among them. I know when we got outside the Capes, we found them very handy, below and aloft.

Just before weighing anchor, Dorsey, the colored steward, who was dear to us all, left the ship, quite broken-hearted. The poor fellow, who could not foresee that all his race were to be made free by the war, felt that the breaking up of the Academy meant additional years of slavery for him. His master, who we understood was not well off, had always generously permitted a large part of Dorsey's pay to go towards the purchase of his freedom, but a considerable sum was still lacking. After we reached Newport, Commodore Blake allowed each of us to subscribe a small amount, which was charged to our accounts, and this, with what he and the other officers gave, enabled Dorsey to rejoin us, a free and grateful man.

What seemed to afford Dorsey a little comfort at parting was the trust reposed in him by Lieutenant Scott, who handed him a quantity of bills and the money to pay them, saying, "Dorsey, we may never meet again, for we can't tell what will happen to us or the country. Please, when you get ashore, settle these accounts for me, and be sure to take receipts, because all people can't be trusted like you, Dorsey."

We started down the Chesapeake, towed by the steamer *R. R. Cuyler* and with the *Harriet Lane* steaming ahead. The latter did not go further than the Capes. Off the Jersey coast we passed over the ground where the *Constitution* was once so closely pursued by the British fleet that she barely escaped by resorting to kedging and towing with her boats.

In later years it has been a source of satisfaction to me to remember that I first saw the open sea from the deck of "Old Ironsides", and that I was on board when the last preparations were made to defend her from an attack. It was from this same anchorage, Annapolis Roads, that the *Constitution* sailed at the beginning of another war—the War of 1812— in which she won such renown.[4] The voyage she made this time was quite uneventful, the only incident I can recall being a sight of the *Niagara* as we went through the Narrows. She and the *General Admiral* were the two largest steam frigates in the world. We found at the Brooklyn Navy Yard two fine vessels of that type, fitting out for the blockade—the *Wabash* and the *Roanoke*.

We were a little disposed to regard ourselves, on our arrival in New York, in the light of returned warriors, and imagining others did the same, enjoyed the sensation hugely. But this dream was rudely dispelled, and we were intensely chagrined, when one of the illustrated papers came out with a picture which showed the 8th Massachusetts charging across the deck of the *Constitution*, driving the rebels over the rail, while we—the imprisoned midshipmen—peered anxiously up through the hatches of the deck below.

I think we must have received our allowance of spending money at this time—the sum of one dollar per month—for I remember our

---

[4] One of the references to the *Oregon* that I most value was that made by the Secretary of the Navy, when he spoke of her in an official dispatch as the *Constitution* of the modern navy. [Author's note]

hurrying in large numbers to the restaurants of lower New York, which we invaded like a swarm of hungry locusts. The months of wholesome but very plain fare at the Academy had given our appetites an extra edge. A dollar must have gone far in those days, or else people were kind in giving us its full value, for even after this raid on the restaurants, we were able to take a ride in the Broadway omnibuses, ending up with a visit to Barnum's Old Museum, which stood at the corner of Broadway and Fulton street. Among its other attractions it contained a theater, to which we at once obtained admission. The principal character in the play was a dashing highwayman, who rode and robbed in England, long before the United States or the Stars and Stripes were even thought of. Historical sequence was not a part of this drama, however, for when its exciting situations did not seem to stir the audience quite enough, a pretty actress, wishing to reassure a little fellow who was fearful about crossing a lonely heath, caught up a small American flag, and throwing it over his shoulders, cried, "Wear this! It will protect you anywhere!" Immediately there was an outburst of patriotism. The whole audience sprang to its feet, shouted, stamped, and cheered.

Sunday morning some one proposed going to hear Henry Ward Beecher, and after much noisy argument nearly all of us put our names down on the list as applicants for permission to attend the services at Plymouth Church. Five or six Southern boys, whose resignations had been sent in, said they would go with us, because they wanted to say when they reached home that they had seen "the accursed Abolitionist."[5] Plymouth Church had to accommodate such crowds that after the pews were filled, seats at their outer ends could be turned down, taking up the space in the aisles. These seats had been reserved for us, so that when Mr. Beecher reached his pulpit, he looked down at two lines of youngsters in blue jackets with brass buttons, and bright anchors on their rolling collars. Whether this addition to his congregation affected his sermon I cannot tell. I only know that I was in a state of patriotic ecstasy, wanting to cry one moment, and cheer the next. When we left the church, and fell into ranks outside, there was an awed silence. At last one of the Southerners said in a husky voice, "Well, fellows, I'm going South, all

---

[5] Henry Ward Beecher (1813–87) was the most influential American preacher of the mid-nineteenth century. During the Civil War, when it appeared that Britain might intervene on the side of the Confederacy, he crossed the Atlantic and "by his famous addresses did what probably no other American could have done to strengthen the spirit in England favourable to the United States, and to convert that which was doubtful or hostile" (*Encyclopedia Britannica*, vol. 3 [New York, 1911], p. 639).

the same. My people are there, and I still believe we are right, but you can bet your life I'll never curse that man again!"

Our shipmates, the soldiers of the 8th Massachusetts, had left us to rejoin their regiment, when we reached the Navy Yard, and the remainder of the first class were detached while we were in New York. On our arrival at our destination, Newport, Rhode Island, the second class was ordered to active service, and a few days later, the third followed. To our great indignation, we learned that we were to be kept—at any rate, until the new appointees were broken in.

At first it was intended to quarter us in Fort Adams, and for some months, though we continued to live on the *Constitution*, we did use the fort's casemates for recitation rooms, and had our infantry drill and artillery tactics on its parade ground, or just outside near the redoubt. As there was no sloop-of-war available for a practice cruise then, and there were not men enough to man a vessel of the *Constitution's* class, we remained that summer in Newport harbor.

In the meantime, the Government had secured the Atlantic House, which fronted on the Old Stone Mill park and Bellevue Avenue, and the beginning of the academic year found us quartered on its second and third floors. Lieutenant Rodgers, now become commandant of midshipmen, occupied rooms on the first floor, while some of the officers who were our instructors had quarters on the second. The *Constitution* had been warped into the inner harbor, and tied up alongside the Goat Island wharf. As two midshipmen had been appointed from each Congressional district for the new fourth class, she had to accommodate nearly two hundred. A little later in the autumn, the frigate *Santee* was sent to Newport, turned into a schoolship, and was moored just ahead of the *Constitution*.[6] By the next season we had as practice and training ships the sloops-of-war, *John Adams, Marion*, and *Macedonian*, which had been replaced on the blockade by vessels having steam power.

At first we used to drill in an open field a little way out on Catherine Street, and later, when the Atlantic House was filled with fourth classmen from the ships, in a larger field off Bath Road, back of the old Ocean House. Much of this ground is now covered by fine residences. Saturday forenoons we sent down spars on the *John Adams* or got the *Marion* under way, and occasionally, when she went aground, had to

---

[6] The *Santee* was laid down in the Portsmouth Navy Yard in 1820 but remained on the stocks until 1855. She was attached to the Academy for almost half a century, finally sinking at her wharf in Annapolis in April 1912. See Carroll Storrs Alden, "The *Santee*: An Appreciation," U.S. Naval Institute *Proceedings* (June 1913), pp. 761–77.

spend our precious Saturday afternoons getting her afloat. Our great gun drills took place on board ship, and our battalion drills on Goat Island.

This island was always particularly suggestive to me of the animal for which it was named, because of an allusion once made to it by a classmate, Prince Pierre d'Orléans. He was writing an excuse for some alleged misconduct in ranks, and began with this truly French construction, "As we were marching over to the Island of the Goat."

D'Orléans, or Pete, as we used to call him, was a grandson of King Louis-Philippe. His father, the Prince de Joinville, wished him to receive a naval education, and as this was impossible in France, during the time of the Second Empire, when all the Bourbons were in exile, our Government had given him permission to enter the United States Naval Academy. He graduated and became an ensign, but resigned soon afterwards. The overthrow of the Empire enabled him to return to France, only to be banished later by a decree of the Republic.[7]

If d'Orleans felt himself a prince in exile, it was never obvious. He neither asked nor expected any different treatment from that given to the other midshipmen. The only luxuries he allowed himself were two great eider-down pillows, and a very superior quality of chocolate, which was sent him from France. We approved of the chocolate; he distributed it generously; but the pillows, which could not be shared, were not looked on with favor. In fact, we felt that like Carthage, they "must be destroyed." To effect this, the class took a mean advantage of Pete's dread of getting demerits. He was very desirous of making a good record while at the Academy, and followed every regulation to the letter.

Evening study hours ended at half-past nine, and for the ensuing twenty-five minutes the corridors of the old Atlantic House swarmed with midshipmen skylarking in light attire. At the stroke of ten, every one was supposed to be in bed, and when five minutes before the hour the drum began to roll, Pete was always the first to make a break for his room and a dive for his bed. One night, while the accustomed frolic was going on, two midshipmen entered Pete's room, tucked the cherished pillows between the sheets, and cutting them open turned them wrong side out. Five minutes later, when the drum rolled, and Pete made his usual home run, he was followed by every member of the class. If he was surprised at

[7] Prince Pierre-Philippe-Jean-Marie d'Orléans, duc de Penthièvre, was born at St.-Cloud, France, on 4 November 1845. After the fall of the Second Empire, he returned to his homeland and lived in Paris and the Château d'Arc-en-Barrois. For another sketch of his Academy years, see Robley D. Evans, *A Sailor's Log: Recollections of Forty Years of Naval Life* (New York, 1901), p. 53.

this attention, he made no comments, but turning his back on the crowd, jumped into bed, and immediately vanished in a swirling cloud of feathers. Even the next day his room was like the center of a snow-storm, and for a week after the servants found employment in chasing the elusive bits of down.

D'Orléans took the loss of his pillows with philosophy. In fact, it is probable he could have borne the loss of many another thing more easily than that of the sense of equality, which enabled him to be the victim of such a jest. That he heartily enjoyed the feeling of being just a boy among other boys was very clearly shown by something that occurred later, during our second practice cruise. While we were in England, d'Orléans was given leave, with permission to rejoin the ship at Lisbon, where he was to visit some of his royal relatives. On our arrival in that port, the King of Portugal, attended by a large retinue, came on board, bringing d'Orléans with him. Pete broke away from his party as soon as he could, and was on his way forward, when he noticed a classmate standing near the mainmast, gazing at royalty, which was making its way along the quarter-deck. As a gentle means of attracting his friend's attention, Pete dealt him a vigorous kick in the rear, and then fled. There was at once a wild pursuit up one gangway and down the other. D'Orléans could easily have escaped by taking refuge with his party upon the quarter-deck, but instead he chose to be caught just where the mauling he received could be seen to the best advantage by the king and the scandalized courtiers.

The instructors of whom I have the clearest recollection during this period at Newport were Lieutenants Alfred T. Mahan and E. O. Mat-thews. Mahan, whose name has now an international reputation as an authority on all matters relating to naval strategy and sea power, was then distinguished as being the only graduate of the Naval Academy who had completed the course in three years. This distinction was later shared by a number of my date, and by a still greater number of the next, who, spurred by the hope of an early promotion, also secured their certificates at the close of the third academic year.[8]

[8] There was a difference, however. Mahan satisfied the requirements of the Academy's plebe (freshman) year curriculum by examination and entered directly into the third (sophomore) class. Although a number of wartime classes have been graduated ahead of schedule, the year or more that they have saved has come from the beginning, not the end, of the curriculum. Mahan remains the only person ever to graduate without experiencing a plebe year. He returned to the Academy to serve as an instructor of seamanship from September 1862 until October 1863.

Midshipmen G. T. Davis, F. A. Cook and C. E. Clark, before leaving the Academy for active service.

Mahan was of a reserved nature, and had a manner that was rather apt to make others feel that they had better keep their distance. I remember my sense of surprise, when I first noticed that he was inclined to favor me in such little ways as an officer could. For instance, on the practice cruise, when he was executive officer, I was released from all other duties during drill except the very easy one of standing near him, and repeating his orders on the gun and berth decks. This position of a sort of aide to him carried with it certain privileges about shore leave, which he assumed I was entitled to, and these practical evidences of kindly feeling inspired a very genuine attachment on my part.

Lieutenant Matthews was of a totally different stamp.[9] We midshipmen found him very companionable, and his only great fault in our estimation was his fatal ability. Languages, mathematics, or navigation—all were the same to him. If one of the regular instructors happened to be absent, there was no hope of missing the recitation. "Pat" Matthews not only could, but did, take the absentee's place. In spite of his intellectual attainments, he was very modest, and if he was ever found at a ball, it was usually behind a group of bashful youngsters, who listened with respectful attention and real enjoyment to his stories of the service. If we had not seen this side of him at Annapolis, we should have thought him a terror, when we were on our way up the Jersey coast in the *Constitution*. Indeed, he was the only officer I ever knew who actually threatened us with personal violence. I can see him now—he was almost diminutive in stature—brandishing a small tin deck trumpet, his thin voice raised into what he fancied was a roar. "Haul away now!" he would shrill. "Never mind looking aloft there! I'll do that, and you do the rest! If you don't haul, I'll break all your heads!"

Or on the gun deck, if he chanced to run against a crowd of us, it was "Gangway there! Gangway! Get out of my way, or I'll knock you all down!" and then as he pushed his way along, breathing threatenings and slaughter, we could see the back of his neck reddening at our affected alarm and only half repressed laughter.

At recitation he required not only correct but prompt answers. Delay, besides affecting the value of the mark, was apt to expose us to sarcastic comment.

"Mr. Clark," he asked me one day, "how do you take in a mainsail, blowing fresh? Promptly now!"

---

[9] A member of the USNA class of 1855, Edmund O. Matthews retired as a rear admiral in October 1898.

"Well, sir, I would man the main-clew garnets and buntlines—" a pause.

"Of course. Go ahead! Go ahead!"

"Yes, sir. Then I would slack off a little of the sheet, and then, then—I—"

"No use doing anything more!" he snapped. "By this time your mainsail's all blown to pieces!"

Such being his style, it may be easily imagined that the following episode was much relished by those who were in the section room at the time. The midshipman who was being questioned on this occasion was invited to consider himself officer of the deck of a full-rigged frigate like the *Wabash*, while "I," continued Matthews, "am her captain. We are walking up and down together, and all the officers except ourselves are two decks below. We are under all plain sail to t'gallant sails, the royals being in, and running ten knots before the wind. Now," with a rush, "I'm overboard! Quick! What'd you do?"

"Why, I'd set the royals, and try to make eleven knots!" was the reply, delivered without a moment's hesitation.

Matthews looked a little nonplussed, but before the general laugh subsided, he had recovered himself.

"Capital!" he cried. "Prompt and decisive! But now suppose it was your roommate who fell overboard! What would you do then?"

My roommates at the Academy during my second year on shore were Francis A. Cook and George Thornton Davis. We were congenial spirits with much the same ideas as to the relative value of study and such pleasure as could be found in a much regulated Academy existence. Our association may not have been profitable as far as our class standing was concerned, but it is pleasant to look back upon, and lasted through the years. Cook and I were comrades at the battle of Santiago, in which it is perhaps superfluous to mention he had command of the flagship *Brooklyn*, and received the surrender of the *Colon*. Davis, whose ill health obliged him to retire some time before the outbreak of the Spanish-American War, yet had the good fortune during our Civil War to be in the largest landing expedition ever organized by our navy, that is, the assault upon Fort Fisher, in which he distinguished himself, being the only regular officer to penetrate beyond the stockade.[10]

---

[10] See reports of Cushman and Parker, Naval War Records. [Author's note]

Chapter 3

THE FIRST CRUISE

We made our first real practice cruise, during the summer of 1862, in the sloop-of-war *John Adams*,[1] with Commander Edward Simpson as captain. We ran first into Gardiner's Bay, for a kind of shake-down, as the saying goes, and then sailed for Hampton Roads. There we felt that we were really in touch with the war, for General McClellan was then making his way up the Peninsula, and Fortress Monroe was a base of operations. The battle of Fair Oaks had just been fought, Norfolk taken possession of, and the once formidable *Merrimac*—after her defeat by the *Monitor*—had been sunk by the Confederates themselves, before making their retreat. We knew that some distance above our anchorage lay the wrecks of the *Congress* and the *Cumberland*, mute witnesses to the gallantry and endurance of our navy.

[1] The original *John Adams* was a twenty-eight-gun frigate built in 1799. Between 1826 and 1829 she was said to have been "converted" into an eighteen-gun ship sloop, but in reality an entirely new vessel was built. Some parts of the old ship may have been used in the construction. The second *John Adams*, designed by Joshua Humphreys, measured 126′6″ in length at 700 tons displacement and carried a crew of 125. A veteran of the Mexican War, she was used by the Naval Academy for the summer cruise of 1862. The following year she was sent to the South Atlantic Blockading Squadron, in which she served for the remainder of the war. Decommissioned in September 1865, she was sold in 1867. (Unless otherwise specified, data on U.S. and Confederate naval vessels has been drawn from the *Dictionary of American Naval Fighting Ships* [Washington, 1958–81]. For the *John Adams*, see also Howard I. Chappelle, *The History of the American Sailing Navy* [New York, 1949], pp. 344, 359.

The one had been burned to the water's edge, and the other had gone down with her flag still flying. Although I had not then read Longfellow's beautiful tribute to the *Cumberland*, I knew that the Prince de Joinville had said on seeing her mastheads, just showing above the surface of the water, "They ought to stand forever, a monument over the graves of the wooden ships!" And it seemed to me—I was even at that age a great lover of Greek history—that the spirits of the heroes who fought at "divine Salamis" must have inspired the defenders of the last of the "wooden walls."

To those who like to trace coincidences, the careers of two officers of the *Cumberland* will present some interesting features. They were Lieutenants Selfridge and Stuyvesant, who graduated at the heads of their respective classes at the Academy, and were on the gun deck of the *Cumberland* when she went down. Selfridge later commanded the *Cairo*. She was destroyed by a torpedo. Then he was sent to the *Conestoga*, and she was sunk by a ram. Stuyvesant became executive of the *Weehawken*, which was blown up by a torpedo while lying off Charleston, then of the *Wateree*, wrecked by an earthquake wave at Arica. After these experiences, they seemed to have exhausted their ill luck, fortunately for the service as well as for themselves.[2]

From Hampton Roads we proceeded to the anchorage off Yorktown, where we visited the fortifications and siege works, and also saw those of the Revolutionary period, and the headquarters of General Cornwallis. The field hospitals were crowded with the sick and the wounded brought back from the front. It was my first sight of the real horrors of war, and made a deep impression; the crowded condition of the hospitals, the heat, the swarms of flies, and the terrible suffering, which there were so few comforts to relieve. If war had its glories, here was the reverse of the medal.

From Yorktown we sailed to Port Royal, South Carolina, keeping outside the line of blockaders. In the Entrance, as the harbor is called, we found the old ship of the line *Vermont* and the steam frigate *Wabash*, the flagship of Admiral Dupont, and commanded by his chief-of-staff, our former commandant, C.R.P. Rodgers.

Returning north, the *John Adams*, a dull sailer, had the advantage of the Gulf Stream nearly all the way. We ran up Long Island Sound as far as

---

[2] Selfridge, class of 1855, retired in flag rank in 1898. He wrote the *Memoirs of Thomas O. Selfridge, Jr., Rear Admiral, USN.* Moses M. Stuyvesant, class of 1860, resigned his commission as a lieutenant commander in 1868.

Oyster Bay, which I particularly remember as the place where the *Great Eastern*—that first experiment in colossal shipbuilding—passed us.[3] We touched at New Haven, where we all went in a body to the home of Rear Admiral Foote, to pay our respects. He was then on leave, recovering from a wound received during his service on the Mississippi, where he had so greatly distinguished himself.[4]

After our return to Newport, we were granted a month's leave.

Our second practice cruise—a more extended one—was in the corvette *Macedonian*, in the summer of 1863. Our captain was Commander Stephen B. Luce, an authority on seamanship, as I have already remarked. We ran across the North Atlantic, making our first port at Plymouth, England, where we stayed several days. D'Orléans' father, the Prince de Joinville, visited the ship while we were there. He was a man of genial manners, and must have had a well developed sense of humor, for I remember his telling with considerable unction of an experience of Prince Alfred's, then a midshipman on board H.M.S. *Euryalus*. The throne of Greece offered to him had been declined, but his messmates, determined the occasion should not pass unmarked, constructed a diadem of tallow and slush, "and," ended the French prince, rubbing his hands gleefully, "they have mount him on a table, and have crown him King of Grease!"[5]

I dare say many things more worthy of recollection during our stay in Plymouth will be forgotten before the memory of her wonderful straw-

---

[3] At the time of her completion in 1858, the *Great Eastern* was four times as large as any other ship afloat. A double-hulled iron steamer designed and built by the English engineering genius Isambard Kingdom Brunel, she was 680 feet in length, displaced 32,160 tons, and could carry 4,000 passengers or 10,000 troops. More than forty years would pass before another vessel approached these dimensions. Unfortunately, the 4,000 passengers never materialized, and the only years in which the great ship covered her astronomical operating costs were those she spent laying the Atlantic cable, 1865–73. She was broken up in 1888.

[4] Commander of the Mississippi Gunboat Flotilla from August 1861 until April 1862, Rear Admiral Andrew H. Foote supported the Union army in the combined operations that broke through the defenses of the central Confederacy. The wounds from which he was convalescing when the midshipmen called on him had been inflicted by shell splinters during the attack on Fort Donelson. He never really recovered and died en route to assume command of the South Atlantic Blockading Squadron in June 1863.

[5] Alfred Ernest Albert (1844–1900), the second son of Queen Victoria and Prince Albert, was offered the crown of Greece upon the ouster of King Otto in 1862. The British government felt that it would be impolitic for him to accept this invitation, but a crown still lay in his future. Following the death of his uncle, Ernest II, in 1893, he ascended the throne of the tiny, central German duchy of Saxe-Coburg-Gotha.

berries and clotted cream. The bumboat women brought these dainties off to the ship in large quantities and never had any trouble in disposing of them.

From Plymouth we ran up the Channel to Portland, and later we went to Spithead. While at Spithead, I was given four or five days' leave to visit London, in company with Midshipman Nicoll Ludlow and the captain's clerk, Harris. Ludlow and I, having only money enough to make the trip, could not afford to purchase citizen's clothes, and were obliged to wear our uniform jackets and caps. We considered this quite an affliction, and were the more pleased to have Mr. Harris with us, as we felt that his years and frock coat gave an air of dignity to the party. We were to find, however, that our brass buttons were our best asset, and procured us an entrance to places that even a golden key would not have unlocked.

At Morley's Hotel, Trafalgar Square, where we took rooms, an elderly Englishman, who overheard us in the coffee-room making our plans for the day, became interested, and coming over to our table, entered into the discussion. Having a thorough acquaintance with London, he was able to lay out a schedule for us that was of the greatest value, and it was largely owing to him that we managed to see as much in our four or five days as many people do in a month.

Our little naval delegation had no idea of calling at the Legation, but the Secretary came to see us, and when we went in return to pay our respects to Mr. Adams, the Minister, he gave us cards of admission to the House of Commons. This was a privilege we had not looked for, but we were to be more fortunate still. We were passing through one of the corridors of the House of Commons, when a young Englishman, whose eye had evidently been caught by the American uniform, stopped us and introduced himself. He told us he was the nephew of a peer—Lord Castlereagh, I think it was—and if we wished to visit the Gallery of the House of Lords he would be glad to get us an invitation. He not only did this, but went with us to the Gallery and made our visit doubly interesting by pointing out the leading statesmen, such as Lords Palmerston. Russell, and Derby, and others whose names I do not now remember.

Of course we visited Madame Tussaud's Wax Works, and one of the relics there which greatly excited our interest was Napoleon's traveling carriage, captured at Waterloo. While we were gazing at it, a custodian invited us to crawl under the rope, and enter the coach if we wished. The seats were arranged to form a bed on one side, when swung about, and I remember wishing Will Rogers could me see, as I stretched myself out on the cushions where the great conqueror used to sleep.

We had another pleasant experience when we went to see Windsor Castle. We climbed the Round Tower there with a number of other people, and there was a general request for permission to ascend the Square Tower, which rose above it. This was refused, but as we were leaving with the others, a gentleman of military bearing, whom we had heard addressed as Colonel Albert, whispered to us to wait, and after the rest had gone, he would take us up the Square Tower. He said we were the first American naval officers he had seen in uniform at Windsor since the officers of the *Niagara* had been entertained there. This was after the laying of the first Atlantic cable by that ship and H.M.S. *Agamemnon*. From the top of the tower he pointed out Eton College, Runnymede, and the church made so famous by Gray's Elegy. His courtesy and kindness converted what might have been an ordinary sightseeing expedition into a living and happy memory.

We had a strong desire to visit the Arsenal at Woolwich, but when we went to the War Office with our request, the official to whom we applied said, "No, you will have to come to-morrow. Tuesdays and Thursdays are the only days visitors are admitted."

We told him that this was our last opportunity, for our leave was up the next day, and we had to return to our ship.

"Where is your ship?" he asked.

"At Spithead."

"Well," said he, after thinking a moment, "you'll have to know about these things some day, at any rate, so perhaps I had better let you go." He made out and signed two cards of admission for us, and we thanked him, and hurried off, but discovered on examining them, outside, that they referred to us as English subjects. We returned and told him of the error, and for a moment he was in quite a rage with us for having been the cause of it. When he finally paused for breath, we ventured to remind him that we had not taken advantage of his mistake, and then the wind veered, and the choleric old gentleman was disposed to give us so much credit for our honesty that we were quite embarrassed, for we perfectly understood that our American uniforms would never have passed unquestioned at the Arsenal. However, our partisan, as he had now become, declared that we should go now if it took a special order to the commandant, and he wrote one for us. Its presentation caused some little excitement and consultation among the officials there, but when they at last decided to admit us, it was in royal fashion, and the Arsenal was practically ours. Several officers were detailed to escort us, and we were frankly told that we must not attempt any sketches. In fact, that our escorts would be held responsible for seeing that we did not. Said one, "We are going to fill you so full of information, you won't know anything about what you have seen," and this was no idle boast. They even started the largest of their trip hammers for us, to show their enormous power, and then cracked filberts beneath them to show how delicately they could strike. It would have taken a trained head to carry away any connected ideas from the amount we saw, and it certainly would have been an ungrateful spirit that could have taken advantage of the more than courteous treatment that we had received both at the War Office and Arsenal.

Naturally, we went to St. Paul's Cathedral, and equally of course our first object of interest there was the tomb of Nelson in the crypt. It pleased us to remark that the "greatest sailor since the world began" occupied the place of honor, rather than the Iron Duke. When we mounted to the cupola to visit the famous Whispering Gallery, the custodian who accompanied us suggested, with a smiling glance at our uniforms, that he could give us an unusual privilege, which as we were used to climbing would not be likely to turn our heads. He then explained that the ball and cross that crowned the dome, at a height of four hundred and four feet above the floor of the cathedral, were being regilded, and if we cared to, he would allow us to climb up and touch the cross. It was not in the nature of boys to refuse such a chance, but I must confess that the experience I had had aloft on the *Macedonian* had not quite prepared me for what was before us. The ex-sailor who was carrying on the work, told us that a few weeks previous, when the Prince and Princess of Wales were married, he had set off fireworks from the cross. He then opened a window for us, and with somewhat cooling ardor, we began to climb by a dangling rope ladder over the eaves of the cupola, which seemed inhospitably trying to crowd us off. The ascent of the little ladder leading to the top of the cross was straightaway work in comparison, and the view of the city spread out at our feet was truly impressive, though the thought of the return trip robbed it of some of its charm.

Years afterwards, when I revisited London as a grizzled rear admiral, I was riding about the city with my family, on what my little grand-daughter called the "roof garden of an omnibus", and was doing my best to point out the places I had seen as a midshipman. A gentleman seated near us kindly undertook to help me, and as we drew near Ludgate Hill, he observed, "Now you will see St. Paul's." Then, as it came in sight, he spoke of the Whispering Gallery, and added that if we wished, we could climb into the cupola above the dome.

"Oh, yes!" I said, "but I have been above that."

With a look that said plainly, "You evidently do not understand," he pointed again to the dome, and remarked, "You can only go as high as those windows."

"But I climbed out of one," I persisted, "and went up above the ball,"—

I never got any farther with my explanation, for at this point he stopped the omnibus and departed, throwing me a glance in which incredulity and disgust were about equally mingled.

We ran over to Cherbourg from Spithead, and there a number of us were given leave to go to Paris. We could not have seen that fair city at a more opportune time. Louis Napoleon was then in the heydey of his fortunes, the empress was remarkable for her beauty, and the court and capital were the most brilliant in Europe.

Our hotel had two names and two entrances. The one fronting on the Rue St. Honoré bore the name of "St. James", while the other, facing the Tuileries, called itself the "Hotel de Rivoli", thus appealing equally to French and English patronage. The French side was most in favor with us, because there we had a fine position for observing the reviews of troops and whatever was going on opposite us at the Tuileries. Our uniforms and generally bad French attracted some attention as we went about, but there was no positive partiality shown us, as in London.

I had always regarded the French language as solely designed to harrow the feelings of midshipmen and to prevent them from securing a good class standing, and I can still remember the vague surprise I felt on coming into contact with it as a practicable tongue, and in finding that even *I* could make myself understood occasionally. This was quite encouraging, but any little pride I may have felt soon had a severe fall. One day, in a small restaurant on one of the boulevards, I fell in with several members of the junior class, who were in trouble. Mine host had charged them with a chicken, which they vowed had never appeared except in the bill. They appealed to me to interpret for them, and I was so flattered at being retained in the case, that I took the matter up at once. The more I talked, the wilder became the protests and gesticulations of the proprietor. At last an Englishman, who had been an amused witness of our difficulties, offered to mediate. The story goes—though I shall not vouch for the truth of it—that the Frenchman had for some time contended that he would rather lose the price of ten chickens than hear me talk French.

Of the sight-seeing that we did in Paris, I remember best one pleasant afternoon at the Invalides, where we all went in a body. At first there was a slight hint of frost in the air which we could not account for, until it occurred to one bright spirit in our party that the old Napoleonic veterans who acted as doorkeepers and guides, and seemed to be the molders of public opinion, supposed that we were Englishmen. When this misunderstanding was cleared up, there was a decided reaction in our favor. One of the repentant veterans even insisted on taking us to the Governor's office and presenting us to him. In the course of a conversation, pursued with some difficulty I must admit, one of our number happened to remark that although Americans, we came from an English ship; one that had been captured by the American frigate *United States*, during the War of 1812.[6] The old Governor immediately became enthusiastic, and was not satisfied until he had heard and recorded in a journal all we could tell him about the battle between the *United States* and the *Macedonian*. He himself went with us to the tomb of Napoleon, which was of course the main object of our visit, and pointing out an English flag that hung among the captured trophies, gave "perfidious Albion" such a broadside of invective, that it was evident Inkerman and Sebastopol had not sufficed to make him forget Waterloo.

It was somehow borne in upon us that the veterans were not loath to accept our franc pieces, and when it came to a survivor of the Old Guard, we felt we could not well offer him less than a crown. I suppose every old fellow turned seventy was run in on us, as a veteran of Austerlitz, Borodino, or Dresden. I do not remember hearing of any from Waterloo or Leipsic, however.

This tribute to valor caused a financial deficit in our party and necessitated the floating of a loan. Two or three of the midshipmen, whose parents were known to Mr. Dayton, the American Minister, and to some of the Paris bankers, contrived to raise several hundred dollars, which were used as a common fund. This enabled us to remain some days longer in Paris, and also got us into trouble with our captain. When we

[6] Thirty-eight years later, the gifted Doctor S. Weir Mitchell gave me a sheave-shaped box, with gold engraved plate, which bore the name *Macedonian*, saying he valued it greatly, and therefore took the more pleasure in presenting it to me. It had been given him sixty years before by Commodore Biddle, and was made of a splinter torn from the side of the *Macedonian* during the battle in which she was captured. [Author's note]

obtained our leave, he had advised us to buy return tickets, and then stay as long as our money lasted, as some of us perhaps would never have a chance to see Paris again. He thought he knew the state of our finances, but with this additional fund we managed to outstay him by a couple of days, and when we did return to the ship, our reception was not altogether pleasant. When we recalled his suggestions, he said we knew perfectly well what he meant, but to avoid further misunderstandings, he would keep us on board ship for the rest of the cruise. So my impressions of Cadiz and Lisbon, where we afterwards touched, were limited to what I could observe from the deck of the *Macedonian*.

While in Paris, we had seen several Confederate officers, who were either on leave from one of their cruisers, or had crossed the Atlantic in blockade runners, and were ready to join anything that might be fitting out. We recognized two or three of our former classmates among them and would gladly have renewed acquaintance, but their senior officer and our captain objected to our associating in any way. Rumor had it that the Confederate cruiser *Florida* had arrived at Brest, and as it was well known that the French harbors were much in use for the refitting of Southern men-of-war, it was natural that Captain Luce in such a neighborhood should feel it necessary to take every precaution. We realized this, even while we felt it a trifle hard that we were not allowed to speak to our old comrades.

As it turned out, neither the *Florida* nor *Alabama* was in European waters at that time, but their possible presence caused a great deal of speculation among the midshipmen, as to the results should one or both of them attack us during a calm, when their steam power would enable them to take an advantageous position. The *Macedonian* had eight 64-pounders and four 32-pounders on her gun deck and two 100-pounder rifled pivot guns on her spar deck. One of these last could be fired right ahead, and the other astern, while two of the 64s could be shifted forward to the bridle ports and two or three to the stern cabin ports. So we felt we could put up a stiff fight, even if the wind failed us.[7] We had fine officers, and Captain Luce could handle the *Macedonian* like

---

[7] Built as a thirty-six gun frigate at the Norfolk Navy Yard in 1832–36, the *Macedonian* was razeed (that is, her upper deck was removed and her freeboard correspondingly reduced) to become a twenty-four-gun corvette in 1852. She measured 164 feet in length and 41 feet abeam and, prior to conversion, displaced 1,341 tons. A member of Commodore Perry's squadron during his expedition to Japan (1852–54), she later served in the North Pacific, the Mediterranean, and the West Indies, ending her career as a practice ship at the Naval Academy (1863–70).

a yacht. Though probably better informed than we of the whereabouts of the enemy's ships, he must have done a little speculating too, for immediately after leaving Cherbourg, he had the royal poles cut off, and some other changes made to give the ship as much the appearance of an English one as possible. If I recollect rightly, we also ran up English colors on one or two occasions. Thus disguised, we might reasonably hope to lure an enemy near enough to pour in one or two effective broadsides at the start.

Late one afternoon, near Cape Finisterre, a steamer with braced-up yards overhauled us slowly, coming up astern. The captain may have had his suspicions of her, or he may have wished to startle us a little—he had a great liking for practical jokes. At any rate, he chose about the time when she might be reckoned on to overtake us, to exercise us at clearing ship for action, and going to night quarters.

After visiting the ports of Lisbon and Cadiz, we ran over to Funchal, Madeira. There, as a party of the unquarantined were leaving the ship, Lieutenant Mahan, seeing me standing near the rail, said with a friendly nod, "Don't forget to be back by sunset," and as I could not logically return without having gone, I waited for no further encouragement, but joyfully joined the others, and had a fine coast in one of the famous sledges of Madeira to add to my experiences.

From Funchal, we steered about southwest, until we struck the trades, and then for days we ran with all sail set, scarcely touching a brace. A storm and thick weather came on, as we neared Sandy Hook— or what we supposed to be Sandy Hook, for we had not been able to take observations for some days—and we ran to the eastward. I did not know—and probably no one else did—how far we were from the land, but as the gale was from the south, Long Island was a lee shore. It was our first experience in carrying sail to escape to windward, and we found it a very thrilling one. We were under reefed topsails, and once, when the ship laid over so far it seemed to us a question if she could right, Mahan, the first lieutenant, was about to slack the lee-topsail sheets, but Captain Luce, who must have known what she could do, and did not want to lose an inch of sea room, told him to hold on, and the good ship justified his belief in her.

We did not remain long in New York and when we left there for Newport, we were towed into Long Island Sound by the steamer *Freeborn*. As a dead calm fell with night, she kept on with us. We were proceeding smoothly, when all at once the silence was broken by a startling crash. A tall mast appeared out of the darkness, and stood for an instant, outlined against our cathead, and braced-up fore and fore-topsail yards. Then a sloop, her men struggling under the sail and falling hamper, scraped along our side, severing the *Freeborn*'s tow topes and cutting her clear. We rescued the crew of the sloop before she sank; and her captain, when asked why he was drifting about in that fashion, with neither lights nor lookouts, answered that he had seen the Sound boats go past, and supposing there would be no more steamers that night, had lashed the helm over, and one and all had gone to sleep.

We worked the *Macedonian* into the harbor of Newport during the midwatch, tacking repeatedly; everybody stood with the gear led out, ready to raise the clews and swing the yards, whenever the lookout on the jib boom end sighted the beach, and shouted "Hard a-lee!"

In spite of being dog-tired, we all felt a thorough sense of enjoyment of such a performance in seamanship. It was virtually the last experience of our academic careers, for our detachments sent by the Department were waiting for us on shore.

The new commandant of midshipmen, from whom we received our detachments, was Commander D. M. Fairfax. He was a Virginian, and it was said, when Virginia seceded, he remarked despondently to his wife, "Well, the State to which we both belong has gone out of the Union." She answered with spirit, taking both his hands in hers—"Donald McNeil Fairfax, we don't belong to any State! You belong to the whole country and I belong to you."

Fairfax was the officer sent by Wilkes on board the *Trent* to take off the commissioners, Mason and Slidell, and transfer them to the *San Jacinto*.[8] They were still on board the *San Jacinto* when she came into the outer harbor of Newport for coal in November, 1861, a fact in which we would have been much more interested if we had known at that time of the bitter feeling that would prevail, when England demanded their release a little later.

---

[8] When Captain John Wilkes took Mason and Slidell, the Confederate envoys to Great Britain and France, prisoner from the British mail steamer *Trent* on 8 November 1861, he precipitated a diplomatic crisis that was resolved only by their release. Fairfax, then executive officer of the *San Jacinto*, had advised Wilkes against the action. For the former's account of the incident, see "Captain Wilkes's Seizure of Mason and Slidell," in R. U. Johnson and C. C. Buell, eds., *Battles & Leaders of the Civil War*, vol. 2 (New York, 1884–88), pp. 135–42. Fairfax retired in the rank of rear admiral.

Chapter 4

ON BOARD THE *OSSIPEE*

After a short leave of absence, spent at home, orders came for me to report to the commandant of the Philadelphia Navy Yard for passage in the supply steamer *Bermuda*,[1] and on her arrival at New Orleans to report for duty on board the U.S.S. *Ossipee*, Western Gulf Blockading Squadron.

I found the *Bermuda* taking in stores. She had only three or four staterooms, and as already about twenty officers, including eight or nine of my class, had reported, her condition was not such as to induce us to take up our quarters on board until we were obliged to. We were temporarily in funds, having just drawn our advances, so we lived in luxury at the Continental Hotel, up-town.

Officers, when they joined a ship, were allowed to draw three months' pay, and could continue to draw what was due them, until the day of sailing, when the working out of the indebtedness began. This advance was very welcome to most of us, for we had just been promoted to the rank of acting ensigns, and new uniforms, swords, storm clothes, and numberless small articles had to be bought. The amount of money in hand—three hundred dollars—might have seemed more dazzling had

---

[1] A screw steamer of 1,238 tons, the *Bermuda* was captured under Confederate colors in the Bahamas in 1862 and served in the West Gulf Blockading Squadron from May 1863 until 1865. She was sold in September of the latter year.

we not known that recruits at that time often received bounties of a thousand dollars and more, to induce them to enlist.

I had pulled out a roll of greenbacks to pay a bill one day, when a classmate, just arrived, said wonderingly, "How did you come by that wad of money?"

"Drew it at the Navy Pay Office," I answered.

Learning that he could do the same by simply showing his orders, he demanded to be led at once to the El Dorado. His outfit had been provided by his father, and future needs did not concern him much. Life might be brief where we were going, so let it be a gay one, while the money lasted. He constituted himself paymaster for our party, and I was especially favored, as the one to whom he was mainly indebted for the bonanza. Afterwards, when our accounts were taken up on board ship, and there was some trouble in meeting the demands for mess and entrance fees, young Lord Bountiful announced that he would meet all obligations. He had not drawn any pay since leaving the Academy, and therefore must have over one hundred dollars due him. This statement caused a sensation, for we all supposed he must know he had overdrawn his account. Before we had time to enlighten him, the paymaster bounced out of his room, excitedly waving a paper.

"See here!" he shouted, "you say you have a hundred dollars due you? Why, man alive! You're two hundred in debt!"

"In debt!" echoed our Croesus. "How can that be?"

"Well, here's the endorsement right on your orders that you were paid three hundred dollars at the Philadelphia Pay Office."

"Was that my pay? Thunder and lightning! I thought that was bounty!"

Our trip south in the *Bermuda* was chiefly remarkable for its extreme discomfort, as we were packed into her about as tightly as sardines. I had my first sight of a Confederate flag just after leaving Pensacola, Florida, which was then in our possession. We had the town under our guns, held the Navy Yard, six miles away, and also the forts at the harbor entrance. The flag I speak of was flying from a small sloop, mounting a fieldpiece, or swivelgun, and captained by a sort of water guerrilla, named Duke. Three schooners loaded with coal, probably for the Navy Yard, had run rather close in shore to the westward, and Duke, noting this fact from his lurking place in the Perdido River, had slipped out, captured one of them, and was just boarding another, when we came upon the scene. We carried a very convincing argument in the shape of a nine-inch pivot gun, which adjusted matters in short order. The schooner was recaptured, and the sloop taken a few minutes later.[2]

On reaching New Orleans, I reported to Commodore H. H. Bell, and was ordered to continue down the coast in the *Bermuda*.

We found the *Ossipee* lying off Galveston, Texas, and I joined her late in the afternoon, the day before Thanksgiving. The *Bermuda* had brought fresh beef, potatoes, onions, and ice, to be issued in place of the salt beef or pork ration, and as I came off with the first boat-load I had a hearty welcome.

The *Ossipee* was one of the lately constructed, bark-rigged, screw sloops.[3] She was supposed to be high-powered, though I never knew her to make more than eleven knots under full pressure of steam, and with topsails, topgallant sails, and foresail set. She carried three pivot guns (an eleven-inch, a 100-pounder rifle, and a 30-pounder rifle) and eight broadside guns (six 32-pounders and two rifled 30-pounders). We thus had seven guns in broadside, and later, during the passing of Fort Morgan, with our starboard battery engaged, we fought nine guns, having shifted two over from the port battery.

The *Ossipee*'s captain was John P. Gillis, who while in command of the *Monticello* and the *Seminole* had acquired the title of "Fighting Gillis."[4] The executive officer was Lieutenant John A. Howell, who graduated at the head of the class of '54, was the inventor of the Howell torpedo, and afterwards, as a rear admiral, commanded the squadron off Matanzas and Havana during the Spanish War. He and the captain were the only regular line officers attached to the ship, until W. A. Van Vleck—a classmate of mine—and I joined her. The others were volunteer officers appointed from the merchant marine, but with two years' experience in the navy to their credit. The chief engineer, indeed, had once been in the regular service, though at this time he held merely an acting appointment. He used to say he had inaugurated two wars, for he was at Point

[2] James Duke's schooner *Mary Campbell* was captured on 14 November 1863. For a more detailed account, see *Official Records of the Union and Confederate Navies*, series 1, vol. 20 (Washington, D.C., 1894–1922), p. 674.

[3] The *Ossipee* was laid down at the Portsmouth Navy Yard in June 1861 and commissioned on 6 November 1862. She was 207 feet in length, 38 feet abeam, displaced 1,240 tons, and carried a crew of 141. After the Civil War she served in the Pacific, the North Atlantic, and the Far East, finally being decommissioned in 1889.

[4] Appointed a midshipman in 1825, Gillis reached the rank of captain after almost thirty-seven years' service in 1862. He retired in September 1864 and was promoted to commodore on the retired list in 1866.

Isabel, within sound of the guns of Palo Alto, at the beginning of the Mexican War, and was on board the *Pocahontas* off Charleston when Fort Sumter was attacked.[5]

He rather enjoyed telling of a command he had once had. It was a steam dispatch boat, or tender, which boasted an armament of two small brass guns, mounted on mahogany carriages. These guns, carefully tended and kept in the highest state of polish, had had names conferred on them, and were known as George Washington and Thomas Jefferson. Their muzzles had never been acquainted with the taste of powder, however, until one Fourth of July it was decided to fire a twenty-one gun salute. At the first discharge George Washington recoiled unexpectedly, and laying a determined course for the main hatch, ploughed over the coaming and disappeared. This was disconcerting, but orders were given to proceed. Thomas Jefferson, not to be outdone, joined George Washington in the hold, and the salute ended with two guns.

Another of the Chief's experiences, which he did not relate himself, happened while the ship was in New Orleans. The occasion was a dinner given by the wardroom officers to the captain, and as the latter was known to have a liking for a particular brand of port, the Chief went ashore to order a case. Rumor did say that the Chief, in his youth, had had a thorough and practical knowledge of all sorts and conditions of wine, and though for years his potations had been very moderate, it is always hard to live down an established reputation. He ordered the case of port and then, reflecting there might be some delay in sending it off, decided to take a couple of bottles with him, that the captain might run no chance of missing his favorite beverage. On reaching the levee, where there was the usual tangled mass of Mississippi steamboats, he climbed to the upper deck of one of them, and began waving to the *Ossipee* to send in a boat. He was so absorbed that he did not notice the steamer had cast off her moorings and backed into the stream. When this did dawn upon him, he made a break for the bridge, which at once became the scene of a heated interview between him and the captain. The latter, however, finally agreed that he would try to hold his ship in the current until the *Ossipee* could send off a boat for his unwilling passenger. The officer who

[5] The officer whom the author's sense of delicacy forbade him to name was James D. Adams. A native of Scotland, Adams entered the navy as a third assistant engineer in May 1847, resigned in the rank of first assistant engineer on 2 August 1862, and returned to the service as an "acting" (temporary) officer of the same rank ten days later. In January 1863 he was promoted to acting chief engineer, the equivalent of captain in the line, and honorably discharged in December 1867.

was pacing the *Ossipee*'s deck noticed the approaching steamer, and a handkerchief in energetic motion at her rail. He looked through his glasses, recognized a friend, and though somewhat surprised, pulled out his own handkerchief and returned the salute. As he made no further move, the Chief, to make matters clearer by recalling his mission, caught up the two bottles of port and waved them frantically. All was now understood. The officer-of-the-deck ran to the wardroom skylight, and thrusting down his head, shouted to those below, "Hurry up on deck, you fellows! Here's the old Chief off on the worst tear yet! He's hired a whole steamboat, and he's capering round the deck with bottle in each hand, just whooping it up! Hurry, or you'll miss it!"

They hurried, and feeling that the poor old Chief had at last irretrievably committed himself, there was a faint cheer, and much shaking of heads, when in final desperation he was seen to smash the bottles on deck, and tear wildly at his hair. He landed at a point some distance above the city, and got back to the ship, footsore and weary, to find the dinner over, and his character in sad need of rehabilitation.

Another of the volunteer officers in the fleet off Galveston, whom I recall very distinctly, was Acting Lieutenant Commander Bem. He was said to be a Hungarian, but I rather cherished the idea that he might be a Pole, and so possibly a relative of the illustrious General Bem,[6] whose great services to Hungary had made many forget the fact that he was Polish by birth. I was so fond of my fancy that I never asked Lieutenant Commander Bem whether he was related to the General. I was afraid he might say he wasn't.[7]

---

[6] When, as a small boy, I used to read rejoicingly of General Bem's escape from the Austrians, I was equally interested in the marvellous exploits of General Görgey, and often wondered if people were right in their condemnation of his final surrender to the combined forces of the Austrians and Russians. In 1906, happening to say before a member of the Hungarian Parliament that I considered Görgey's surrender entirely justifiable, owing to the hopelessness of further resistance in an open country, and against overpowering numbers, I was surprised indeed when he asked me if I would write a letter to General Görgey, repeating what I had said. It seemed almost incredible that Görgey, who led the Hungarians to victory nearly sixty years before, was still alive. [Author's note]

[7] The officer in question, naval registers being innocent of a Bem, must be Charles F. W. Behm, who was commissioned an acting volunteer lieutenant on 26 August 1861 and promoted acting volunteer lieutenant commander on 22 December 1864. Commanding officer of the sidewheel steamer *Cornubia* in the West Gulf Blockading Squadron from 17 March 1864 until the war's end, he was honorably discharged on 28 November 1865. According to the navy register he was a native of Pennsylvania.

Bem did not have the appearance of belonging to a family of heroes. He was so fat as to be almost unwieldy, and neither spoke our language fluently, nor understood it very well. We were told that one day, when his ship—a side-wheeler—was pushing up a narrow river in North Carolina, a sailor, putting his head into one of the paddle boxes, which made his voice seem to come from the opposite river bank, began to shout, in the most pitiful fashion, "Save me! Oh, save me! the Rebs are after me!"

Bem was instantly alert. "Yes, stop her!" he cried. "Lower ter boat to once quick, undt safe dot refugee!"

"Yes, hurry! Oh, hurry!" came the call from the bank. "Hurry, you chaw-mouthed, thick-waisted, Hungarian son of a sea cook!"

"Yes, mine cracious!" yelled the now madly excited Bem. "Hurry up! It iss sompoddy vot knows me!"

Captain Gillis was the officer next in rank to Farragut and Bell, although there were four or five ships in the fleet larger than the *Ossipee*. He was in command of everything west of the Mississippi, so we did not spend all our time at the Galveston station, although we did remain there once for a stretch of one hundred days, heading to the southwest current and rolling in the sea from the southeast, except when a norther came to our relief.

One trip we made was down the coast as far as the mouth of the Rio Grande, where a large number of English steamers were loading with cotton which had been carried across the river from Texas into Mexico; but as they kept well to the southward of the river's mouth and within three miles of the Mexican coast, we, of course, could not touch them.

Another time, on our way to Pensacola, we ran in to communicate with the senior officer off Mobile, Captain Jenkins of the *Richmond*. As this was at night, we had our distinguishing lights showing, burnt our signal number, and could see the vessels to the eastward repeating our flag number to the *Richmond*. In spite of all this, Captain Jenkins was determined that we should anchor until daylight. He excused himself afterward for this extreme caution by citing the case of Captain Preble, who had been dismissed for allowing the Confederate steamer *Oreto* to come close up to the line, and then run by. A blank cartridge was first fired in our direction, then a solid shot, and finally there was the threat of a broadside. Captain Gillis was furious, but could only comply with the signal to anchor, solacing himself with the retaliatory message, "Save your shot and shell for your enemies, and not for your friends, who you know cannot fire back."

Captain Jenkins came on board promptly the next morning, and I rather expected to see the fur fly, but the two captains went aft to the cabin quietly enough, where they may have had it out with each other, or else decided to bury the hatchet.

Galveston had been a name long associated in the minds of officers and men with defeat and disaster. Of our two vessels, the *Harriet Lane* and the *Westfield*, one was captured, and the other destroyed in its harbor, and their captains, Wainwright and Renshaw, and executive officers Lea and Zimmerman, had all been killed.[8] Just outside the *Hatteras* had been sunk by the Confederate cruiser *Alabama*. Even the brilliant capture of the armed Confederate yacht, *General Rusk*, so heroically conducted by Lieutenant James E. Jouett, ended ineffectively, for the fires he lighted to destroy her were afterwards extinguished by the Confederates.[9]

A few days before we left Galveston for New Orleans, we saw the blockade broken in broad daylight by a sailing vessel. The weather was slightly hazy, and as she had kept close to the land, she was nearly up to the South Battery before being discovered. Her captain, certainly a man of superb courage, had taken desperate chances, and was rewarded by success. We had five or six ships, and all ran in promptly, opening fire upon him. He kept close to the breakers, and in such shoal water that an attempt to ram him would have meant the loss of an armed vessel. The South Battery, Fort Magruder, and the Pelican Spit batteries opened on us, to cover him as much as possible, but I do not think our shots could have troubled him greatly. They were almost bound to be inaccurate, for the ships were rolling deeply in the trough of a heavy sea, running from the southeast. I was at the forecastle pivot gun at this time, and one of the training levers coming adrift, I nearly went overboard with it, in a violent roll of the ship. I had no idea until then that guns could be fought in such a seaway.

Soon after this Captain Gillis was detached, and Captain William M. Walker took his place. This officer had found there was quite a comfort-

[8] Both of these vessels were lost in a Confederate surprise attack on Galveston on New Year's Day, 1863. The *Harriet Lane* was captured by a boarding party from the "cottonclad" gunboat *Bayou City*. The *Westfield* ran aground while getting to sea, was set on fire to prevent her from falling into enemy hands, and exploded prematurely.

[9] The account of this episode is somewhat in error. Although Jouett set out to attack the *General Rusk*, his boat party, which was discovered before reaching her, boarded and burned the privateer *Royal Yacht* instead. For further information, see *Official Records of the Union and Confederate Navies*, series 1, vol. 16, pp. 755–58. Jouett retired as a rear admiral in 1890.

able revenue to be derived from the capture of blockade runners, and kept a sharp watch for them. One day, off Mobile, he went a step further and laid a plan to lure them out. He sent nearly all the ships under his command off in column to the southwest, hoping to persuade the enemy that an attack was to be made upon some Texan port, and that the coast would be comparatively clear for the cotton steamers, waiting behind Fort Morgan. It was planned, however, that our ships should turn as soon as they were below the horizon, and take their stations on two concentric arcs, so that any steamer running out would be seen about daylight.

Admiral Farragut was in Pensacola with both the *Hartford* and *Richmond*, and when word came to him of this manœuvre he was in a fever of apprehension lest the Confederate gunboats inside Mobile harbor should take advantage of the absence of so many vessels to overpower, or drive away, the few that were left on the blockade. This would mean that it was legally raised and could not be reëstablished until after sixty days. Farragut's flagship, the *Hartford*, was rushed away from the Pensacola Yard, where she was undergoing slight repairs, and the *Itasca*, commanded by Captain Brown, was sent out to order the offending cruisers to return to their stations. Rear Admiral Chester, then an ensign on the *Richmond*, says in his interesting account of this incident,[10] that at Brown's suggestion the Admiral had a few tons of soft coal tumbled on board the *Itasca*, and she went off, sending up a column of black smoke. As the blockade runners, unable to obtain anthracite, always used soft coal, black smoke was what our ships made for, whenever it was sighted. Consequently, it was only a matter of a few hours before Brown had all of Walker's ships corralled.

Captain Walker was at once sent for, to go on board the flagship, where he must have passed a very bad half hour. If the Admiral did not relieve him at once, I have no doubt that it was only because there was no other officer then available. That was his last performance at sea, and I never heard of his employment on any duty again.[11] When he returned

---

[10] Rear Admiral Colby M. Chester, "Chasing the Blockaders," *District of Columbia Commandery, Military Order of the Loyal Legion of the United States War Papers No. 94* (Washington, 1914).

[11] Captain Walker did not go to sea again during the Civil War, but by a curious coincidence he had just been assigned to command the sidewheel steamer *De Soto*, a vessel he had brought into commission in 1861, at the time of his death in August 1866.

from the *Hartford*, he was in a towering rage, and vented his wrath on Mr. Howell, the executive officer, for some neglect of duty, actually mine, but for which the executive was at least partially responsible. Howell, as soon as the captain disappeared, naturally fell upon me, but I was not disposed to accept the entire blame, and fortunately I had heard him refer some point in the matter to the chief engineer, merely to make sure of his ground, I suppose. So when he began some sarcastic remarks about my recent Naval Academy knowledge, I answered that not only did it fail to shed light on that particular point, but that I also had not had the advantage of instruction by the chief engineer. Howell looked at me for a moment as if he would enjoy licking me more than anything else in the world, but he was broad-minded, as well as broad-shouldered, and the matter ended there between us. This was not the end of my troubles, however, in connection with Captain Walker's strategic operations.

The *Ossipee* was for some time out of favor with the Admiral. He regarded—or affected to—every one on board her as members of a trust attempting to control the output of cotton. Having been sent over to the *Hartford* one day, with a requisition, I was told to go to the cabin, where Captain Drayton and Flag Lieutenant John C. Watson began to question me about the articles required. It was a little difficult for me to keep my mind on the business in hand, I was so interested in watching the Admiral, who was seated at his desk farther aft. I had never before had as close a view of this man, whom the *London Times* had spoken of as "the doughty Admiral, whose deeds in war had placed him at the head of the nautical profession upon the earth." So it was not surprising that I, who was not then of age, and expected soon to follow him into battle, should have been gazing at his strong, yet kindly face with admiration and affection. All at once he glanced in my direction, and broke in with, "Brass plate, eh? What's that for?"

"To cover the socket of the after eleven-inch pivot, sir," I explained, greatly pleased that he had spoken to me.

"There's nothing in the Ordnance Manual providing for that," he remarked.

"No, sir, but you see, on board the *Ossipee*—

"What?" he interrupted, "so that's where you come from, is it? There's a great deal too much brass already on board that *Ossipee*, young man!"

He ended his speech with a threatening gesture and a wave of his hand, as if to clear me out. Somehow, he did not look exactly dangerous, and I had to account to my own captain for the success of my mission, so I persisted. "But, Admiral, you see, Captain Walker—" The mention of that name finished my case. I suddenly found myself making for the companionway, hastened by the knowledge that my ears were to be cut off, pulled, or in some way sacrificed. This was the only marked attention I ever received from the great Admiral. Probably he only meant to let our captain understand that any request coming from him would be summarily dealt with. At any rate, when Commander William E. LeRoy relieved Captain Walker a few days later, the ban was removed.

I once heard a speaker at a banquet in Philadelphia refer to me as one of Farragut's eaglets, and was inwardly amused as I reflected that I might at least lay claim to having been pushed from the nest of the parent bird.

LeRoy, who was afterwards Admiral Farragut's chief-of-staff during his European cruise, was a perfect example of a gentleman of the old school.[12] Once, when he was about to ram an enemy's ship, an officer remarked to another, standing near him, "There goes Lord Chesterfield at the Reb. I'll wager he's getting ready to apologize now for being obliged to hit him so hard."

The term Lord Chesterfield could only be applied to LeRoy's deportment, for his disposition in no way resembled that cold diplomat's. I remember once, when he saw an inferior contemptuously treated, hearing him say, with a fine scorn, "Sir, in my opinion, a gentleman is one who is a gentleman to everybody."

In spite of this broad view of good breeding, LeRoy was quite a stickler for convention, and his feeling in this respect was often severely tried by the bearing of a good-natured but poorly trained servant whom he found in the position of cabin boy, when he took command of our ship.

"Do you know," he would say, appealing to the general sympathy, "That worthless fellow Tripp will drive me distracted. Why, I can't thank him when he helps me to put on my coat, or hands me a glass of

[12] William E. Le Roy reached the rank of commander in July 1861, after twenty-nine and a half years' service. Although this seems like a long time, it was not unusual by prewar standards. Thereafter the pace of his advancement accelerated. Promoted captain in 1866 and commodore in 1870, he became a rear admiral in 1874, in which rank he held command on both the South Atlantic and European stations. He retired in 1880 and died in 1884.

water, but he strikes an attitude and says, 'You are entirely welcome, Captain LeRoy.'"

The climax came when Tripp, who was to be sent north for discharge, asked for a letter of recommendation. The captain was genuinely perturbed. "Good heavens!" said he. "Suppose I give him a letter such as he wants, what is his employer going to think of *me?*"

When the detachment to which Tripp belonged was mustered, before leaving the ship, LeRoy came on deck, nervously handling an envelope. As he motioned Tripp to his side, some one near me was heard to observe that "the skipper must be putting up a job on Tripp, to judge from his guilty expression."

"Tripp," began the captain, "you asked me for a letter, and I am giving you this. I have done the best I can for you, but remember, you must not open it until you reach New York."

A few weeks later, the captain's steward received a letter from Tripp, in which he said that there was no recommendation in that envelope, but he did find a fifty-dollar bill. It must be added here that LeRoy had little beside his salary.

Among other mannerisms, our captain had a bow that was so very low and sweeping, it was suspected he took much secret satisfaction in it. The deepest one I ever saw him make, however, I am sure gave me more pleasure than it did him. We were at quarters, one day, firing at a stranded blockade runner in order to prevent the enemy from landing her cargo. Suddenly, from a battery on shore, came the screech of a projectile. It came as if it meant business and was evidently headed straight for me. I instantly doubled up like a jackknife, and just as quickly came the feeling of anger and shame at the exhibition I must be making before all hands, from my elevated position at the forecastle. As I straightened up, I stole a covert glance aft, to see if the captain had by any chance failed to observe me. To my enormous relief, I saw he too was slowly getting back to the perpendicular, and I heard him say to the executive officer, "By Jove, Howell! that was an awfully close shave! That confounded thing only went about a foot clear of our heads."

I had no mind to question the captain's claim, but the words were hardly out of his mouth, when a wild Irishman stationed in the gangway midway between us shouted, "Begorry, b'ys, I cud have caught thot in me hat!"

The fate of the vessel we were firing at was settled a night or two later by Flag Lieutenant Watson, who boarded and practically destroyed her, setting fire to everything that the enemy might use. There was no force to oppose him, so the conflict he was prepared for did not take place. [13]

[13] John C. Watson was Farragut's personal aide and was with him in all his battles. He was the officer who threw a line about the Admiral, when he sprang over the rail and outside the mizzen rigging just as the *Hartford* struck the *Tennessee*, at that moment so well shown in the painting, "An August Morning with Farragut."

It was the second time during the battle that the Admiral's activity and absolute fearlessness had caused this precaution to be taken. On the first occasion, it was Quartermaster Knowles who at Captain Drayton's suggestion followed Farragut up the main rigging, which he climbed almost to the top, in order to be able to see above the smoke. Though protesting at first, he finally allowed Knowles to lash him to the rigging, when it was pointed out to him that a wound not necessarily fatal might yet be enough to make him lose his footing and fall overboard. This is mentioned here, because the two incidents have occasioned some confusion, and a good deal of discussion as to who really lashed Farragut to the rigging at Mobile. [Author's note]

Chapter 5

WITH FARRAGUT AT MOBILE

It was the morning of August fifth when we fell into line to pass the forts and attack the Confederate fleet at the entrance of Mobile Bay. The Admiral had inspected our ship a few days before. He had shown particular anxiety to have the guns trained as far forward as possible, and when the eleven-inch pivot gun had been trained forward until it was almost against the side of the port, he was still not quite satisfied, and in his impetuous fashion, again called, "Haul away!"

"But if it's fired in that position, it's liable to blow away the main chains, Admiral," objected the officer in command.

"Well, blow them away, then! Any way to get a shot in first thing!"

The eleven-inch pivot did not belong in my division, but I overheard this remark of the Admiral's because, with a desire to keep as near him as possible, I had joined the little group of officers following him about the ship. A look of recognition in his eye as it happened to glance in my direction almost tempted me to say, "That gun would have trained easier, Admiral, if you had allowed us the brass plate for the socket," but the captain and executive were both standing near, and I did not have the courage.

In my own division I had four guns—the forecastle pivot, two 30-pounder rifles, and one 32-pounder, which was under and just abaft the forecastle.

The *Brooklyn* led the line that memorable morning, the *Hartford* second, with Farragut's blue pennant at her mizzen. The *Ossipee* had sixth place, there being only one ship after her. All our ships had their largest flags floating from peak, staff, and every masthead. From my position on the forecastle, I counted nearly sixty. It was a beautiful and inspiring sight. The monitors were to starboard of the line of ships and a little in advance, the *Tecumseh* leading and opening the ball. The plan was for each ship to keep a little on the starboard quarter of the next ahead, until nearly up to the forts and batteries, so as to get into action at the earliest possible moment.

The forecastle pivot was the first gun fired on the *Ossipee*, and a moment later another of my guns in the bridle port let go. The men aft began cheering as wildly as if we were putting down the Confederacy, then and there. When one of our leading ships sheered a little and poured in a whole broadside, there were cheers for the *Brooklyn, Richmond*, or whichever vessel it was. All at once, an officer who had climbed into the rigging, called out something about the *Tecumseh*. Those below, catching only the name of the ship, started another cheer, but Mr. Howell, waving his trumpet, shouted "Great heavens, men! Are you cheering, when your own companions are lost?"

Some one has well described the moment when, after the sinking of the *Tecumseh*, Farragut took the lead:

"One ship is gone, but the wooden walls
    Defy the walls of stone,
And proudly steaming past, give back
    The greetings fiercely thrown.
Beyond, their ships and iron-clad
    Loom in the dawning gray,
But Farragut is leading us,
    And we shall win the day."

I believe the statement has been made that the fire of Fort Morgan and the water batteries slackened when the *Brooklyn, Hartford,* and *Richmond*, with their powerful broadside batteries, were just opposite, but if this were so, they had certainly recovered by the time we came along. Before we fairly got into action, our smokestack guys were shot away, and when I remarked upon this to our game little boatswain, Mr. Milne, he shrugged his shoulders, and said, "That doesn't trouble me. The engineers will have to attend to it."

"How about that?" I asked, as a shot struck the forestays. He became very vehement then about the appearance they would make when spliced. I thought, myself, we had come off very luckily, for one stay, entirely cut through, was only held by the snaking, while of the other but a single strand remained, and this was all that kept the whole length of them from crushing down upon us, on the forecastle.

Our consort, the gunboat lashed to our port side to carry us through, if disabled, was the *Itasca*; her commander that same George Brown[1] who had once decoyed our ships with black smoke. As we approached Fort Morgan, Brown began firing to the westward, over towards Dauphin Island, and Captain LeRoy shouted to him from the bridge, "Do you think, Brown, you're going to reach Fort Gaines from here?"

"No," was the answer, "but I can add to the smoke and bother Fort Morgan for you."

A little later, a shot that came through our side, just at the angle of the deck and waterways, sent a lot of splinters flying, and one of them landed on board the *Itasca*, striking Brown on the leg. Fortunately the flat side hit him, so he escaped with only a painful bruise. LeRoy saw him jumping about the bridge, and called out, "Did one of those splinters hit you, Brown?"

"Well, you might call it a splinter on board your big ship," returned the aggrieved Brown, "but over here, it ranks as a log of wood."

The smoke lifted a little, as we were passing the water batteries, and their men could plainly be seen, frantically loading and training the guns. Our fire at point-blank range must have confused them somewhat, for they only succeeded in hulling us a couple of times with nine or ten-inch round shot. Even with this small percentage of hits, however, the casualties at our Number 5 gun were enough to silence it for a time.

Just after we passed the forts, the ironclad *Tennessee*[2] came out of the smoke on our starboard bow. Before I could report her, the captain and Mr. Howell had taken in the situation, and a critical one it was. It seemed to me there was really no escape for us. Howell, who was on the

---

[1] Lieutenant Commander George Brown, USNA 1855, retired as a rear admiral in 1897 and died in 1913.

[2] The *Tennessee* was the flagship of Rear Admiral Franklin Buchanan and the only ironclad in his squadron. One of the largest warships built by the Confederacy, 209 feet in length and 48 abeam, she displaced 1,273 tons. Her casemate, which mounted two 7-inch and eight 6-inch guns, was protected by six inches of armor on the forward section and five inches on the broadside and stern. Like every Southern ironclad, however, she was seriously underpowered and slow to answer her helm. Her best speed, fully laden, was six knots.

bridge, shouted to the captain, "shall we port, and ram?" but LeRoy, who was aft, coolly answered, "No, steady! I think we'll go clear."

That question having been officially settled, and as none of my guns would bear until the *Tennessee* came farther aft, my attention centered on a big rifle gun that was projecting from her bow, the hole in it looking ominously large. The projectile, when it came, raked our berth deck and as the big ironclad was almost alongside by that time, we returned it with the muzzles of our guns depressed, but I imagine all our shot simply struck her casemate and bounded off. I was glad to see that she had the rammer in one of her broadside guns, and could therefore only give us one more in passing. It fortunately missed the boilers, going through just forward of them. Her stern gun, which could have raked us, was not fired, and Lieutenant Wharton, the officer who was training it, told me afterwards that the primers failed. Our narrowest escape was from a ten-inch shot that grazed our main steam pipe, tearing off the fearnaught and wooden battens in which it was encased.

Our ships having run up the bay, beyond the range of the forts, several had anchored, and their captains were preparing to go on board the flagship. I believe the thought had come to many of us—and it was not a comforting one—that the *Tennessee*, which had proved that she could fight her way through our fleet from van to rear, might, when darkness fell, steam up into our midst, and while we were hampered by the fear of injuring our friends, she would feel free to ram and fire in any direction. We learned afterwards that Farragut, fully aware of the advantages his enemy would have in a night battle, had determined, after a short respite, to attack the *Tennessee*, even though it had to be under the guns of Fort Morgan. The gunboat *Morgan* was still with her, but we had destroyed the *Gaines*, and the *Selma*[3] had been captured after a running fight with the *Metacomet*, commanded by Captain Jouett, the officer who had boarded the *General Rusk* at Galveston.

Those of us who did not know of Farragut's decision were still wondering what was to come next, when all uncertainty was ended by Admiral Buchanan, who resolved to attack at once. When it was seen that the *Tennessee* was steaming back up the bay, Farragut hoisted his famous signal, "Run down the enemy's principal vessel at full speed." The distinguishing pennants of three ships followed this signal, the

---

[3] The *Tennessee*'s three consorts, little sidewheel steamers mounting four to six guns each, were no match for the vessels of Farragut's squadron. The *Morgan* escaped up the bay to Mobile.

David Glasgow Farragut.

Monongahela's, the *Lackawanna*'s and our own. Farragut, after referring to the signal in his detailed report, calls the combat that followed, "One of the fiercest on record."

The first to attack was the *Monongahela*. I saw her strike the *Tennessee* going at full speed, and then pass on, her bow badly crushed. The *Lackawanna* made the next attempt, dashing against the ironclad with a force that it seemed must fairly ride her down, but the *Tennessee* shook her off as a baited bull might one of the dogs tormenting him. Then the grand old *Hartford* rushed at her, but the blow was a glancing one, and broadsides were exchanged with the muzzles of the guns almost touching. The guns of the *Hartford* went off at less than two-second intervals, a salute never to be forgotten.

The monitor *Chickasaw*, Commander Perkins, had been dogging the *Tennessee* everywhere, battering her casemate at close quarters. Her colors had been shot away, and as the *Richmond* or the *Brooklyn* passed, letting go a whole broadside, overboard went her smokestack. In the rush, as the ships were circling about, the *Lackawanna* struck the *Hartford*, cutting her down almost to the water's edge. We were then preparing to ram, but our captain, fearing the *Hartford* might go down altogether, was about to check his ship to go to her assistance, when the Admiral, who was storming at the rail, observed his intention, and waved him on. We were pointed straight for the *Tennessee* with throttle wide open.

All at once, I saw an officer with a white flag appear above her casemate. Facing about, I started aft, shouting "The ram has surrendered! She's showing a white flag!"

Perhaps the captain and executive saw this as soon as I did, but it was my duty to report anything ahead, and I was, of course, excited. As I ran forward again from the break of the forecastle, I heard our boatswain, Mr. Andrew Milne, calling to the Confederate officer, "Put your helm to starboard!" This direction, if complied with, would have thrown the *Tennessee*'s stern off, and made the blow a glancing one. Seeing that the officer either had not heard, or did not understand, I repeated, "Put your helm to starboard!" adding, "Ours is to port!"

He answered, "I cannot. Our wheel ropes are shot away."

So it happened that I was the first to communicate with the enemy's flagship, when she surrendered at the close of America's greatest naval battle.

The order to back our engines and put the helm over had been promptly given and obeyed but it is doubtful if there was time for the *Tennessee* to have aided in averting the collision. Our captain and executive reached the forecastle just as the ships struck, and began to swing alongside. It seemed to me as if the whole ship's company were on deck by that time. They came swarming up from below, wild with excitement. An Irishman from the fireroom, in a perfectly frenzied state—and little else—dashed forward, yelling, "Board her! Board her!" I caught him by his undershirt, knowing if he leaped the rail, he would slide down the slope of the casemate and be crushed between the two ships, and with some assistance, dragged him back and down on deck.

As soon as order could be restored, Captain LeRoy hailed, and asked, "Do you surrender?"

The officer answered, "Yes, we surrender. This is the Confederate States ship *Tennessee*. I am the commanding officer. Admiral Buchanan is wounded."[4]

Captain LeRoy replied, "This is the United States steamer *Ossipee*. I accept the surrender for Admiral Farragut."

We lowered and sent over a boat for the Confederate captain. As he came on board, he was nervously handling his sword, but LeRoy, ignoring this, shook him warmly by the hand, and said in his cordial way, "My poor fellow, have a glass of ice water. You see, my steward has it ready for you. Wasn't it fortunate our supply steamer came in a day or two ago?"

The other bowed his head to hide his emotion, and taking LeRoy's arm, the two went aft to the cabin.

In arranging to take over the surrendered *Tennessee*, Captain LeRoy, so habitually thoughtful and considerate of others, did a great wrong to Lieutenant Howell, which he immediately and deeply regretted. To that officer naturally belonged the honor of taking possession of the ram, and no one had as much reason as LeRoy for feeling that he was highly deserving of it. At the moment of sending off our boat however, other vessels were closing in, and in the haste and excitement LeRoy, seeing Acting Lieutenant Girard standing near, asked him to go over and take charge. Girard, a zealous officer, was not a regular member of our ship's company. He had been very desirous of coming in with the fleet, and having received permission from the Admiral, had applied to LeRoy to be taken aboard the *Ossipee*, where he had not been assigned to any duty. When questioned afterwards about this matter, LeRoy said he knew that

---

[4] The *Tennessee* was surrendered by Buchanan's flag captain, Commander James D. Johnston. He and Le Roy were old friends. For Johnston's account of the action, see "The Ram *Tennessee* at Mobile Bay," in *Battles & Leaders of the Civil War*, vol. 4, pp. 401–6.

our ships had drifted down nearer the forts, and fearing the battle might be renewed, he felt that Mr. Howell could ill be spared from the *Ossipee*. He acted on this thought before other considerations had entered his mind.

Our temporarily crazed fireman was not the only one who became drunk with the excitement of battle. An acting officer commanding the tug *Philippi*, whose application to accompany the fleet past the forts had naturally been rejected, suddenly decided after the other ships were well on their way, that he would force the passage alone. The audacity of this proceeding was so great that he was some distance up the channel before the garrison at Fort Morgan realized what he was trying to do. Then the gunners began to pour fire upon what they doubtless supposed was a laggard. Of course his little craft was quickly obliterated, and as might have been expected from such an idiot, he neglected to throw his signal book overboard. Having it in their possession, the enemy could read every signal made while our fleet was in the bay. To those who have never seen a signal book, it should be explained that its sides are faced with sheet-lead plates, heavy enough to sink it instantly, and it is understood by all nations that it is the one thing a conquered foe may destroy, when resistance has ceased, and forbearance is expected.[5]

The *Morgan*, the only Confederate vessel that had escaped destruction or capture, and which had taken refuge under the guns of Fort Morgan, slipped away in the night, and keeping well over to the eastward in shallow water, reached Mobile in safety.

Grant's Pass, a shallow entrance to Mobile Bay from the west, had depended for its defense upon a small fortification in midchannel, which must have been built on piles, and was called Fort Powell. It had withstood repeated attacks from our light-draught gunboats in Mississippi Sound, and our prisoners from the *Selma* and *Tennessee* were confident of its ability to hold out. We were now behind it, however, and the small garrison soon learning what it meant to be shelled from the rear, it was abandoned and blown up during the night. This not only opened a door for us to receive supplies, but cut off the solitary chance of escape for the garrison of Fort Gaines on Dauphin Island. A Union force under General Gordon Granger had landed to besiege this fort, and as we too could easily reach it with our guns, Colonel Anderson, who was in

---

[5] For these antics, the *Philippi*'s commanding officer, Acting Master James T. Seaver, was court-martialed and sentenced to be dismissed from the service. For details, see *Official Records of the Union and Confederate Navies*, series 1, vol. 21, pp. 505–7.

Ossipee.

command, recognized the hopelessness of the case, and surrendered with over eight hundred men.

This left only Fort Morgan to be dealt with, and accordingly our troops were landed on Mobile Point, in its rear. As their flanks could be protected by our ships, and any attack upon their rear fully guarded against, the reduction of the fort was only a question of time. The troops were backed by heavy guns, which were landed on the Point. A number were sent from the ships, in charge of Lieutenant Tyson of the *Hartford*. The soldiers ran zigzag trenches up towards the fort, and the riflemen, to protect themselves while shooting, placed sandbags in pairs a few inches apart, with a third bag on top, on the edge of the trench towards the enemy. Pushing their rifles through the openings between the bags, they were able to pick off those of the garrison who ventured to show themselves in an embrasure, or above the parapet. During the last few days of the siege, these approaches were carried close up to the ditch of the fort.

By keeping low in the trenches, operations could be observed with reasonable safety, and a number of officers from the fleet landed for this purpose. One of them, Acting Ensign Charles Putnam, had been a former shipmate of ours on the *Ossipee*. He used to tell of an instance which showed the sharpshooting was not confined to one side. A soldier near him in the trenches confided that he was after a marksman in the fort who had been sending bullets into his particular aperture with unfailing regularity. "I've just fired, so he's got the turn on me now," said the soldier, "but after he's had it, he'll have to take to cover, you bet!" He had hardly finished his sentence when a bullet came singing through the orifice, and on the instant he bent forward, sighting his rifle, but almost as quickly fell back with another bullet through his cheek. The idea that his adversary might employ a partner in this little game had not occurred to him.

The commander of Fort Morgan was General Randolph Page, formerly an officer in our navy, where he had been known as "Ramrod" Page.[6] He put on a bold front during the siege, but one of his assump-

---

[6] Page's first name was Richard, not Randolph. He entered the navy at the age of fourteen in 1824. By the time the secession of his native Virginia led him to resign his commission, he had reached the rank of commander and become recognized as one of the navy's foremost ordnance experts. From June 1861 until May 1862, he was ordnance officer at the Norfolk Navy Yard. He then established the ordnance and construction depot in Charlotte, North Carolina, which contributed greatly to the Southern war effort. In March 1864 he was detailed to command the outer defenses of Mobile Bay, and though already a commander, CSN, was given the additional commission of brigadier general, CSA. He was a first cousin of Robert E. Lee.

tions amused us greatly. Admiral Farragut one day sent in a flag of truce, asking for permission to despatch some of our seriously wounded men in the *Metacomet* to Pensacola, where they could be cared for in the hospital. General Page humanely acceded to this request, but also stipulated that the *Metacomet* should return at once from Pensacola, since he regarded all the ships in the bay as his prizes and the crews as his prisoners. We did not use the expression "bluff" in those days, but this was certainly a superb instance of it.

On August 22, the army was ready to open with its batteries, and several ships—the *Ossipee* among them—took position in Bon Secour Bay to assist in the bombardment. At this time I was in command of the quarter-deck division, Lieutenant Chew, who had formerly held that position, having just been promoted to that of navigator. We expected to be more severely punished than on the fifth, for then the ships had simply run past the batteries, while we knew that the Admiral meant to make this a stand-up fight to a finish. To our surprise, the guns of the fort, on this occasion, did comparatively little execution. Either the fire from our ships and shore batteries combined was overpowering, or else the Northern sharpshooters may have made it almost impossible for the Confederates to work their guns. At night our ships ceased action, but as a fire which had broken out in the fort made it a glowing mark, the shore batteries kept on more furiously than ever. There was an inside work, called the citadel, which was completely burned out, and the garrison, unable to extinguish the flames, was forced to retire into the casemates. The column of fire, rising straight up toward heaven, and the flashes and roar of the guns made the scene an appalling one, and as I watched it from the deck of our ship, I wondered what means the poor fellows in that inferno could take to communicate with their enemies, had they wished to surrender. In the morning, a white flag waving from the ramparts bore witness that the last of the fortifications that had guarded Mobile Bay, and formed the first line of defenses for the city, had fallen.

The consideration that would have been shown the vanquished was at first withheld, when it was found that they had spiked their guns, and that General Page and several of his officers had either broken their swords, or thrown them into the fort's well. The commander of the *Lackawanna*, Marchand,[7] had been a former shipmate of the general, and had asked permission of Admiral Farragut to take him as a guest on board his ship, until the prisoners were sent north, or to New Orleans; but learning of this violation of the laws of war, he said, "Admiral, if you

---

[7] For a sketch of Marchand, see the introduction in Craig L. Symonds, ed., *Charleston Blockade: the Journals of John B. Marchand, USN, 1861–62* (Newport, R.I., 1976).

send General Page to me now, I shall put him in irons in the coal bunker."

This feeling of indignation gradually wore away. At least I never heard that the Fort Morgan prisoners were subjected to any unusually rigorous treatment.

This period of stirring action was followed by a little outside cruising and another tour of blockading duty, at our former station off Galveston. We then returned to Mobile Bay. Its upper portion was still held by the enemy, but as we were in possession of the entrance and the anchorage inside, no great exercise of vigilance was required, and the men had little to occupy them. It was rumored that when the Northern troops departed, after the fall of Fort Morgan, they had been obliged to leave behind them several barrels of commissary whiskey, which they had buried, for safe keeping, behind one of the sand dunes on the Point. The grog ration had been lately abolished in the navy, and the anxiety our sailors displayed to get ashore and dig for that whiskey was only equalled by the energy and perseverance with which they spaded up every place that looked at all promising. Their weary and dejected air when they returned from these excursions was sufficiently good evidence that the treasure had not been found.

Captain LeRoy actually made use of this devotion to the "demon Rum" to improve the religious tone of the ship. It was his custom to read prayers in the evening when, the crew having been called to stand by their hammocks, he was sure of having two long lines of quiet, if not very attentive, listeners. But on Sundays, when the quarterdeck was transformed into something like a chapel, and the bell was tolled, the captain was apt to read the service to almost empty benches. One afternoon, remarking a crowd of eager faces in the starboard gangway, he asked Mr. Howell what it was the men wanted.

"Oh, they're wild to get their names down on the liberty list so they can be off to the diggings," explained Howell.

"Indeed!" said LeRoy. "Well, Mr. Howell, will you please only allow those to go who came to church this morning?"

The next Sunday he read to a full congregation.

During the last few months of the war, the men accepted by the recruiting officers, or those for whom the government paid bounties, were often physically weak or too aged to be serviceable. One day a draft of men came on board the *Ossipee* to fill vacancies, and our captain, recognizing one of them, exclaimed, "Well, if there isn't old Paul Jones! How could they have allowed him to leave the Naval Asylum? Why, I remember his being called 'old Paul Jones' when I was a midshipman!"

As some occupation had to be provided for this ancient mariner, Mr. Howell made him captain of the starboard watch of the afterguard, a position which gave him little to do, but plenty of opportunity to be in evidence. He used to toddle about the deck at all hours, with a paint swab and bucket, cursing—for the benefit of the officer-of-the-deck—all the lazy lubbers who had been assigned to him, and whose work he was obliged to do. If you offered to send for the "lazy lubbers," he promptly objected, swearing he would rather do all the work himself, then have to instruct such haymakers. There was always a most piratical expression in his bleared old eyes as he made these complaints, which showed he particularly enjoyed breaking the regulations about profanity in the presence of an officer.

I once tried to stem the tide of complaint by asking him if he had ever seen the Admiral in any of his cruises.

"Seen him?" he sneered contemptuously. "Knowed him when he was a cussed little squirt of a midshipman, dependin' on me and other smart topmen to steer him straight!" and with this tribute to Farragut's early abilities, our conversation ended.

Of course it was not long before old Jones went under the surgeon's care. His cot was swung under the light poop deck, where the officers often gathered to smoke after dinner.

"What you got there?" would be his greeting to the steward, coming from the cabin, a dish in his hand.

"Just a little pudding, Jones, that the captain has sent you."

"What the hell's the matter with it, that he can't eat it?" If the steward, on this, showed a disposition to sheer off, he would be rounded to, with, "Here! put that down. I'll see about it by and by." Jones had no idea of giving up the pudding, but wished to have it thoroughly understood that nothing like gratitude or obligation was entailed. He was soon shipped back to the Asylum at Philadelphia, later known as the Naval Home.

Just before the final surrender of the Confederate armies, the *Ossipee* was sent to New Orleans, where we had a chance to observe what a great relief a little blood letting may be to a strongly felt hatred. New Orleans, which had not suffered the hardships of four years' virtual siege, like Richmond, Mobile, Charleston, and Savannah, was more inclined than those cities to show her dislike of the hated North. I remember hearing of a tremendous commotion one evening at the Varieties Theater, because after "The Bonny Blue Flag" had been played, some one rose and asked for "The Star Spangled Banner." There was such a riot that the performance had to stop. Finally the manager came out on the stage, stated that the money paid for admission that night would be refunded, and assured his audience that no Yankee air would ever be played in the Varieties Theater. His announcement was followed the next day by an order from Butler, who was then military governor: "The orchestra of the Varieties Theater will henceforth open with the 'Star Spangled Banner,' close with 'Hail Columbia,' and 'Yankee Doodle' must be played at least once during the evening."

One of the first things I had noticed on coming to New Orleans was the inscription on the pedestal of the Jackson statue, "The Union must, and shall, be preserved." I expressed my surprise that the Confederates had allowed these words to remain, and was informed that Butler had ordered them to be chiseled in, when he took over the governorship.

In spite of the detestation of New Orleans for the Yankees, no other city, north or south, made such a display of mourning for the death of Lincoln. We did not receive news of the assassination until the morning after it had occurred, and as we heard that Secretary Seward had also been attacked, the idea for the moment prevailed that there was a wide-spread plot. Four or five wretches—it is safe to say they had never been near the firing line—ventured to call for cheers for this crime against the nation, and were promptly shot, or cut down. So great was the excitement and resentment that for a time it seemed as if the soldiers would break loose from all restraint. I remember some army officers asked me and my companions, "Where are your side arms? There will be no arrests made for slashing any scoundrel to-day. This comes straight from the Provost Marshal's."

Of course, there were many citizens who deplored the atrocity that had taken place, not only because it was a crime, but because they felt too great provocation might convert a merciful into a merciless North. They needed no suggestion to hang out mourning, but even those not so inclined were very quick to take a hint from the bands of soldiery pervading the streets, keenly on the alert for any lapses of this sort. Indeed, by sunset, there probably never was a city more thoroughly draped in black than New Orleans. Care was taken that there should be no object to offend a Northern eye. Even the gallant survivors of the Washington Artillery whose war-worn uniforms were not only regarded with respect by our veterans but were the delight of the fair sex, went into temporary retirement.

It was while at New Orleans that we heard the last shot fired by the navy in the Civil War. We congratulated our chief engineer, Adams, on thus rounding out his career, for, as I have mentioned, he had heard the opening guns at Palo Alto and Fort Sumter. It was after resistance had apparently ceased everywhere that "Savez" Reed, the Cushing of the Southern navy,[8] conceived the idea of loading the ram *Webb* with cotton, and escaping with her to Havana. There he hoped to be able to dispose of her and her cargo to the benefit of himself and his daring associates.

I do not know whether the *Webb* had any protection beyond the cotton piled up around her boilers and machinery. Reed had fitted some sort of torpedo to her, with which he thought he might dispose of one adversary, and with this slight preparation he proposed to run past ships, forts, and batteries on the lower Mississippi, from the mouth of the Red River to the sea. He managed to slip by the *Manhattan* and *Tennessee* ironclads, and a little farther on successfully passed the *Selma* and *Quaker City*; but although he had taken the precaution of cutting the telegraph wires, a rumor of his attempt had reached New Orleans. Captain Maxwell of the *Pembina*, seeing a steamer rapidly approaching, shouted to Captain Emmons of the *Lackawanna*, "That's the *Webb*! I know her! She's the only doublewalking-beam steamer on the river!"

The *Lackawanna* opened fire, and the *Ossipee* followed suit, but the *Webb*, apparently uninjured, dashed through, and down the river out of sight. The *Hollyhock* and the *Quaker City* were soon in pursuit, and then the *Ossipee*, a little delayed by a collision with a heavy coal barge lying at the levee at Algiers, opposite the city.

Late in the afternoon, we sighted the *Hollyhock* returning. She signalled the *Webb* had been run ashore and was on fire. It seems the *Richmond*, which was on her way up river, had anchored to repair her machinery. Reed naturally supposed she was lying in wait for him, and if she failed to sink him with her heavy broadside battery of nine-inch guns, she would certainly drive him down to the forts, thus shattering his only hope, which had been to pass them in the dark. So, yielding to what he thought was the inevitable, Reed destroyed his ship. As the Rebellion had been absolutely crushed, I think there was a general sense of disappointment that this daring venture against such heavy odds had not won through.

---

[8] The exploits of William B. Cushing, especially the sinking of the ironclad ram *Albemarle*, made him one of the romantic heroes of the war. The services of his Annapolis classmate, Mississippian Charles W. Read (not Reed), were equally adventurous. Probably the most daring of his deeds was the capture of the U.S. revenue cutter *Caleb Cushing* in the harbor at Portland, Maine, in June 1864. For information on Cushing, see Ralph J. Roske and Charles Van Doren, *Lincoln's Commando: The Biography of Commander W. B. Cushing, USN* (New York, 1957).

Soon after this, the *Ossipee* was sent north, as were nearly all the other ships in the Western Gulf Blockading Squadron. Admiral Farragut had been succeeded some time before by Rear Admiral H. K. Thatcher. We left Lieutenant Howell in the hospital at New Orleans, and Lieutenant Chew became executive officer. I was then second watch and division officer, having been advanced gradually from the fifth. When we reached Philadelphia, I was detached and ordered home. It was a year and eight months since I had sailed from that port to join the *Ossipee*.

Chapter 6

THE BOMBARDMENT
OF VALPARAISO

The month of September saw me again at the Philadelphia Navy Yard. I had orders to report for duty on board the *Vanderbilt*, which was fitting out for a cruise around South America. The situation in Mexico was then engaging the public attention. Our attitude had made it clear to Louis Napoleon that he must either decide to fight us, or else withdraw the French troops from Mexico and leave his dupe Maximilian to his fate. The newspapers, of course, were full of rumors of war, and I remember some verses the London *Punch* published at this time that were widely quoted, especially their refrain, which was in the form of a duet between the Emperor and Secretary Seward, and ran,

"I can't"

"You must" (get out of Mexico)

"I won't—"

"You will."

The French naval force on the Pacific coast was superior to ours, and in view of this fact, our Government had determined to send out to that station the double turreted monitor *Monadnock*, then considered one of the four most formidable vessels in the world. She was to be convoyed by the *Vanderbilt* which, with the *Powhatan* and *Tuscarora*, made up a squadron commanded by Commodore John Rodgers. The *Vanderbilt* was chosen for the flagship. Her captain was Commander J. H. Sanford,[1] and among her officers I was pleased to find Ensign F. A. Cook, my roommate at the Academy, and Ensign W. A. Van Vleck, who had been with me in the *Ossipee*.

Our Commodore, under whom we were proud to serve, came of navy stock. His father, also a Commodore John Rodgers, commanded the only cruising squadron during the War of 1812, and his severe handling of the English sloop-of-war *Little Belt*, though quite unpremeditated, afforded some satisfaction to a people sorely indignant at that time over the attack of the *Leopard* upon the frigate *Chesapeake*. The record of the elder Rodgers has been somewhat obscured by the better known achievements of his son, whose great services to the country, at that dark period when the Army of the Potomac was falling back from Richmond, can scarcely be overestimated.[2] Their importance can perhaps be best understood by a few quotations from his own dispatches. He writes in one, "To save the army as far as we can, demands all our disposable force. The fighting has been continual, the losses very great. We fall back in admirable order, disputing every inch of the way. . . . If, as I hope, we can get the army upon a plain, on the river bank, and then protect each flank by gun-boats, it can have a chance for rest." And again, "Now, if ever, is a chance for the navy to render a signal service, but it must not delay."[3]

When the first monitor foundered off Hatteras, there was a general feeling among the wooden-wall seamen of the navy that an iron craft, heavily armored, and floating only two feet out of water, was nothing but a death trap. Rodgers, sure that it would require a practical proof to

[1] Joseph P. Sanford entered the navy in 1832 and resigned as a lieutenant in 1853. Rejoining the service at the outbreak of the Civil War, he was appointed an acting lieutenant on 13 May 1861 and received a regular commission as a commander on June 6 of the same year. Promoted to the rank of captain while aboard the *Vanderbilt* in September 1866, he resigned for good on 1 March 1869.

[2] Commodore John Rodgers was born at Havre de Grace, Maryland, in August 1812 and became an acting midshipman in February 1829. The "great services" to which the author refers took place in the closing weeks of the Peninsula Campaign in June and July 1862, when the gunboats of the James River Flotilla, of which Rodgers was senior officer, helped to frustrate Lee's attempt to destroy McClellan's army. For details, see Robert Erwin Johnson, *Rear Admiral John Rodgers, 1812–1882* (Annapolis, 1967), pp. 191–221.

[3] Rodgers to Commodore L. N. Goldsborough, 1 July 1862, in *Official Records of the Union and Confederate Navies*, series 1, vol. 7, pp. 533–34. The quotation is not quite verbatim, but the discrepancies are insignificant.

Commodore John Rodgers.

dispel this feeling, took the monitor *Weehawken* to sea in a gale, and having shown that a vessel of her type could survive a storm, confidence was restored, not only in the navy, but also in the country. A little later he won a signal victory in this very ship, compelling the Confederate ironclad *Atlanta* to strike her colors, after an engagement so sharp and decisive that the *Weehawken*'s consort, the *Nahant*, was not even obliged to open fire. It was a triumph the more marked, because so many of the citizens of Savannah were spectators, having come to see and rejoice over what they supposed would be a Confederate victory.

A belief in the monitor type was an article of faith with the Commodore. His officers soon discovered this. We left Philadelphia with the *Monadnock* in November, and the *Powhatan* and *Tuscarora* joined us at Hampton Roads, but to all intents and purposes there was but one ship in the squadron for the Commodore, and that the *Monadnock*. When he spoke of "that ship," we knew without inquiring that he meant the *Monadnock*.[4] He had this habit of concentrating one of the most magnificent minds I ever knew on some particular object, to the exclusion of all others. He used to make me think of a walker who, with eyes fixed on some noble and distant view, is quite heedless of any obstacles that may lie in his path. Mrs. Rodgers, knowing his indifference to the affairs of everyday life, had sent to sea with him a servant called David who, although the Commodore would have scorned the idea of needing a valet, really filled that office. Sometimes the Commodore got away from David, and then there would be noticeable oddities in his attire. Mrs. Rodgers used to say that after her husband's behavior on their wedding day, she was prepared for any eccentricity on his part, for on that momentous occasion, when all the friends and relatives were assembled and the bride was ready and waiting, the groom was not to be found. After an awkward and trying delay, he was finally discovered in the kitchen, entirely absorbed in the mysteries of a cookbook.

Often when he was pacing the deck during my watch, his fine head

---

[4] The *Monadnock* was one of the four *Miantonomoh*-class double-turreted monitors, which were generally regarded as the best ships of their type built during the Civil War. Armed with four 15-inch smoothbore Dahlgren guns, the *Monadnock* was 258 feet 6 inches in length, 52 feet 9 inches abeam, displaced approximately 3,400 tons, and had a speed of 9 knots. Her turrets were protected by 10 inches of armor. The only ship of her class completed before the end of the war, she was commissioned in September 1864. On the voyage described by Admiral Clark, she became the first monitor to round Cape Horn.

sunk in thought, I have seen his face suddenly light up, and beckoning me over to the rail, and resting his arms comfortably upon it, he would fix his eye upon me, and begin, "Now, this officer—" and ramble along, until I interrupted him with, "Really, Commodore, I haven't the slightest idea of whom you are talking."

When he alluded to "*that* officer", the rest of us soon learned that he meant Cook, whom he had chosen for his flag-lieutenant, and who ran him a close second as to heedlessness. Having sent for "that officer" one day at his request, I overheard the following conversation between them.

"Mr. Cook," began the Commodore, "did you make the signal I spoke of, to 'that ship' at daylight this morning?"

Cook, of course, knew "that ship" referred to the *Monadnock*, but he was equally certain that he had not been ordered to make any signal to her at that particular time. There ensued quite an animated discussion, the Commodore very positive he had given the order, and Cook as stoutly declaring if he had been told, he should have at least recollected something about it. At last the Commodore brought the argument to an end by remarking somewhat wearily, "I say I told you to make the signal. You say I did not. Well,—we never shall know." And he turned sadly away.

Our chief engineer, John Germain, regarded the *Vanderbilt* in much the same light that the Commodore did the *Monadnock*. With the exception of one voyage across the Atlantic, he had been her chief engineer ever since her construction, and when Commodore Vanderbilt, her builder and owner, turned her over to the navy, he requested that Germain should continue with her. To effect this, Germain and two or three of his assistants were made acting officers, the chief with the rank of lieutenant commander. They all served through the war and went with us to the Pacific. Germain had many stories to tell of Commodore Vanderbilt; among others of his interview with President Lincoln, which had resulted in the transfer of the ship to the government. It was when the country was in a state of alarm over the exploits of the *Merrimac*. Vanderbilt had the idea that she might be effectively attacked by steamers, so strengthened at the bows that they could be used as rams, and he offered one of his own ships to make the trial. Mr. Lincoln suggested calling in the Secretary of the Navy to discuss the project, but Vanderbilt objected, saying in his blunt way that he wouldn't trust him with a flatboat on the Connecticut River. The President, who never allowed personal feeling to interfere with what might be of service to the country, overlooked this criticism of his cabinet officer and heard Vanderbilt through, remarking, however, at the end, "But suppose your fine steamer is lost; what will the Government have to pay?"

"Don't worry about that, Mr. President!" answered Vanderbilt. Then in his impulsive fashion, he seized a sheet of paper and wrote a receipt of five dollars for the ship, saying, "There, Mr. President, keep that, and if she's lost, the country pays five dollars for her, and if she isn't, she'll be worth more to me than ever." After telling of this offer, he used to add, "But old Welles got ahead of me, after all, for having heard what I had said and done, he had a bill introduced, giving me the thanks of Congress for the *gift* of the ship, and of course, after such an honor, I couldn't have the face to say that I had only meant to give her temporarily, for a time of need."

I have often wondered whether, when it was decided to sell the *Vanderbilt,* her former owner's wishes were consulted. The purchasers took out her engines and boilers, making her a four-masted sailing ship, with the name of *The Three Brothers.* I last saw her in the harbor of Gibraltar, in the year 1906. She had been turned into a mastless coal hulk, and yet in her ancient timbers there still remained something of the old beauty of line and proportion, so pleasing to a sailor's eye.[5]

Germain was a man of enormous strength. His assistants used to tell with great unction of their chief's encounter with the prize fighter, Billy Mulligan, who took passage in the *Vanderbilt* when he crossed to England to attend the international prize fight between Heenan and Sayers. The two countries were in a ferment of excitement over this match. I recollect, as a boy, hearing my teacher, Roswell Farnham, say that he wished our people had taken as much interest in the contest between Buchanan and Fremont for the presidency as in that of Heenan and Sayers for the championship belt. With this feeling in the air, it was natural that Mulligan, a celebrity in his profession, should consider himself unhampered by the regulations that governed ordinary people. Germain found him in the engine room one morning, complacently breaking some rule of the ship. Germain called his attention to this, and added

[5] The sidewheel steamer *Vanderbilt* was originally the flagship of Commodore Cornelius Vanderbilt's North Atlantic Mail Steamship Line (hence her nickname, Vanderbilt's Yacht). Built in 1856–57, she measured 331 feet in length, 47 feet 6 inches abeam, displaced 3,360 tons, and had a speed, very respectable for the era, of 14 knots. She was chartered by the army in April 1861 and transferred to the navy a year later. This cruise was her last commission. Placed in reserve in 1867, she was sold to Howe & Company of San Francisco in 1873. Her career as *The Three Brothers* was spent mostly carrying grain to northern Europe.

Vanderbilt.

that he was the chief engineer. "Are you really?" answered Mulligan, "Well, I'm Billy Mulligan, and I'd have you know that when it comes to chiefs, I'm the Big Chief, wherever I happen—" Just here, something like a circular storm struck him, and he was outside in the gangway when he came to a realizing sense that he had been interrupted. He often visited the engine room after that, coming to the door and inquiring for "Mr. Chief", and when invited within, would enter and bask in the presence. Heenan was a passenger on the return trip, and one of his first proceedings after coming on board was to present himself at the door of the engine room, and ask for Mr. Mulligan's friend.

Germain and our executive officer, Franklin,[6] got on well together, though it was known that the former, when he entered the service, had proclaimed that "no first mate should ever give him orders when the skipper was aboard."

On leaving Hampton Roads, we headed for the port of St. Thomas. Our order of sailing was in the form of a diamond, the *Monadnock* on our starboard quarter, the *Tuscarora* on our port quarter, and the *Powhatan* right astern. In good weather the *Monadnock* could make about seven knots, which of course became the speed of the squadron. Quite early in the voyage, we struck a heavy gale, and she parted her wheel ropes. For hours we waited, watching her, where she lay in the trough of the sea, the waves making a clear break across her. We lost sight of the *Powhatan* and *Tuscarora*, but with his eyes fixed on the distressing plight of "that ship," I doubt if the Commodore was hardly aware of their disappearance. We found them riding at anchor when we reached St. Thomas, where the Commodore had a mast stepped on the forecastle of the *Monadnock*, which fitted with yards and sails from the *Vanderbilt* and *Tuscarora*, gave her a course, topsail, and jib.

Our next stop was at the Isles de Salut, near Cayenne, where we coaled. One of this group, Devil's Island, became well known later as the scene of Dreyfus' imprisonment. At the time of our visit, there were about a thousand convicts on the islands, with a force of marines in charge of them. Among them was a prisoner who excited our interest and speculation, because he was on such a different footing from the others. He lived apart in a pretty cottage, and we noticed that his guards treated him with respect. The night before we sailed from the Isles de Salut, a

---

[6] Charles L. Franklin graduated third (two places above George Dewey) in the Academy's class of 1858. Commander Franklin died on active duty in 1874.

French officer who was dining on board the *Monadnock* volunteered the information that this prisoner was Felice Orsini, supposed to have been guillotined with his confederate Pieri for their attempted assassination of the Emperor Napoleon III, in January, 1858. We never had any means of knowing whether this statement was an indiscreet betrayal of the truth, or a flight of fancy on the part of its author. It is not an impossible supposition, however, that Louis Napoleon was so alarmed by the threats of the Italian secret societies, of which he and Orsini were both members, that he had agreed to a merely apparent execution of the latter, and contrived that some common criminal should suffer in his place.[7]

We visited the ports of Cira, Bahia, Rio de Janeiro, and Montevideo on our way to the Straits of Magellan, but the only occurrence I can recall in connection with any of these places was a visit made by the Emperor of Brazil, Dom Pedro, to the *Monadnock*, and the very thorough inspection he gave her.

Speaking of thoroughness reminds me that few could equal our Commodore in that respect. He had a passion for research, and would go to almost any lengths to satisfy himself. When we were off the mouth of the Rio de la Plata, it happened that an odd looking fish was caught by one of the men. A volunteer officer on board, whom the Commodore considered an authority in such matters, unfortunately remarked that this fish was luminous. The Commodore was interested at once and bent upon having light. He retired to the cabin with his treasure, and there followed a great commotion of closing ports and skylights. The captain presently made an explosive exit, declaring the darkness and lack of air unbearable. A little later the Commodore appeared, baffled and perspiring, but still hopeful. It had occurred to him that there were empty water tanks on board. Inside one of these, with the plate on, he thought absolute darkness might be secured. But Franklin, the executive, discouraged this project. "You know, Commodore," he protested, "you are really too large to crawl through that manhole, and even if you did manage to squeeze in, we might have to cut the tank open to get you out again."

The chief engineer was next appealed to. How about that after boiler, in which steam had not been gotten up? Germain was even more

---

[7] See Orsini, Encyclopædia Britannica. It states that Louis Napoleon's apprehensions impelled him to attack Austria. [Author's note]

emphatic in his disapproval than Franklin. "Good heavens, Commodore! There's not only the risk of getting caught in the manhole, but it's dangerous to get inside one boiler when there's steam up in another."

What scheme the Commodore would have evolved next will never be known, for just then our pilot, a fat, important little Englishman, came mincing along the deck, and his acquaintance with that part of the coast prompted the Commodore to ask if he could give the local name for the luminous fish, which was placidly swimming round and round in the narrow confines of a bucket. The pilot looked, thrust his hand into the bucket, drew out the fish, and uttering the one word, "Squid!" tossed it over the rail and strutted away.

The Commodore stared indignantly after the retreating figure, and then turned to those of us who were gathered about him, for we were always interested in him, if not in his works.

"Did you ever see anything to equal that?" he complained. "A man gets a rare—I may say an almost unique specimen—and some infernal fool comes along, calls it a 'squid', and throws it overboard!"

We anchored four times while going through the Straits of Magellan, in Possession Bay, off Sandy Point, at Port Gallant, and in York Roads. Sandy Point, with less than one hundred inhabitants, was the only settlement south of the Argentine frontier, one thousand miles away. During our stay there, the Commodore heard that coal had been found only a few miles inland. He instantly conceived the idea that with this supply to draw on, heavy tugs might be stationed in Possession Bay to tow sailing ships through the Straits and to a good offing in the Pacific, thus affording them an escape from the dangers, losses, and hardships of beating to the westward around Cape Horn, the severest task imposed upon a seaman.

Of course before a report could be made on the subject, samples of the coal must be secured and tested, and the Commodore determined on a visit to the reputed mine. A few horses were obtained, and a small party, of which I was a member, started on the expedition. Our route, for part of the way, lay up the dry bed of a stream, strewn with boulders and overhung with low stunted trees. It must have been one of these trees that knocked the Commodore from his saddle. At any rate, the first thing we knew, he was on the ground, being dragged over the loose rocks and boulders, his foot having caught in the stirrup. It seemed an age before some one, seizing his horse's bridle, pulled him out of the way of trampling hoofs, and we were all much excited save the Commodore himself, who was heard to calmly express the wish, as he was jerked and bumped along, that some one would be kind enough to "extricate" his foot.

We returned to the ship with several bags of specimens, and various experiments were made in the cabin, as in the case of the luminous fish, and equally to the captain's exasperation. The Commodore came to the conclusion that the coal was too poor for steaming purposes, and so dropped the matter, but many of us thought it was a plan that should have been perfected, even had it entailed the shipping of coal to the Straits. Had the Commodore's idea been carried out, it might have delayed the construction of the Panama Canal a number of years.

I am afraid Captain Sanford had little sympathy from the rest of us when he showed impatience with the Commodore's pursuit of hobbies, and absent-minded ways. To us, his eccentricities were a part of his character, and therefore all lovable. If we had lived right up against them as the captain did, we might have been a little better able to share his viewpoint, but I am inclined to doubt it. I did see the skipper on one occasion, however, when I really felt sorry for him. He and the Commodore were standing together on deck, the captain anxiously watching the weather signs—for there was a stiff gale blowing—and the Commodore going through the contents of his pockets. From one of these he suddenly released a quantity of fine tobacco dust, and sent it up into the wind's eye, whence it promptly blew back into the captain's. His cry of pain roused the Commodore's attention and sympathy, but as his first move was to blunder on to the captain's feet and almost crush one of them, his next attempt to approach was violently deprecated by Sanford, who hopping wildly about, his foot in one hand, and holding his eyes with the other, implored the Commodore for Heaven's sake to keep away from him.

At York Roads, one of our officers, while hunting on shore, accidentally shot a Fuegean through the leg. It is to be feared his family would willingly have sacrificed him again, for after the wound had been dressed by the surgeon, they departed laden with what they regarded as a fortune in cloth, flannel, and tobacco.

Our ship and the *Powhatan* made their way out of the Straits into the Pacific at the western entrance, and proceeded up the coast to San Estevan Bay in the Gulf of Penas. There the *Monadnock* and the *Tuscarora*—to which the Commodore had temporarily transferred his flag—joined us, having come up through the inside channel. The *Monadnock* and the other ships had coaled, while at Sandy Point, from a sailing ship which had been sent there to meet us, and at San Estevan Bay we again coaled the *Monadnock* from our own bunkers. We then sailed in company for Valparaiso. When we left Hampton Roads, the strength of the French fleet was the question that engrossed us. On our way down the east coast of South America, we had found Brazil and Argentine—or Buenos Ayres, as it was then called—at war with Paraguay, and we knew that Chile, Peru, and Bolivia, on the west coast, were at war with Spain,[8] but we had not dreamed that this latter conflict could affect us vitally until we reached Valparaiso, and found ourselves part of a situation which threatened to become more tensely exciting than any prospect of an encounter with the French fleet.

The Spanish fleet, under Admiral Mendez Nuñez, was lying in the harbor of Valparaiso when we arrived, waiting for orders concerning the bombardment of the city. The fleet under Nuñez consisted of his flagship, the *Numantia*, a broadside ironclad mounting thirty-four guns, four fine wooden frigates—the *Villa de Madrid, Resolucion, Blanca*, and *Beranguela*—and the gunboat *Vincidora*, all these together carrying about two hundred guns.

The English fleet lying at Valparaiso, to which with ours, the residents anxiously looked to prevent the bombardment of an unfortified and defenseless town, had three ships, the *Sutlej* and *Leander* frigates, and the gunboat *Shearwater*, mounting in all about one hundred and ten guns. To these we could add sixty, having found the *Mohongo*, one of our double-enders, in port on our arrival.

The *Sutlej* was flying the flag of Rear Admiral Denman, and on board the *Leander* was Commodore DeCourcey. Two greater contrasts in type could not have been imagined. Denman was tall and spare, having what his officers—to use a favorite British adjective—called a "cruel" nose, while DeCourcey, so short and stout that he looked like the jack of clubs, was said to have a "cruel" paunch.

Lord Charles Beresford,[9] who was a midshipman on the *Sutlej* at this time, seems to hint that court influence had played its part in Denman's selection for flag rank, for he speaks in his memoirs of Admiral, the

---

[8] The conflict whose closing scenes Admiral Clark relates was Spain's last war with her former colonies. The South American alliance actually consisted of Chile, Peru, and Ecuador.

[9] In after years Lord Beresford, then a noted admiral, referred to the *Oregon* in a way that a sailor particularly values when coming from one of his own profession. He spoke as a seaman of the feeling of pride he had in the ship, and in regard to her achievement remarked with emphasis, "When any of our officers say, 'We have ships that could do it,' I answer, 'Yes, but we have not done it.' " [Author's note]

Honorable Joseph Denman, succeeding to his position, "after the enjoyment of twenty-five years of profound peace in command of the Queen's yacht."[10]

The bluff DeCourcey was not adapted for the command of royal yachts, if one can judge by a story that was told us by his officers. Some ancient sovereign, whose treasury was not perhaps in a state that would permit of more substantial rewards, had conferred on the DeCourcey family the rather curious privilege of standing with covered heads in the presence of royalty. Queen Victoria, who was well posted in all family traditions, one day noticed a broad-beamed craft in naval uniform, including the cocked hat, drifting about at one of her levees, and placed him immediately. "I see, Commodore," she remarked, as he was presented, "that you are availing yourself—and justly—of the privilege of your distinguished family."

"Yes, Your Majesty," acknowledged DeCourcey, with a low bow, but no sign of removing his headgear.

"Having done so," added the queen, "should you not remove your hat in the presence of ladies?"

"Assuredly, except when Your Majesty is present. As the subject, I must remain covered in the presence of my sovereign."

The Spanish admiral, Mendez Nuñez—or Mondays Tuesdays, as we used to call him—had a most attractive personality. He had reached the rank of admiral at a comparatively early age. His reputation, not only as an officer but as a man, was of the highest, nor was it clouded because Queen Isabella, of whose character the same could not be said, was devoted to his interests. No one felt more deeply than he the alternative of either yielding to the threats of the American and English commanders, or bombarding a defenseless city, as his orders from Madrid demanded.

The interval of waiting for these orders was filled with the wildest speculations. Would they or would they not come, and if they did, would the English and American squadrons interfere? I venture to say that there were few in our squadron who were particularly pleased with the prospect of interference and the resulting conflict with the Spanish fleet. Fresh from one war, and with the expectation of going into another, we were not hungering for additional fighting. Still it was all in the day's work for us, and it amused us to affect much sympathy for Chief Engineer Germain and our acting chaplain, Mr. Bush, for being in-

[10] *The Memoirs of Admiral Lord Charles Beresford* (London, 1914), p. 65.

volved in such a position. Germain, who had served through our Civil War, would have resigned at the end of it had not Commodore Vanderbilt urged him to stay by his ship until our fleet reached San Francisco. When we condoled with him on being caught, as it were, between the two commodores, he would answer rather grimly, "Never mind about that! If there's a battle, just you get this ship pointed right, and I'll drive her through the *Numantia* herself."

Mr. Bush was the pastor of the church Commodore Rodgers attended in Orange, New Jersey. As he was out of health, his parishioners had given him leave for a year, and flag officers being then allowed to appoint civilian secretaries, Commodore Rodgers had been able to obtain one of these positions for him. Greatly benefited by the voyage, he had up to this time often congratulated himself on his good fortune, but now he could only smile sadly when asked about the advantages of Valparaiso as a health resort.

When it became known that Valparaiso was actually to be bombarded, the excitement, not only on shore, but afloat, was intense. Millions of dollars' worth of property belonging to foreigners would undoubtedly be destroyed, and while the English stood to lose the largest amount, yet the *Vanderbilt* was besieged by ministers and consuls from many other nations, all appealing to the Commodore to interpose. There were meetings and councils both in Santiago and Valparaiso. Our minister, General Kilpatrick, was noisily demonstrative, urging the Commodore to interfere, and treating the whole affair as if it were some light undertaking. He declared if it came to a battle, he wanted to be on board the *Vanderbilt* and have a hand in it. He bore the reputation—no doubt deservedly—of being a dashing cavalry officer,[11] but I can remember, when he made this speech, seeing the Commodore turn and look at him in a half amused, half contemptuous way.

There was, I think, a general feeling among our officers and crews that the affair was really none of our business. Chile was at war with a nation possessing a navy, and could scarcely look to others to save her sea-ports from contribution or destruction. So far as property was concerned, there was little or nothing belonging to Americans to protect. Of course, the

[11] A graduate of the U.S. Military Academy class of 1861, Hugh Judson Kilpatrick became one of the boy generals of the Civil War. His most responsible command was as chief of Sherman's cavalry on the "March to the Sea." At the end of the war, a major general at the age of twenty-nine, he resigned from the army and accepted the appointment of U.S. minister to Chile, which he held until 1868. Later he became active in politics. In 1881 he was reappointed minister to Chile, where he died later that year.

worst feature of the bombardment was the misery it would occasion in a city of one hundred thousand people, among whom there would certainly be numbers too sick or helpless to be moved, and the many homes that would be destroyed.

Commodore Rodgers was undoubtedly influenced by these last considerations, for it was evident from the outset that he meant to interfere, if he could induce the English admiral to take part with him. There were a few of our officers—Captain Sanford was one of them—who attributed this readiness on the Commodore's part to his desire to see a fight between the American monitor and the Spanish ironclad. I think the Commodore must have had some knowledge of this talk, but if so, he gave no indications, but kept steadily on his course, with his eyes on the main issue. I discovered, however, during this period of waiting, that he was not indifferent to the opinions of his officers, even of my rank, though in this case there may have been some personal regard involved. He had always shown a very kindly feeling for me, and often during the cruise had passed an hour or two of the midwatch talking with me, much to the irritation of the captain, who evidently felt I could not attend to my duties properly when absorbed by what the Commodore was saying. One afternoon during my watch, a square-rigged ship was sighted to the northward of Valparaiso, and after looking at her some time through a glass, I said, "That's a man-of-war. Let's hope it's the *Lancaster!*"

The Commodore, who had overheard me, asked at once, "Why do you hope it is the *Lancaster?*"

I knew immediately what was in his mind, for the *Lancaster* was the flagship of Admiral Pearson, and his arrival would mean that he would take command of our fleet. This change would have been pleasing to those who did not approve of the Commodore's policy and who hoped that Pearson's might be different.

I hastened to disabuse him of this idea and explain my own thought, by saying, "Because she carries twenty-six nine-inch guns, sir."

His face brightened, and he said, "Yes, that would be a help," and after a pause, he added, "of course, the *Monadnock* would be triumphant in the end."

"Yes, Commodore," I answered, "I suppose so; but don't you think a little assistance would give us a better chance of seeing the triumph?"

It was said by some that he meant to transfer his flag to the *Monadnock*, if a battle took place, but this rumor was disposed of by his statement that Bunce, her captain, could fight her all right, and he would look on from the paddle box of the *Vanderbilt*.

The Commodore became strongly attached to Nuñez. I remember hearing him say one night, when he returned from a conference on the *Numantia*, "Nuñez is brave and true. He will do his duty. My heart warmed towards him while he spoke."

I learned that Nuñez had thoroughly won the Commodore's approval by the frank way in which he stated his intentions. "Commodore," said he, "you have a reputation in your country, and you too, General Kilpatrick, but I also have one in mine, and I shall try to keep it. I shall bombard Valparaiso. Of course, you know," he added, "that this matter could be adjusted. I have plenipotentiary powers, and if the Chileans would just stop blowing their bugles in my face and salute our flag, at the very first gun I would hoist their flag and return the salute, then go on shore and settle all troubles. As they are not willing to do this, I must carry out my orders. If you feel it your duty to interfere, Commodore, your *Monadnock* may be too strong for my *Numantia*, but I think I can dispose of everything else, and then if I find I can't whip the *Monadnock*, I will leave."

It was this calm certainty of being able to "dispose of everything else" that troubled all of us except the Commodore, and even he may have had his misgivings. Meantime the preparations for battle went forward. Twelve hundred bags of coal were stored in the gangways of the *Vanderbilt* to shelter the most exposed parts of her boilers and machinery. The *Tuscarora* plated her sides with chain cables, and on board the *Powhatan* the light spar-deck cabin used when she was a flagship was removed, and a pivot gun mounted in its place.

Beresford, in his memoirs, alludes to the American fleet and especially to the *Monadnock*, whose identity however he confuses with the *Miantonomoh*, her sister ship.

He says, on page sixty-six:

"The European residents in Valparaiso, who owned an immense amount of valuable property, stored in the custom houses, were terrified at the prospect of a bombardment, and petitioned Admiral Denman to prevent it. An American fleet of war-ships was also lying in the bay. Among them was the 'Miantonomoh', the second screw iron-clad that ever came through the Straits of Magellan, the first being the Spanish iron-clad 'Numantia.'

"When the 'Miantonomoh' crossed the Atlantic in 1866, the *Times* kindly remarked that the existing British Navy was henceforth useless, and that most of its vessels were only fit to be laid up and painted that dirty yellow, which is universally adopted to mark treachery, failure and crime.

"The British and American Admirals consulted together as to the advisability of preventing a bombardment. The prospect of a fight cheered us all, and we entered into elaborate calculations of the relative strength of the Spanish fleet and the British-American force. As a matter of fact, they were about equal."

In the midst of these preparations, the English admiral, Denman, suddenly announced that he had orders from home which positively forbade him to interfere. Then all was confusion and dismay. The English residents, realizing that their property was likely to be lost, or injured, were furious because their admiral would not, in violation of his instructions, give an order that meant a battle of the most sanguinary description. They sent him a wooden sword, and talked of "our fancy squadron, Lady Denman commanding." The squat and truculent DeCourcey went on the warpath. He declared—so we heard—that if we decided to fight, he would be with us. If any shot came his way, he was going to fire back. Of course this stand made him generally popular, and the contrast with Denman the more telling. Nevertheless, if Admiral Denman, aware from the first that he was powerless to interfere felt that by threatening to unite with us he might force the Spaniard to spare the city, he took a chance that involved his reputation, and braved what many would regard as worse than death. Cables and wireless telegraphy practically ensure against such a situation in the present day.

The Valparaisans still cherished a faint hope that the Spaniards might relent, or that we might be induced to interpose. In fact, we were regarded for a time with enthusiasm, in the light of their sole defenders, and I remember seeing illuminations in the plaza of Valparaiso in honor of the squadron "de los Estados Unidos." Commodore Rodgers now felt that the time had come to dispel these false hopes, and spoke out decisively. A large delegation of foreign residents had come on board the *Vanderbilt*, stating that as far as lay in their power they made the Commodore official protector of the rights of their respective countries. The insistent urging of General Kilpatrick was supported by an Englishman, one who had been an ardent Southern sympathizer just a few months before. He drew an animated picture of the gratitude his countrymen would feel towards Americans, winding up with the phrase, "blood is thicker than water."

"Yes," retorted the Commodore, losing his hitherto unruffled serenity, "but I notice that you would have America contribute all the blood!"

Then turning to the minister and delegation, "We are not afraid to fight, even against great odds; but England must be involved. All I ask is a cutter with the English flag flying, to tow astern of the *Vanderbilt!* The gratitude you speak of would not prevent certain Englishmen from fitting out new *Alabamas* and *Floridas* to destroy what little commerce we have left, should we get into a war with Spain."

It must be said of the Chileans that when they saw there was no longer any hope of protection, they showed no intention of submitting. When Nuñez announced the bombardment for four days later, he declared his intention of firing only upon the public buildings, but as they extended all the way from the bonded warehouses at Reeftopsail Point to the Naval Academy and railroad station at the northern end of the city, it was evident that no quarter would be really out of reach of shot and shell. So, on the day before the bombardment, the sad exodus began. I was on shore that day, and saw men and women carrying their sick and aged, and hurrying crying children before them, abandoning their homes to take refuge in the country, or on the high hills that overlooked the town. On the fateful morning, these hills were black with people. Many of them had come from Santiago as spectators, and that city had also sent all her fire companies to assist in checking the flames, after the bombardment was over.

A little after eight o'clock, the Spanish frigates and the *Vincidora* stood in, and took their stations near the shore. About nine o'clock, a signal was hoisted on the *Numantia*, lying just to the northward of our ships, and her consorts opened fire. At first, except when a slanting roof was struck, we could not see that much damage was being done, for nearly all the buildings were of stone, but soon smoke began to rise above the bonded warehouses, and it was evident fires had started. Very shortly these began to spread, especially in the southern portion of the city. The firing from the ships was erratic. Sometimes a frigate would let go a whole broadside, and again the shots would be intermittent. A little after eleven, the *Numantia* hoisted another signal, upon which the ships ceased firing, and stood out past us to their former anchorage. We immediately ran in, and sent large fire parties from all our ships. As we pulled in to the mole—as the landing place in front of the custom house was called—we could see that it was torn up in every direction. The building from the front showed only holes where the projectiles had entered, but the moment we passed through the arched gateway we found a complete wreck, and the square between it and the Intendencia was filled with débris. The building itself was ruined. The fires were soon under control, and late in the afternoon our fire parties were withdrawn. We did not hear of any loss of life, which was not extraordinary, as the city was deserted. It was said that property amounting to many millions of dollars was destroyed, but there was never, to my knowledge, any careful estimate made.

Beresford says, after writing of the bombardment:

"I accompanied a landing party to help extinguish the conflagration. We put the fires out, but the inhabitants were so angry with us because we had not prevented the bombardment that they requested that the landing party should be sent back to their ships. Then the flames broke out afresh. For years the resentment of the Valparaisans remained so hot that it was inadvisable to land in the town, men from the British ships."

A correspondent from the *Herald*, Mr. Carpenter, who later became the secretary of our legation in Chile, had been living aboard the *Vanderbilt* until the day before the bombardment. He went ashore then, and took up his quarters in the Hotel de Chile, whose proprietor, Landais, was a Frenchman. Early the next morning Carpenter started for a post of observation and safety on the hills, urging his host to accompany him. The Frenchman emphatically refused, declaring that if the Spaniards dared fire a single shot at the Hotel de Chile, he would let loose the Emperor Napoleon and all "la belle France" upon them. Carpenter said about ten minutes after the firing began he saw a shot strike the tiled roof of Landais' imperially protected hotel, and go glancing up it, spreading destruction as it went. In a flash, out rode Landais on a big donkey, a mattress lashed to his back to ward off projectiles. He headed for the hills, and as he rushed past Carpenter, his eyes bulging to such an extent they could have been brushed off with a hat, the latter called to him to stop, as the danger line was passed, but he paid no attention. He knew if he could only get the Andes between him and the guns, his safety would be assured, and he kept on.

In fact, there was only one citizen who weathered the storm in Valparaiso that day, and as he was dumb, he could never tell of his experience. When we first anchored at Valparaiso, the officers of the *Mohongo* told us of a dog who had taken up his quarters on the mole, and levied a tariff on American officers in uniform. He required silver coin, disdaining copper. When he had secured the proper coin, he trotted off to a certain butcher's and exchanged his money for meat. It was even said—though I will not vouch for the truth of this—that when contributions had been unusually generous, he used to bury his bank roll, drawing upon it when necessary.

Collector, or Revenue Jack, as he was sometimes called, fearless of Her Catholic Majesty's squadron, was at his usual post on the mole when the storm broke. Our boats had been in early to bring off any Americans who preferred viewing the bombardment from the water instead of the hills, and after they had returned to the ships, Collector was remembered, and keen were the regrets that he had not been taken aboard. Mr. Carpenter, who was armed with a powerful glass, said afterwards that before the whole scene was obscured by smoke, he could make out the old dog, jumping about on the mole as it was raked and torn by shot and bursting shells. When our boats with fire parties pulled swiftly for the landing, some one shouted, "There he is!" and in a few minutes we were greeting and rejoicing over the excited and lone defender of Valparaiso.

Not long after this, the *Vanderbilt* and *Monadnock* sailed for Callao, leaving the *Powhatan* and *Tuscarora* behind to await orders from Admiral Pearson. For hours after leaving port, we kept Aconcagua, the loftiest of the Andes, in sight over our starboard quarter, though it was already distant one hundred and ten land miles from our starting point. We had left the Spanish fleet at Valparaiso, but owing to the *Monadnock*'s slow rate of speed, it must have caught up with us on the way north, for just after we made San Lorenzo, the high island outside of Callao, it was seen in the offing. It was then the custom in our service, dating perhaps from the attack upon the unprepared *Chesapeake*, to carry guns loaded while at sea, removing the charges when in port, and so, as we neared Callao, the first lieutenant came up to ask the captain's permission to send the crew to quarters. Captain Sanford turned upon him sharply. "What! unload the guns now, with the Spanish fleet close aboard?"

The Commodore, who was standing near, half jokingly, half reproachfully asked, "Did you have them loaded, Captain, at Valparaiso?"

This was the only time I ever heard him show any feeling about the captain's protests and opposition.

In coming to Callao, we had known that we should probably witness another bombardment, but in this case the object of attack was very far from being defenseless. In fact, so well prepared were the Peruvians that it was said that Nuñez had received an intimation from home not to jeopardize his fleet in an action with shore batteries, but he felt that his country had lost honor in the eyes of other nations by the bombardment of Valparaiso, and Castilian pride demanded that he should fight at Callao.

The Spanish fleet anchored under San Lorenzo, while ours took up a position nearer the town. Callao, which was really the port of the capital city, Lima, a few miles inland, was much less populous than Valparaiso, and was defended by a citadel and heavy batteries. We found the Peruvians had about sixty guns of the average caliber already mounted, and were working desperately upon six heavy Armstrong rifle guns, but I think only two of these—three-hundred pounders—were in readiness when the battle began. They also had a small monitor, but she was neither heavily armed nor armored. We heard that they had among their forces several officers who had served in our Union and Confederate armies. There were also two or three ex-Confederate naval officers in Callao at this time, but whether the Peruvians made use of their services I do not know.

The battle of Callao commenced a little after noon, on the second of May, 1866. The ironclad *Numantia* led the right wing, her companions being the frigates *Blanca* and *Resolucion*. The frigates *Villa de Madrid*, *Beranguela*, and the newly arrived *Almanza* formed the left wing. All the merchant shipping had been shifted to the northward of its usual anchorage, and the *Monadnock* and the *Vanderbilt* lay off the town, a position that gave us an excellent view of the battle, and was—the Commodore considered—out of gunshot of the smooth-bores, while as the only two rifled guns were mounted at the northern end of the line of batteries, we were well to the right of their line of fire.

The *Numantia*, or one of the Peruvian batteries just beyond her—we could not tell which—opened the engagement, and immediately sixty guns on shore and half of the two hundred and seventy-five afloat came into action. A thick pall of smoke hung over the bay, pierced by flashes from the guns, whose steady roar was almost appalling. Presently the cloud began to drift away in spots, and our attention centered on the *Beranguela*, which seemed to be entirely enveloped in smoke or dust. As it gradually cleared, we could see a large opening in her side, amidships. She headed out at once, and as she passed us, steaming at full speed for San Lorenzo, she was listed well over to keep afloat. A boat from our ship, carrying both surgeons, pulled under her bows to offer medical assistance, but the captain, shouting that he must save his ship, would not stop. Ten minutes later, the *Villa de Madrid* made signals, and the gunboat *Vincidora* steamed in, and gave her a line, so it was evident that her boilers or machinery were disabled. With such a heavy battery as she had, it might have been expected that she would take the gunboat alongside and remain in action, and we were somewhat surprised when we saw her being towed over to San Lorenzo.

The *Resolucion* hauled out after two o'clock, but later returned and fought for nearly an hour, when she again retired. The *Blanca* held out until almost four o'clock. Her captain, Topete, who was badly wounded in this action, later became Minister of Marine, and when in command at

Cadiz, started the revolution that overthrew Queen Isabella. The *Numantia* and her brave consort, the *Almanza*, fought until sunset, when the battle ended. The *Numantia* was practically uninjured, but the intrepid Nuñez, who had refused to go behind her armor, because he wished to share the dangers to which his companions on the wooden ships were exposed, was severely wounded. We were told that Prado, the President of Peru, had been helping to serve the guns on shore, and his Secretary of War had been killed in one of the batteries.

About four o'clock, we had seen a boat pull over from the *Almanza* to the flagship, and were informed that she was taking the *Almanza*'s captain, Sanchez, over to confer with the Admiral. The conference ended, Sanchez returned to his ship and continued the fight.

It was my outspoken admiration for this bravely fought ship and her captain that was the occasion for a talk with Commodore Rodgers that made an indelible impression on me. Mr. Bush had told us once that the positions the Commodore took in an argument, which so often surprised us, came in many instances from a desire to get the viewpoints of others. But sometimes there was more beneath the surface, as I learned on this occasion, to my sorrow. I had just given vent to an outburst of enthusiasm for the gallant Sanchez, when the Commodore, overhearing me, made some remark about "the pride and obstinacy of a Spaniard." Although I felt this opinion might have been advanced for argument's sake, I was still considerably nettled because the enthusiasm I had shown had been quenched in such an unlooked-for manner, and seeing what I thought a vulnerable point that I could seize on, I said, "Well, to my mind, the *Almanza* is a nobly fought ship, and I know of none in our war, except one, that was more determinedly kept in action."

"Indeed!" said the Commodore, much interested in such a positive statement. "What ship was it?"

"The *Galena* in the James River," I answered promptly.

In an instant the Commodore's face, which had been all eager inquiry, clouded over. He turned away, motioning for me to follow. It was not till we were quite alone that he began, so slowly and seriously that his words have never been forgotten, "The *Galena* was a mistake. The monitor was the right principle. We could not afford mistakes, fighting in such a war, and with the danger of foreign interference. I had to prove the *Galena* a mistake. The poor fellows who died on board her that day did not die in vain."

My satisfaction in what I had thought a smart rejoinder had totally crumbled by this time, and I could only brokenly express my regret, but the regret was even then tempered by the feeling that I had gained a still clearer idea of the character of the man before me, and a new knowledge of life's values. The deep sadness of the Commodore's face, as he uttered those few words, taught me that what the world regards as glory may weigh but slightly against the heavy responsibility such a man must face, when he communes with himself.[12]

---

[12] At the beginning of the Civil War, the North built three ironclads of differing design: the *Monitor*, John Ericsson's revolutionary "cheesebox on a raft"; the *New Ironsides*, a heavily armored but otherwise conventional screw steamer; and the ill-fated *Galena*, a lightly armored screw steamer. The latter's unique feature was the pronounced tumblehome (curvature) of her sides, which was intended to compensate for her thin skin by deflecting hits. That this intention had not been realized became evident in the engagement to which Admiral Clark referred, on the James River below Richmond on 15 May 1862. In the course of sharp action with the Confederate batteries at Drewry's Bluff, thirteen of the forty shells that struck the *Galena* penetrated her plating, killing twelve of her crewmen and wounding twenty-one. The following year her armor was removed, and she served out the war as a wooden ship.

Chapter 7

THE WRECK OF THE *SUWANEE*

Many of us, knowing how well and devotedly Commodore Rodgers had served his country and how great were his natural abilities, felt that he had been insufficiently rewarded, and that he should at least have been advanced a grade. But once, when this subject was touched upon, he said that he considered the country had treated him generously. Contact with such an officer and his ideals could not but have its effect upon the young men serving under him, making them feel that good and even heroic services should be rendered, not for the sake of rewards, but in return for the education given them and for their honorable life positions.

Commodore Rodgers has not been the only officer to express these views. Admiral John C. Watson, the personal aide and favorite of Farragut, when claims were being made for his advancement, requested that they be not urged; the intrepid Cassel entered his protest against the promotion given him over his brother officers; and even the wonderful Cushing, whose exploits were said "to have spoiled romance," never complained of their meager recognition by an advance of one grade.

These truly chivalric men felt that a promotion nobly earned, nobly inspired, but that an advance undeserved brought dishonor to the recipient, depressed the worthy who were passed over, and encouraged the selfish and unscrupulous who possessed regrettable influence.

It has been this spirit permeating our naval service that has made it what it is—able to keep its efficiency through long periods of peace, and to give a fine account of itself when the hour for action has arrived.

From Callao we sailed for San Francisco, stopping at Panama, Acapulco, Magdalena Bay, and San Diego on our way. This was my first acquaintance with the magnificent mountain scenery of the west coasts of Central America and Mexico. Later in life, many of the mountain peaks seemed as familiar as the faces of old friends, I used their summits so often in triangulation work. Colima, Isalco, and Ometepe wore feathery plumes of smoke on their superb heads, for they were active volcanoes. We passed close enough to the spot where the *Golden Gate* lay beached to have a good look at the remains of that ill-fated steamer. She was wrecked when on her way from San Francisco to Panama, her treasure room full, and many of her passengers going home with fortunes from the gold fields. We had been told that when the catastrophe occurred, and some of these people in their rage and despair were flinging on deck the bags of dust and nuggets so useless to them then, one man who was known to be a powerful swimmer went about picking up the golden harvest and loading his pockets with it. When the steamer had nearly reached the beach, the flames swept aft, driving all before them into the sea. This man leaped with the rest, but was so heavily weighted with his precious freight that he went down like a stone, a victim to his greed.[1]

A San Francisco wrecker who looted the treasure room of this steamer met with better fortune. He sailed with his gains to his home city, where he immediately became involved in a dispute with the courts over the question of ownership. But while the public attention was thus centered on him in San Francisco, another of his schooners was busily working away at the wreck, and before the lawyers had finished wrangling, she had secured over a million in gold, which was sent abroad.

When we reached San Francisco, Commodore Rodgers left us. Danger of a war with France was practically over by that time, Louis Napoleon having agreed that his troops should be withdrawn from Mexico, a third at a time. The Commodore went home overland, but as

---

[1] The sidewheel steamer *Golden Gate*, built in 1851, belonged to the Aspinwall Line. A relatively large vessel by contemporary standards, she displaced 2,850 tons and could carry 1,250 passengers. In July 1862 she caught fire at sea three and a half miles off Manzanillo, Mexico. The flames spread rapidly, and though her captain succeeded in beaching her, there was heavy loss of life. Of the 337 persons aboard, only around 80 survived. She was carrying $1,400,000 in gold, much of which was salvaged.

the Union Pacific Railroad was not then completed, I believe he had to make a part of the journey on horseback, under the escort of a United States troop of cavalry. Admiral Henry Knox Thatcher took his place.

San Francisco, though by no means the metropolis of the present day, was the first American city of any size that we had seen since leaving Philadelphia. It was stirring with picturesque life and movement, and most of this was concentrated on the water front. Montgomery Street was then the principal thoroughfare, and there were very few business buildings beyond Kearney Street. The only large hotels I can remember were the Occidental, the Cosmopolitan, and the What Cheer House, the last catering almost entirely to miners. It was always crowded to the doors, and one could pass an entertaining half hour at any time, standing in its lobby and watching its patrons as they came in to register, often with their fortunes and all their personal effects in their belts and upon their backs.

I recollect two theaters, the Metropolitan and Maguire's Opera House, though there may have been others. I had a very slight acquaintance with their interiors, for theater tickets, like many other things, were very high priced in San Francisco in those days, and our pay proportionately low, when we came to exchange our greenbacks for gold on shore. My month's salary as an ensign—one hundred dollars in greenbacks—shrank to about half when exchanged for specie. However, as we were in three watches, our shoregoing was naturally limited, and our forced economies did not trouble us much. I remember one of the things that impressed me most, in a city so full of a rough and adventurous element, was the scarcity of policemen. I was told that there were only about two hundred in all, but my informant added meaningly that the Vigilance Committee was still a name to conjure with, and that lamp-posts and rope made an effective combination in the hands of peace-loving citizens.

The greater part of the time that I remained on the *Vanderbilt* was spent in San Francisco harbor, with the exception of one trip which we made to Honolulu. Queen Emma, the wife of Kamehameha V,[2] had just returned to this country from a visit to England, and we were detailed to give her a passage home. Admiral Thatcher turned over his cabin to her and an Englishwoman in her suite, a Miss Spurgeon. The queen was an agreeable and cultivated woman, but the English companion was a good

[2] Queen Emma was actually the consort of Kamehameha IV, who reigned from 1855 to 1863. Kamehameha V (1863–72) was king of Hawaii at the time of which Admiral Clark writes.

deal of a trial to the Admiral. She generally contrived to lead the conversation at meals to "odious" comparisons between the North and South, always assuming that every one must concede the latter to be immensely superior, though of course if she were wrong in these views she was amiably anxious that the "dear Admiral" should set her right. The restraint which the Admiral's chivalry put upon him, while in the cabin, was usually followed by a terrific outburst as soon as he reached the deck.

During the month we were anchored in the harbor of Honolulu, Queen Emma kept the ship's company generously supplied with fresh provisions, ranging from vegetables to cattle. One day, a young bull managed to break loose, after being hoisted on board, and as he was an active animal, he soon cleared the forecastle. The crew came rushing down the port gangway. I was officer of the deck at the time, and hearing the tumult, I came hurrying over to check it. The men, more concerned about the bull than my orders, paid no attention, but swept on, and luckily I got a clue to their behavior by a sight of horns and tail flourishing in the rear. In a second I had joined the rout. I made a jump for the rail, which was low and had a molding outboard, and there I clung, watching the triumph of his Bullship, who for a brief space had the entire deck to himself. He was finally entangled with ropes dropped from the rigging, and being thrown down, was dragged off, still snorting defiance.

Among the quantities of fowls sent off by Queen Emma were a number of gamecocks, or so the men chose to consider them. Each mess in the ship's company had its champion, of which it proudly boasted, while the cocks themselves crowed a challenge to all comers. One afternoon, a sailor who had been amusing himself fishing for gulls with the usual outfit of cord and salt pork, happened to catch one. He put his captive in a vacant chicken coop, and some one suggested introducing a gamecock to see if a fight could be brought off. The rooster was ready. As soon as he landed in the coop and discovered the other bird, he uttered a shrill crow, and ruffling his neck feathers for war, flew at the gull and spurred him severely. The gull was visibly surprised. He was lonely and strange in his new surroundings, and had rather welcomed the advent of the cock as a companion in misery. He drew back into his corner to meditate on this turn of affairs, but the little feathered bomb flew up again and hit him another smart clip. When this happened a third time, it seemed to occur to him that this other bird actually meant to be unpleasant. He suddenly darted forward, and seizing the rooster by the head, made a valiant and determined attempt to swallow him entire. When he finally gave up, and that gamecock got his head out of chancery, he was absolutely quelled, and his only idea was to find a space between the slats of the coop wide enough to squeeze through.

A second and a third champion entered the lists and were disposed of in the same way. The gull did not wait for them to declare war. He had found that "watchful waiting" did not pay.[3] I then insisted that the victor should be freed.

Prince—afterwards King—Kalakaua was a frequent visitor to the *Vanderbilt*. He came off one day for lunch, bringing with him, as a contribution to that meal, a roast dog, a highly rated native delicacy. He explained that it was poy fed, and I think was a little disappointed that we did not take to it with more enthusiasm.

The heir to the throne, Prince Billy, as he was called, spent nearly all his time at Waikiki, swimming among the breakers like a fish, or drinking like one, on shore. I never remember seeing him.

About seven months after we left Honolulu, I and several other officers were transferred from the *Vanderbilt* to the *Suwanee*, a double-ender, whose captain was Commander Young.[4] He died soon after we joined the ship and was succeeded by Commander Richard L. Law. We were lying at Panama at this time, where we had just relieved the *Dacotah*. A massacre, which had taken place at Panama, and in which a number of Americans returning from California had been killed, caused our Government to keep a vessel of the Pacific squadron at that port, except at those times when an English man-of-war could undertake the duty.[5] On several occasions it had been necessary to land an armed force, but as a rule the presence of the ship was enough to protect foreigners and

---

[3] "Watchful waiting" were the words used in 1913 by President Woodrow Wilson to describe his policy towards the Mexican government of General Victoriano Huerta, whom he hoped to oust by a combination of diplomatic pressure and an arms embargo. The failure of these means to achieve that goal resulted in the occupation of Veracruz, to which Admiral Clark refers in chapter 8, note 2 (p. 106). For details, see Jack Sweetman, *The Landing at Veracruz: 1914* (Annapolis, 1968).

[4] An iron-hulled, sidewheel gunboat of 1,030-ton displacement, the *Suwanee* was commissioned in January 1865. She measured 255 feet × 35 feet and carried a complement of 159 officers and men. Her speed was 15 knots.

[5] Admiral Clark was probably thinking of the disturbances in the summer of 1856, although they were far from constituting a massacre. Order was restored after 160 men from the *Independence* and the *St. Mary's* were landed at Panama City under the command of Captain Addison Garland, USMC. The *St. Mary's* put her marines, who were soon reinforced by a detachment from HMS *Clio*, ashore again in 1860.

their property. Yellow fever was much dreaded in those days, and with reason. One of our ships, the *Resaca*, during her stay at Panama, had lost twenty-five men out of a crew numbering less than two hundred, and when she passed us near Acapulco on her way up the coast, she still had many sick on board. Under these conditions, of course, very little shore leave was granted. One day, however, two of our officers, Lieutenant Commander Wood and Ensign Wilson, with their boat's crew, were given permission to go ashore. They wanted to visit the ruins of the old tower, the only vestige left to mark the site of Old Panama, the city destroyed two centuries before by Morgan and his buccaneers. It came near being a fatal visit for them.

The party, having made a landing, left one man to look out for the boat, which was drawn up on the beach. Unfortunately, this man, or rather boy, was an inexperienced landsman, and took a crazy notion to experiment with his charge in the absence of the others. They had not gone far when they heard wild cries for help, and rushing back to the beach, saw their boat, her bow pointed to sea and her jib set, already some distance from the shore. Her panic-stricken occupant, in answer to repeated shouts to "haul down the jib," threw himself down in the stern sheets and stretched his arms despairingly to the little group on the beach. Seeing it was useless to expect anything from him, Wood and Wilson began to look about for some means of pursuit, and finally found an old native canoe, hollowed out from a single log. In this frail and treacherous craft they courageously put off, and as they became more accustomed to the use of the paddle, were gradually gaining on the boat, when the breeze freshened, and she began to draw away from them. It was then that the desperate nature of their venture came upon them, for with the breeze, the sea was getting up, and it was doubtful if they could have returned to the shore, even had they been willing to give up all hope of rescuing the author of their troubles. They continued to shout to him to lower the sail, but with absolutely no effect.

The sailors left upon the beach watched pursuers and pursued out of sight, and then began the six-mile walk into Panama. It was nearly evening before they reached their ship, and as all knew it would be a matter of several hours before she could get up steam, and the breeze was carrying the two boats to the eastward all the time, off the track of the few steamers coming to Panama, it was felt that there was practically no hope of a rescue.

The improbable occurred however, as it sometimes does. An English man-of-war, the *Malacca*, commanded by Captain Oldfields, was coming up the coast under sail and stood well over to the eastward. She was just putting about when cries for assistance were heard in the darkness. She rounded to, and in a few minutes a canoe manned by two almost exhausted but very thankful young men came alongside. A little later the boat with its prostrate occupant was sighted and hoisted on board, and before the night was over, the *Suwanee* had her full complement again.

I had had two promotions while on the *Vanderbilt*. I was promoted to the grade of master,[6] in '66, and to that of lieutenant in '67. When we went north to San Francisco in the *Suwanee*, I passed my examination for lieutenant commander, reaching this grade at the age of twenty-four. We did not remain long in San Francisco, having received orders to proceed to Alaska, which had only recently come into our possession. We went first to Victoria, Vancouver, and after a short stay, started on our way to Sitka.

We got no farther than the northern end of Vancouver Island. We were running out of Johnson's Straits the morning of July 7. It was about six o'clock, and I had the deck. We were traveling at full speed, with the current adding two or three knots, when the ship struck an unknown rock, and almost instantly became a complete wreck. The impact was so great that men were thrown from their feet, and those of the crew who were sleeping were pitched from their hammocks. A few who were temporarily demoralized ran to the boats, but the watch on deck behaved admirably. The marines went promptly to their stations at the boat-falls, and by the time the captain and officers reached the deck, and Sanders, the executive, relieved me, comparative quiet was restored. The engine was stopped at once, so there was a full head of steam to blow off. The captain—whom the shock had thrown from the transom where he was sleeping—called to me as he came up the companionway to know if I had sounded the pumps. I answered, "Why, Captain, the whole bottom is torn out of her, from bow to amidships." Indeed she had already started to break in two. The bow was settling, and the deck planking beginning to separate. All at once, with a splintering crash, she parted through the gun ports, just forward of the hurricane deck. About thirty men were left on the forecastle, and the captain asked if I could get across and join them. I managed it easily enough, and though the bow of the ship had completely gone under, the rest of her was so high upon the rock that we were able to get at the storerooms and broke

---

[6] This grade, established in 1837, was replaced by that of lieutenant (junior grade) in 1883.

out a number of barrels of beef and pork. The executive shouted across to us to cut away the rigging, so that the foremast would fall over the side, but as the mast and rigging would have been our only refuge if the ship slipped from her position into deep water, I protested against this. Even then the deck was so steeply inclined that we had to use the cleats and ropes to keep our footing.

A grating that chanced to drop overboard was instantly seized by the force of the current, and sucked under the ship, and this was too much for the nerves of our chief boatswain's mate. I had already suspected this man of cowardice, and now I saw him making a stealthy attempt to reach the after part of the ship. I was about to call attention to him, when Chapman, one of our petty officers, intervened. "Let him go, Mr. Clark! The cur is demoralizing the men!"

A little later, when the provisions we had broken out had been hauled over by lines to the hurricane deck, all hands assembled there, and the boats were manned and loaded. The after end of the ship was by this time well under water also, and as I had had no opportunity to go to my stateroom, I should have lost all my effects, had it not been for the thoughtfulness of Ensign Perry, and a sergeant of marines named Burke. They had snatched the blankets from my bunk, and emptying the contents of drawers and stowage places into them, had tied them into a bundle by the four corners. So nearly all my things were saved.

We were near Hope Island, and the boats were able to land behind a point, but in spite of its protection, the sea was running heavily enough to capsize the first three or four. When it came my turn to shove off, the captain asked me to take charge of his kit, saying he was going to trust it to my management, or luck. When we pulled in, it looked at first as if we were really to make a successful landing, but a few moments after our bow touched the beach, a heavy roller caught us under the quarter, and turned the boat over, only two or three of us managing to jump clear. Luckily, the water was deep enough to keep us from being crushed among the rocks when the boat rolled over us. The captain's faith was justified, for his effects had been pitched ashore at once and landed high and dry, but mine were submerged with me. As they floated to the surface, an Indian—there were a number of them hovering about in canoes—seized the bundle and started to make off with it, but one of our people who saw what was happening pulled a rifle on him, and compelled him to restore my property.

Everybody having landed safely, the captain that same day sent Lieutenant Commander Frank Wildes, in charge of one of the ship's boats, with orders to proceed through the Gulf of Georgia to get help from Victoria, or one of the Puget Sound ports. He had not gone far when he fortunately fell in with H.M.S. *Sparrowhawk*. Her captain, Commander Porcher, took him and his crew on board, and started for Hope Island at full speed, arriving the second day after the wreck. The *Sparrowhawk*'s prompt arrival was most welcome, for although we had built the best tents we could of awnings and sails, they were very inadequate protection from the heavy rains.

As the *Sparrowhawk*'s capacity was limited, we soon realized that a number of us would have to be left behind. When the captain informed me that he meant to leave me in charge of this party, my feelings were somewhat mixed. The prospect of being stranded on Hope Island for an uncertain length of time was not particularly pleasing, and yet I was rather flattered that the captain had chosen me for a position of trust which he might have offered to any one of the three officers who were my seniors. He allowed me to select my men, those who volunteered to be preferred. Ensign Thomas Wilson, assistant engineers Greenleaf and Chasmar, and thirty-three men—all volunteers—were detailed. The captain's only instructions were that everything possible was to be saved from the wreck, and that a constant watch must be kept upon the Indians, who were gathering in great numbers. They were well armed, many of them having breech-loading rifles, like our own. The principal chief in the vicinity was called Cheap, and he looked upon the English as his natural enemies.

The officers and men of the *Sparrowhawk* did everything possible for our people who were embarking with them, and also for those remaining behind. Lieutenant Reginald Townsend came ashore repeatedly, bringing everything he could think of for my comfort, both from his personal effects, and what could be drawn from the ship's stores. We soon had our tents quite comfortable and rainproof, except for the heaviest downpours.

When Chasmar volunteered to be one of the party left with me, I was quite concerned, for he was seemingly wasted with consumption, and during the year I had been with him he had had eight or ten hemorrhages. I felt that the constant dampness and exposure would be almost fatal to one with his complaint. To my great surprise he seemed to benefit rather than otherwise by the camp life. There were five staff officers on the *Suwanee*, and as Chasmar outlived them all, I think he may be regarded as one of the earliest examples of what the open-air treatment can accomplish.

The instant the departing *Sparrowhawk* had turned a point, Cheap, the "bad Indian," came out from behind another where he had been lurking. By good fortune, one of the marines in my party knew the Siwash dialect, so we had a powwow. Cheap proclaimed sovereignty over all the islands and waters in the neighborhood, and complained that the presence of the British gunboat had kept him from exacting his rightful tribute from the wreck. This must now be made good to him. I replied, through our interpreter, that there could be no question of tribute, for while I was on the island I was the one and only chief. The water in front was also under my jurisdiction. I would graciously permit the Indians to come into the bay however, provided they kept away from the beach in front of the camp, and did not approach it from the woods in the rear. That since we were not "King George men" with whom he was engaged in war, I would be glad to trade with him, and if he brought, or sent to the camp, every day, a deer, or a large salmon, tobacco, flannel, and blankets would be generously returned.

Cheap seemed satisfied with these terms, and as he was a wily individual, and quite alive to his own interests, I really believe he used all his influence while we were there to keep the peace but as the Indians continued to gather, and we knew that the fresh arrivals were avaricious, we still felt that there was some danger of an outbreak. One day, when several hundred of them had congregated in front of our camp, and were showing a constant disposition to edge closer, we ran out a twelve-pound howitzer from its hiding-place in the woods. Having neither shrapnel nor canister, we had—this was the suggestion of Ingraham, a boatswain's mate—filled it nearly full of small cans packed with pebbles. We motioned the Indians to stand aside, giving them to understand in sign language that every living thing in our line of fire would cease to exist. When we had finally secured a clear field and let go, it seemed as if a perfect storm of hail had burst upon the waters of the bay. After the gun had been run back to its lair, we beckoned the aborigines to return, but very few accepted the invitation. Even our friend Cheap at his next visit seemed very ill at ease. In spite of the respect this manœuver had inspired, we kept up all precautions. One commissioned officer, with a petty officer and four men, were on guard, day and night. I still had in reserve the threat of uncorking a bottle of smallpox, so effective, as Washington Irving tells us, in "Astoria."

One morning, we found that a small steamer, the *Otter*, belonging to the Hudson Bay Company, had come to anchor off our camp. I had an interview with her captain and contracted with him to take us and such stores as were saved to Victoria. He was rather inclined to take advantage of our situation, we thought, and I consequently enjoyed his confusion and rueful protests, when I made him include among his receipts a quantity of brass tubes, which he had stowed away as part of his own cargo. We had intended to take them out of the wreck at low tide, but discovered the morning before we sailed that the captain had forestalled us at this work.

On our way south in the *Otter* we met the *Sparrowhawk* coming north, just at the upper end of Seymour's Narrows. Her captain brought word from Admiral Thatcher that he was sending a small steamer, the *Forward*, to the scene of the wreck to bring us away, and that the *Suwanee's* guns must be saved if possible. I concluded that I might as well continue in the *Otter* until we should meet the *Forward*, and it was not long after this that we sighted a large bay steamer, the *New World*, which it seemed had been sent in her place. On board was our navigator, Lieutenant Commander George Wood, Ensign Thomas Perry, and twenty of our men. The admiral had sent me permission to travel south at the first opportunity, but Greenleaf, Chasmar, Wilson, and I decided to transfer to the *New World* and return with Wood to Hope Island. Perry took Wilson's place in the *Otter*.

The *New World* had brought diving apparatus, and a professional diver, rejoicing in the euphonious title of "Billy the Bug", but when this gentleman saw the position of the wreck, he decided the risks were too great and declined the job. Hearing of this, Mirch, our gunner's mate, immediately volunteered his services. The day he began operations everything was favorable, and though the current was strong, the water was so clear that the hatches of the storeroom on the second deck could be plainly seen. While Mirch's armor and helmet were being adjusted on the hurricane deck, the Indians, who had flocked to the scene in their canoes, were in a fever of excitement, which even their stoicism failed to conceal. A number of them, shepherded by Cheap, were roosting along that part of the ship's rail which had not been submerged. They kept a tight clutch on their canoes, and it was perfectly evident they would have jumped into them and viewed what was going on at a safer distance, if Cheap had not commanded them by motions to remain. He was a public character with a reputation to maintain, and could not afford to show any signs of fear. There were a few moments of terrible tension, when Mirch, who had been lowered to the spar deck, walked slowly along it, remaining an unnatural length of time beneath the water, as it seemed to them. But when he approached the steerage hatch, and began his descent into the deeper darkness below, flesh and blood could bear it no longer. It was too much even for Cheap. With a cry of terror, he leaped for his canoe and led the flight. We could see him and his followers still spattering water, as they rounded the point, and it was several days before they again honored us with a visit.

Usually we would have been glad enough to have them keep away, but at this time it happened that Wood wanted to get some information from Cheap, and after waiting in vain for him to put in an appearance, finally decided to make a visit to his village. Wood and I were the only officers in the party, and we had our revolvers in our belts, but none of the men in our boat's crew were armed, as we considered that we were making a friendly call. We discovered soon after landing that the friendliness was all on one side. Cheap was not at home, and in his absence we found we were distinctly unwelcome. An ugly-looking half-breed, who was manifestly trying to foment the ill feeling against us, came up to me, gesturing and muttering excitedly, and before I knew what he was about, snatched the revolver from my belt. Quick as the action was, Wood was quicker. Before the half-breed could free my revolver of its leather guard, Wood's was at his head, and the cool contact of its muzzle caused him to hand back my weapon with almost comical rapidity. The other Indians, who had surged forward on this movement of their leader's, retreated, and Wood, lowering his revolver slowly, motioned the half-breed to go, and he slunk off completely cowed. It occurred to me that it would have been prudent to have held him as a hostage until we were safely in our boat, but Wood's contemptuous treatment of him so impressed the other Indians that they gave us no further trouble.

We saved all the ammunition in the after part of the *Suwanee* and her guns, with the exception of the forward one-hundred pounder. That the Indians did a little salvage work on their own account was proved in a curious way, some twenty years later. Commander Hitchcock of our service was at that time recovering from an illness in a hospital at Victoria. One day, when his dinner was brought to him, he noticed that the silver spoon and fork lying on the tray were marked "Thomas Perry, U.S.N." He questioned the nurse and found that the two articles had been left at the hospital by a poor Indian who had been treated there, and who had insisted on bestowing the only valuables he had, in gratitude for kindnesses received. Commander Hitchcock was able to purchase the fork and spoon and sent them to their original owner, now a rear admiral on the retired list.

On our way to Victoria, we had occasion to prove the power of the current in Seymour's Narrows, where a few years later the U.S.S. *Saranac* was lost.[7] We were caught in the narrows by the full force of the ebb, and despite our utmost efforts, we were not able to win through. The chart states that the current there runs from six to nine knots, but although the *New World* could make eleven knots, she was unable to overcome it. Two or three times, by bottling up our steam until we came to the worst place, we managed to bring her bow almost to the end of the gorge, where she hung quivering for an instant, only to be swept back by the relentless force of the water. Finally we gave it up and ran into Plumper Bay, some distance above the entrance, where we waited for the flood tide.

On our arrival at Victoria, we were somewhat disturbed to learn that this *New World*, in which by wording of the contract we were to continue our way to San Francisco, had been condemned as unsafe for even the enclosed waters of Puget Sound. There was no telegraphic communication then with either Washington or San Francisco, which left Lieutenant Commander Wood in an embarrassing position. He had to choose between entailing on the Government the extra expense of our passage on another steamer, an expenditure it might refuse to recognize, or the distressing alternative of risking more than fifty lives under his charge. The English admiral, Hastings, whose flagship the *Zealous* was lying at Esquimalt, showed much concern over our situation. He expressed the opinion that our admiral, Thatcher, could certainly not have known when he made the contract what a rotten hulk the *New World* was, and when he heard that Wood had decided he must try to get through in her to San Francisco, he strongly advised the engaging of another steamer. If our Navy Department censured such a course, which appeared unlikely, he would be glad to state that he had been responsible for the action as far as a superior officer in another service could be. Finally, during a visit he made to the *New World*, he declared that rather than see nearly sixty American officers and men put to sea in such a death trap, he would transport them in his own ship. It was a pity Wood did not feel himself in a position to accept this generous and considerate offer, for coming to public notice at a time when the *Alabama* claims were being adjusted, it might have helped to bring about a kindlier feeling between the two countries.

After all, our old "death trap" took us safely to San Francisco, but that

[7] The sloop-of-war *Saranac*, a sidewheel steamer commissioned in 1850, was lost in the Seymour Narrows, off Vancouver, British Columbia, on 18 June 1875.

was merely good luck, because for seven hundred miles, and during seventy hours, we ran over an absolutely glassy sea. Only once, in a long swell off Cape Mendocino, did she roll to her guards, and that roll brought everybody up on deck, ready to take to the boats at an instant's notice.

Chapter 8

AN ASIATIC CRUISE

Detached from the Pacific fleet and ordered home, I took passage on the steamer *Golden City* for Panama. At Aspinwall, now called Colon, I transferred to the *Alaska*. She was just casting off her lines to leave the dock, when a messenger came running down it with orders for the captain to make fast again, and wait for passengers just arrived at Panama by a South Pacific steamer. They proved to be officers and men from the *Dacotah*, and the survivors of the *Wateree* and *Fredonia*, vessels destroyed by the earthquake wave at Arica;[1] nearly three hundred in all. Among them was my classmate, George T. Davis. He asked me to visit his home, in Greenfield, Massachusetts, on the way to my own in Montpelier. I was very easily persuaded to do so, as I had a strong desire to see what changes five years had made in the features or the expression of his youngest sister Louisa, who when I had last seen her was a young girl. The visit resulted in our engagement, and we were married on April 8, 1869. The Greenfield paper, in announcing the event, gave me a higher rank than I have ever attained since, referring to me as Charles E. Clark, Lieutenant *Commanding* the United States Navy. The usual announcement about presents "numerous and valuable" was not quoted. I should add that our marriage followed orders suddenly received by me

[1] The latter two vessels were among those lost when Arica, Peru, was struck by an earthquake and tidal wave on the afternoon of 13 August 1868.

Rear Admiral Clark and granddaughter, Louisa Russell Hughes.

to a ship, and that Mary, the next older daughter, wife of Senator Conness and mother of Lady Rich, had married one week earlier. Louisa Russell Davis, mother of Mrs. Clark and Mrs. Conness, was born at 34 Beacon St., now the office of the publishers of this book.

We have two daughters, Mary Louise, married to Captain S. S. Robison, U.S.N., and Caroline Russell, married to Captain C. F. Hughes, U.S.N., and one granddaughter, Louisa Russell Hughes.[2]

In September, 1870, I became navigator of the monitor *Dictator*—the *Richard Murphy* as the sailors used to call her.[3] She was then the largest of our ironclads, and also the most heavily armored, but through some mistake in her construction she had only one turret, and her battery consequently was only half that of the *Monadnock*.[4] Her overhang was nowhere less than four feet wide, and because of her great length, she would, when pitching in a heavy sea, strike this projecting part with such force that it seemed as if the next shock must inevitably tear her open, and founder her. Many of her crew never went below in rough weather, saying they did not propose to be caught like rats in a trap, without even the chance for a swim. I remember a pilot who joined us at Tybee Roads, just below Savannah, who spent the greater part of two days and nights on the sloping awning above the turret, and vowed if he were ever fortunate enough to get on shore again, he meant to stay there.

On our way south from Hampton Roads, during what was generally known in the service as the first Cubic War, we encountered a gale while in the Gulf Stream and our wheel ropes parted. The space between deck and boilers was less than two feet, and as it was therefore impossible for men to repair the damage to the ropes with steam up, we were obliged to haul fires. So for hours we lay in the trough of a heavy sea, which swept

[2] Captain S. S. Robison took part in the battle of Manila Bay and now commands the battleship *South Carolina*.

Captain C. F. Hughes now commands the battleship *New York*. He was Chief of Staff of the battleship fleet with Rear Admiral Charles J. Badger, when that officer, under orders to Tampico, proceeded to Vera Cruz instead, arriving a few hours after the fighting began, landing reënforcements, and being in responsible command from that time on and when our heaviest losses were incurred. [Author's note]

[3] Prior to this cruise, the author was briefly assigned to the receiving ship *Vandalia* at Portsmouth and the decommissioned screw sloop *Seminole* at Boston.

[4] The navy's first true seagoing monitor, the *Dictator* was commissioned on 11 November 1864. She was a sizeable vessel for the period, 312 feet in length and 50 abeam, with a displacement of 3,033 tons. The armament of which Admiral Clark complains consisted of the two 15-inch smoothbore Dahlgren guns common to single-turreted monitors.

our decks, submerging everything but the turret and the light deck extending from it to the smoke-stack. The tugs which were with us as consorts, the *Standish* and *Triana*, were absolutely useless. The first lost her rudder, and the engines of the second broke down. We saw nothing of the *Standish* during all that troubled night, and the one glimpse we had of the *Triana* we would have been very glad to forego. She came drifting down upon us out of the darkness, and for a moment it looked as if she were going to get caught under our overhang, which would have been fatal to us both, but luckily we had enough steam at the time to go ahead, and she just cleared us astern. When morning dawned, neither tug was visible, so we made for the Savannah River. We heard afterwards that they fortunately met, and effecting a combination like the blind man and the cripple, one towing and the other steering, they got into Charleston Harbor.

Our captain, Edmund R. Calhoun, had had much experience with ironclads. He had served in monitors off Charleston during all the engagements there, and was in command of the *Wehawken*, when having grounded at night, she was exposed the next day to a cross fire from Sumter and Moultrie. One of our young officers, who was conspicuous for his coolness and courage in all the emergencies of this trying cruise, was Wilson McGunnigle, a brother of the Lieutenant McGunnigle I reported to on board the *Constitution* when I entered the service. It was a loss to the navy when he resigned later to go into the banking business.[5]

Before ending this cruise, we went to Port au Prince, Hayti, in company with the flagship *Severn* and the *Saugus*. Santo Domingo was then considering annexation to the United States, and as there was some idea that Hayti might wish to interfere, we were sent there to bully her into keeping her hands off.

From Port au Prince, we went to Samana Bay, Santo Domingo, where the sentiment of the party in power seemed strongly in favor of annexation. I remember that the mulatto pilot who tried to induce our captain to let him take the ship into port was an enthusiastic partisan. He had voted several times already, he told us, and meant to vote again when he got ashore, and when we inquired about the proportion of those who were against the measure, he assured us that they were not allowed to vote at all. If there were truth in his account of affairs, it must be

---

[5] He was one of the guests invited by the Navy Department to take passage on the *Oregon*, when it was proposed to have her lead the international fleets at the opening of the Panama Canal. [Author's note]

concluded that the eventual decision against annexing Santo Domingo must have come from the United States.[6]

All during our stay the authorities showed a great desire to ingratiate themselves with us. Captain Bunce of the *Nantasket* had a rather startling proof of this. He had sent a complaint to Governor Baez, whose brother was then president of Santo Domingo, about the insolence of one of the native boatmen. The governor promptly replied that he had identified the man, and had despatched him under guard to his brother, the president, with the request that he be shot at once. Bunce was obliged to send a horseman posthaste to prevent this too obliging evidence of national good will.

My first shore duty was at the Naval Academy, Annapolis. I was there from 1870 to 1873 as an instructor and assistant to the commandant of midshipmen. I made one practice cruise on the *Saratoga* in company with the *Constellation*. On board the *Saratoga* was a boatswain's mate by the name of Brady, who will doubtless be remembered by others beside myself because of his absolute devotion to one of the officers. For this young man he desired all things good in the official line and was jealous of any distinction conferred on others. One Sunday, while the ship was in port, a letter from the Secretary of the Navy was read at general quarters, highly commending the gallantry of an officer who had saved the life of a man who had fallen overboard. That evening Brady rolled aft, and sidling up to his idol, who was pacing the deck, began a long dissertation on what a fine thing it was for a young officer to have "one of them 'condemnatory' letters from the Secretary of the Navy, sir."

"Of course it's a fine thing," agreed the officer, rather puzzled to know what the old man could be driving at, "but if you have any reference to me, Brady, I can't quite see how one is coming my way."

"Why, I'll tell you, sir," said Brady, sinking his voice to a hoarse confidential whisper. "To-morrow I gets leave and comes back alongside, just after pipe-down, when you has the deck. As I steps for the gangway, I misses my footing and overboard I goes. And you in after me," he ended triumphantly.

"That's a wonderful plan, Brady," said the young officer, smiling, "but you see it has one fatal drawback. I don't know how to swim."

[6] The possibility of annexing the Dominican Republic arose in 1868, when the Dominican president, in a surprising response to Secretary of State Seward's offer to purchase a naval base there, invited him to have the whole country. Seward and President Andrew Johnson welcomed the idea, but Congress did not. The following year President Grant actually obtained a treaty of annexation, which, despite his strong support, was overwhelmingly rejected by the Senate.

"Lord, sir! that don't make no difference. Don't you be afeard to jump. I'll hold you up till the boat comes."

After my three years at the Academy I was ordered as executive to another monitor, the *Mahopac*,[7] lying at Norfolk. They were rush orders, for war was again threatened with Spain on account of the *Virginius* affair,[8] and all was hurry and hustle. I reached New York City in a driving snowstorm, too late to catch any night train south, and crossed over to Jersey City to be sure of the first train in the morning. It was a case of "much haste, less speed." The hotel clerk with whom I left word to be called chose that occasion to indulge in a fit, and I slumbered peacefully on through part of the next day. The hotel clerk's fit reminds me of a telegram that was sent by an officer to his wife, when his ship arrived at Hampton Roads after a European cruise. He had picked up many English expressions while abroad, and his telegram, when it reached the little resort in the Adirondacks where she was spending the summer, was worded "Arrived Hampton Roads ten A.M. Friday. Am fit." Of course the country operator knew that the last sentence must be incorrect, and when it came to the lady's hands it read, "Arrived Hampton Roads ten A.M. Had a fit." She very nearly had one herself, and her husband's unfortunate phrase cost him something in explanatory telegrams.

The *Mahopac* got off the day after her officers reported, some workmen from the navy yard going in her as far as Hampton Roads and working to the last minute to stop the leaks which would have been fatal to a vessel of her class. Of course, in the general rush it had not been possible to make arrangements for anything like ordinary comfort in our living conditions. All stores had been tumbled aboard in the greatest haste and without any regard to order, and the four negroes shipped as wardroom

---

[7] The *Mahopac* was one of nine *Canonicus*-class single-turreted monitors. These were the first monitors whose design and construction benefitted from the operating experience of their predecessors. Commissioned on 22 September 1864, she measured 223 feet in length and 43 feet 4 inches abeam, displaced 2,100 tons, and carried a crew of approximately 100 officers and men. The design speed of her class was 13 knots.

[8] In October 1873 the former blockade-runner *Virginius*, falsely registered under American ownership, was captured by the Spanish cruiser *Tornado* while carrying munitions and insurgents to Cuba. Her passengers and crew were condemned to death by a military court in Havana, and before American and British protests brought an end to the executions, fifty-three of the unfortunate prisoners were shot. This number included several Americans, among them the *Virginius*' captain, Joseph Fry, late lieutenant, USN and CSN. The indignation this news aroused in the United States was so great that for some months war with Spain appeared likely. The Spanish government eventually agreed to pay an indemnity to the families of the men executed.

boys must have been taken right out of the corn fields. They were quite hopeless as far as proper service was concerned, but we did contrive to get a little amusement out of them. Lieutenant Joseph Jones, a volunteer officer, much older than the rest of us, stage-managed the entertainment. A pitcher, with features painted on its smooth surface and a sheet dangling limply from its neck, hanging by its handle in a darkened stateroom, made a "ghost" weird enough to inspire terror in the breasts of Salt, Mustard, Vinegar, and Pepper, as Jones had named our outfit in the order of their complexions. The knowledge that the "ghost" was the creation of Jones never seemed to help them at all. A boy told to go and get something from a certain room, would approach its curtain with eyes bulging, and the muttered protest, "I'se powerful skeered, sah, Missah Jones done been in dah," while his mates waited in a sort of fearful ecstacy for the moment when he would burst through the door, with his wool standing on end.

One day Salt, the pantry boy, was so absorbed in watching the mental struggles of Pepper, who had been told to fetch something from the doctor's room, that he ventured too far from his own base, and Jones, slipping by him, set up a ghost to face him on his return. The wild yell and crash that meant the loss of a good part of our crockery told us that the flank movement had been only too successful.

On our arrival at Key West, we found nearly everything we possessed in the way of a navy assembled there, the European and South Atlantic fleets having been recalled. Our all was not much at that date,[9] but the Spaniards were no better off than we, so I imagine a fight would have seen us on the winning side. Nearly all our ships were fitted with spar torpedoes, and these were expected to inflict great damage on the enemy, always providing he would stay quiet until we got alongside, and that we were not "hoist first" through the spar breaking, or the guys carrying away.

But of course our chief concern was target practice, and a board of three officers was created to superintend it. They decided that six hundred yards was the proper distance to begin with, but our captain, O'Kane, agreed with me that this would bring the target absurdly close. He told me to set ours at two thousand yards, and he would go aboard the flagship and take up the matter with the authorities. He had scarcely pulled away when the three officers composing the board arrived. They

[9] The squadrons assembled at Key West in February 1874 constituted the largest concentration of American naval force since the Civil War. In the ensuing maneuvers it was found that the fleet speed, determined by the slowest vessels, was a stately 4.5 knots.

made themselves quite disagreeable over our failure to adopt the distance they had suggested, and I had to send out a boat to bring the target in to the six-hundred-yard line. Executives of monitors in those days often fired the guns themselves, and I was generally regarded as a good shot. Allowing for the vessel to sheer a little, I pointed ahead, waited for the contact, and fired, hoping my luck would stand by me. I knew it had when I saw the men crowding their heads into the port as the gun recoiled. "There ain't any target, sir!" cried one, as I stepped outside and was greeted by the long faces of the board.

I put on an injured look and said regretfully, "Well, you see how it is. We can only get one shot a day, and our material for targets will have to be increased."

Indeed, the little tent-shaped target was absolutely obliterated, its center stick having been struck at the base, and the Board, which had been eloquent about getting the admiral's ear and O'Kane's scalp, made a silent and solemn departure.

The war flurry over, and the fleet dispersed, I went home for a short leave, at the end of which I received orders to the Asiatic station. As I was to go out by steamer from San Francisco, my wife and our two little girls, then nearly five and three years of age, were able to accompany me.

An overland trip took longer then than it does now, but we were prepared for that and did not find it tedious. I remember there was a little ripple of excitement at one of the stations on the plains where the east and west bound trains met, when some one pointed out Rochefort, the titled French Radical, among the passengers on the platform. He had just made his escape from the penal colony of New Caledonia, and having landed in San Francisco, was on his way east.[10]

[10] A vitriolic pen and a passion for controversy kept the editor and dramatist Henri Rochefort, Marquis de Rochefort-Luçay (1830–1913), in the storm center of French politics for almost half a century. In 1868 his newspaper, La Lanterne, was suppressed after its eleventh edition, and he was sentenced to a year's imprisonment for its criticisms of the government of the Second Empire. Rochefort fled to Belgium, where he continued publication of his paper, but was allowed to return to France following his election to the National Assembly in 1869. He then founded a new journal, La Marseillaise, whose editorials earned him another prison term. Freed upon the fall of the empire, he became a member of the Government of National Defense and later a supporter of the Paris Commune. His identification as a communard led to a sentence of life imprisonment in New Caledonia, from which he escaped on an American ship in 1874. Permitted to return to France by the proclamation of a general amnesty for political offenders in 1880, he established a third newspaper, aptly entitled L'Intransigeant, which helped create the Boulanger crisis. Still later he became a leader of the right-wing forces in the Dreyfus Affair. His autobiography, Les Adventures de ma vie, was published in five volumes in 1896.

We became much interested in two of our fellow passengers, a Mr. Power and his cousin, Mr. Codd. They were Irishmen and were making a world tour for the sake of Mr. Power's health. He had recently lost his seat in the House of Commons and was nervously used up and depressed. His cousin was supposed to supply the good spirits for the party, and as he had a lively fancy, I am sure that at times he managed to make Mr. Power forget his other troubles. Whenever the train stopped long at a station, it was Mr. Codd's habit to march up and down its platform with my children, having first effected a change of hats with one of them. His solemn air as he paraded along, the blue ribbons of his absurd headgear hanging over one eye, and a radiant youngster clinging to each hand, delighted the crowd and horrified Mr. Power, but his protests were only answered by, "We're from Dublin, after all, my dear fellow. Not quite English, you know."

When we reached San Francisco and were confronted at the ferry by the long line of hackmen with their dangling whips, Mr. Codd exclaimed, "They all know my name, by Jove! See how they're fishing for me!"

He and Mr. Power engaged one of these discerning fellows for the next afternoon and took us all for a drive out to the Cliff House and Seal Rocks. Besides being pleasant in itself, this excursion was actually the means of putting money in my pocket, or perhaps I should say keeping it there. We chanced to meet the agent for the Pacific Mail Company that afternoon, and after watching my little girls who, dressed in sailor suits, were playing on the beach, he remarked that it would be a shame to charge those young mariners for their trip to China, and the Company would consider it sufficient if I bought tickets for Mrs. Clark and myself.

The good ship *Colorado* took us through to Yokohama in twenty-three days. She was a side-wheeler with a single engine, and had opened the line to China and Japan when I was in San Francisco eight years before. During the whole trip of five thousand miles we encountered neither gale nor sail.

I reported to Admiral Pennock in Yokohama, where he was flying his flag on the *Hartford*, whose cabin I entered for the first time since my memorable interview with Farragut. Pennock was a connection of Farragut's, by the way. He assigned me to the *Yantic* as executive.[11] She was

---

[11] The *Yantic* was a wooden-hulled screw gunboat of 836-ton displacement commissioned in August 1864. She was 179 feet in length, 30 feet abeam, and carried a crew of 154. Following more than three decades' service in the Far East, the West Indies, and

Hartford, with topgallant masts housed, and without covered spar deck. Rig during the Civil War.

then lying at Shanghai, so I continued my trip on the *Colorado*, my wife and children disembarking at Nagasaki, to remain for the rest of the summer.

Soon after I had joined the *Yantic*, we were sent to Amoy, where we arrested General Legendre, who without authority from the United States had accepted the position of military adviser to the Japanese in their first expedition to Formosa. He had been a general in our army, and had come out of the Civil War with little remaining of his natural self, for in addition to a glass eye and wooden leg, he had a wig and false teeth.[12] It was said that he once tried to make an impression on the natives of Formosa by reducing himself to his lowest terms in their presence, but no interest was shown until he removed his glass eye, when the assembly suddenly waked up, and expressed—through an interpreter—a desire to see him take out the other one.

It was while we were at Amoy that our captain received some cabled instructions from Admiral Pennock, ending with the words, "Clark's family all right." Of course I knew that there must be some reason for this statement of what seemed to me an obvious fact, and a few hours later, when we heard that Nagasaki had been swept by the most terrific typhoon that had been remembered in years, I was grateful indeed for the admiral's thoughtfulness. The destruction had been almost unprecedented, and among the houses blown down was the one standing next the hotel where my family was staying.

After seven months in the *Yantic* I was ordered to the *Hartford* as executive, and when she sailed for home, to the *Kearsarge*. The *Kearsarge* was then the largest ship left on the station, so when I offered to exchange with Craven, who was my senior, and who was attached to the

---

home waters, she was loaned to the Michigan Naval Militia in 1898. Recommissioned during World War I, she sailed the Great Lakes as a training ship until 1926, when she was returned to the State of Michigan. Her long career ended when she sank at her dock at Detroit in October 1929.

[12] Charles William Le Gendre was among the more bizarre of the soldiers of fortune who enjoyed a golden age in the later nineteenth century. Born in France in 1830, he rose to the rank of brevet brigadier general, U.S. Volunteers, during the Civil War, in the course of which he lost part of his jaw, the bridge of his nose, and his left eye. In 1866 he was appointed U.S. consul at Amoy, China, and subsequently accepted employment as military advisor to the Japanese government (1872–75), which, as Admiral Clark relates, led him into difficulties. These had no lasting effect on his activities, however, and in 1890 he became an advisor to the Korean Royal Household, a position he held until his death in Seoul in 1899.

Monocacy, I suppose I got credit for magnanimity to which I was not entitled. I did not feel bound to confess that the change appealed to me, because I felt sure the *Monocacy* would soon go to Shanghai for extensive repairs. The rest of my cruise was spent on this ship, which was so long identified with the Asiatic Station that when she was sold, only a few years ago, it must have seemed to the old seamen who had shipped on her, over and over again, as if it were their home that was being broken up. She had the light draft necessary for river work, and the Chinese, with reference to her paddle wheels, used to call her "two side walkee."[13] When I joined her, Captain Joseph Fyffe was in command. This officer claimed descent from "the first families of America", or in other words, the noble red man. He was inordinately proud of his ancestry, and any suggestion on the part of an Englishman or Scotchman that he might be connected with the ducal family of Fife was always warmly resented. "Belong to that Flute family!" he would exclaim. "No, sir! I spell my name F-y-f-f-e, and come of a race whose ancestors were out for scalps, when those Scotchmen were stealing sheep from over the border!"

Though inclined to take himself and his family affairs rather seriously as a rule, he would often amuse us with accounts of his father-in-law, who was no other than Moody, the fighting parson of the Ohio Valley. Fyffe used to speak with enthusiasm of the fashion in which Mr. Moody conducted his meetings, jumping sometimes from his improvised pulpit—a plank resting on two barrels—to beat the heads of a couple of rowdies into a pulp, then hopping back like a rooster to his perch to lead the singing. When these energies were turned on the little country place his son-in-law was trying to beautify, however, they did not seem so admirable. There was quite a degree of pathos mixed with the humor with which the captain told how a lawn on which he had expended both time and love had been ploughed and turned into a hayfield by the forcible old gentleman, and the young shade trees he had grouped with such care, uprooted and planted in straight rows.

"The old cuss would walk up to one of them," said he, "put his arm around it as an elephant would his trunk, yank it out, and march off with it. Things got to such a pass that one day I just sailed out of my gate and

---

[13] The *Monocacy* was a naval fixture in the Far East, where she represented the United States for thirty-six years. Sometimes called the "jinricksha of the navy," she was commissioned in Baltimore in 1866 and joined the Asiatic Squadron late in 1867. She was 265 feet in length, 35 feet abeam, displaced 1,370 tons, and carried six guns and a complement of 159. Sold in 1903, her name was given to a second *Monocacy* (PG 20), which served on the Yangtze from 1914 until 1939.

shouted, 'Brown County, ahoy! What will you give me for the whole blamed outfit! Farm, fertilizers, father-in-law, and all!'"[14]

I never had occasion to regret my move to the *Monacacy*, for the duty in connection with her was thoroughly agreeable. We were in Shanghai for lengthy periods, did quite a bit of cruising about Japan, including some delightful weeks in the wonderful Inland Sea, and made one trip north to Tientsin, where luckily we did not tarry long.

The hospitality in the Orient at that time was princely. Had Mrs. Clark and I been willing, we could have made our three years on the station one long visit from house to house. In fact we did once spend three months in Shanghai at the home of our Consul General, Mr. George F. Seward, a nephew of the great statesman of the same name. At this time he had just received his appointment as Minister to China, and as he was consequently obliged to pass a part of the winter in Peking, he urged us to stay on with Mrs. Seward, knowing that she and Mrs. Clark were devoted friends. Another Shanghai home that became familiar to us was that of Mr. and Mrs. Harrison. He was the manager of the Oriental Bank, then the largest banking concern in the Far East. If it had not been for the hospitable spirit that pervaded this home, it would have seemed a little too much like living in a palace, marble halls and all. The rooms were so stately that furniture had to be made especially with reference to them, and I remember the beds in the suite of rooms we occupied were so colossal that a family of giants could have slept in them very comfortably. Those were the days of long-drawn-out dinners, a regiment of wine glasses standing by each plate, and your own Chinese "boy" behind your chair, to see that you were served exactly as you would have been at home. I believe these customs are things of the past. In China, as elsewhere, it has ceased to be good form to play with food and wine through an entire evening, and though many in the Orient still put everything except their souls in the keeping of their "boys", they no longer consider it necessary to be served by them in a friend's house.

There is a general impression that the Chinaman is a soulless machine in his relations with other races, dependable and even honorable in business matters, but with no sentiment towards his employer, however well he may have been treated.[15] And yet you will come across an

---

[14] As the narrative makes clear, Joseph F. Fyffe, USNA 1853, was one of the most colorful naval characters of his generation. For a sketch of his life, see R. W. Daly, "Joe Fyffe—Officer and Gentleman," U.S. Naval Institute *Proceedings*, April 1956, pp. 417–25. He retired in the rank of rear admiral in 1894.

[15] It should be recalled that during the Boxer war there were Chinese converts who braved injuries and even death in defense of their foreign friends. [Author's note]

exception occasionally, as in the case of the comprador, Ah Tee, in Hong Kong. During our stay in that port, I made a point of having my little girls meet this old Chinaman, with the hope that they would remember him as one who had been a friend to their country at a time when she needed friends. It was touching to see the old man's pleasure in the recollection of his services, which can perhaps be best described by the insertion here of a few verses, purporting to be written by a poor relation of Truthful James.[16]

AH TEE

By "Truthful Jack"

My story begins in the year sixty-four,
Which was durin' the time of our late Civil War.
(And just by the way, which ter me its a mys'try
That ain't never been cleared by my knowledge of hist'ry.
When people are fightin' themselves like the devil,
Why in 'nation should sech goin's-on be tarmed civil?)
Well, this ain't my tale, but its reely surprisin'
How durned easy it is to start in moralizin'.

'Twas our ship *Saginaw*, ter meander along,
In her v'ygin' around had brung up at Hong Kong.
A city in which if the heathen gits skittish
They're put down mighty quick by the red-coated British,
Who, if given to land-grabbin', yet I've hearn tell
When they once git a country, kin govern it well.
And to whatever part of this wide earth they go.
They will make that same portion, "quite English, you know."

Now the *Saginaw's* crew, Cap'n McD. commandin','[17]
Was powerful glad in a port to be landin'.
For pervisions were low, and their grog it was slacker,
And they hadn't no coal, and still less of terbacker.
But when Cap'n McD. hurried quick to the shore,
For to buy out the town, and a leetle bit more,
He found—and to him 'twas a long ways from funny,—
He couldn't git no one to look at his money.

[16] The allusion is to Bret Harte's poem, "Plain Language from Truthful James," first published in 1871, whose narrator is plucked by a Chinese cardsharp, Ar Sen.

[17] There is some confusion here. Commander David S. McDougal commanded the screw sloop *Wyoming* in Asian waters from 1862 to 1864. The sidewheel steamer *Saginaw* served in the same area from 1860 to 1862 under Commander James F. Schenk.

The slim little bank clerks remarked with a grin,
It was yet on the cards that the Rebels might win.
When the captain to this swore blank, blank, and dash, dash,
They replied, "That may be, but we can't risk our cash."
At the chandler's and grocer's he couldn't git trusted,
For they "feared", which meant "hoped", that the North might go
    busted.
And poor Cap'n McD. was reduced to despair,
For his crew warn't the kind as could hold out on air;
He was tired of being rebuffed an' rejected,
When he run across help, in a way unexpected.

'Twas a little old shop, in a dirty side street,
And the odors about,—well, the same wasn't sweet.
But within, grouped about in keg, bottle and can,
Was all that could comfort the in'nards of man.
In letters promiskus, swung over the door,
The name of Ah Tee, U. S. Ship's Comprador,
An' Cap'n McD., with a very deep sigh,
Thought before givin' up, he would make one last try.

At the first look around at walls, counter and shelf,
You'd have said that the shop was a-keepin' itself.
But there presently came from the dark at the rear,
A voice, which remarked in a gibberish queer,
"Ah! you, Melican man, my long time no have see!
All Melican off'cer he savy Ah Tee!"
And a little old heathen, his hair in a queue,
And a welcomin' smile on his lips, stepped in view.

Thinks McD. to himself,—"When I come to show down
My paper, that smile will be changed to a frown."
But Ah Tee looked at things in a different way,
"Long time Melican sailor, he plenty good pay,
"He my velly good fiend, all time speakee me tlue;
"S'pose this time losee money, maskee,[18] my can do."
This trust from a heathen, the captain unmanned.
Somethin' swelled in his throat, and he put out his hand.

And that warn't all neither, for when he'd supplied
The wants of the ship, and her crew satisfied,

---

[18] Maskee = Never mind, no matter. [Author's note]

The day they weighed anchor to sail for Shanghai,
Ah Tee paddled off for to tell 'em good-bye.
Six big strappin' coolies in line followed him,
And each carried a bag filled with "plunks" to the brim,
Which they dropped on the deck at Ah Tee's invitation,
While the old man proceeded to make an oration.

Which the substance was this,—In all ports they would find
As to money the "Blitish" of much the same mind,
Banks and stores in Shanghai, "allee same" as Hong Kong;
So he'd brought "littee cumsha"[19] to help'em along.
The speech rather sudden-like came to an end
With this explanation, "You b'long my good fliend."
And the very last sound, as the ship put to sea,
Was the sailor-men shoutin', "Three cheers for Ah Tee!"

Which is why I remark that our virtues and sins
Don't always match up with the shade of our skins,
And the somethin' that preachers tarm speeritchul grace
Ain't confined to the people that own a white face.
And if ever it happens that you, sir, and I
Should enter them mansions they talks of, on high,
Where the crooked comes straight, and wrong is made right,
We'll find that old Chinaman's record is white.[20]

M.L.R.

When we made our trip through the Inland Sea, Captain Fyffe, who was well acquainted with our Minister to Japan, Mr. Bingham—they both came from the state of Ohio—invited him to go with us. The

---

[19] Cumsha = a present. [Author's note]

[20] This was not the only occasion on which Ah Tee lent a helping hand to the *Saginaw* and her commanding officer. Oddly enough, this vessel happened to be in Hong Kong some time later, when it was felt that war might break out between the United States and England on account of the *Trent* difficulty. The *Saginaw*, which had been laid up at that time, and her crew—reduced to two or three men—would have been an easy prize for the English, and McDougal, who had been left in charge, determined to remove her to the Portuguese port of Macao, if he could manage it. His first step was to send for Ah Tee and explain the situation to him. Ah Tee came off at nightfall with fifty coolies, and great was the astonishment of the English officers who had been joking McDougal about the amount of prize money that might come to them from the capture of his vessel, to see this ship, without a crew as they supposed, get under way and steam out of the harbor. [Author's note]

presidential contest was on at home, and Mr. Bingham was exceedingly anxious to learn whom the Republicans had nominated for President and Vice President. He began to get positively feverish about this at the time we were visiting the island of Miajima, one of the most beautiful spots in the Inland Sea. Its picturesque temples, its torii running out into the clear water, and the graceful, spotted deer wandering about its village streets were all indifferent to Mr. Bingham. Nothing would do but we must run across to some small settlement, where it was reported that a telegraph station had been established. After a long struggle with the native operator, a telegram was despatched, and the answer awaited with suspense. Finally the instrument commenced to tick, and the operator handed over a slip with the names "Crawford and Mulcahy" inscribed on it. Mr. Bingham was reduced to despair. "That ends it!" he said despondently. "If the party is that scared it doesn't dare run anybody that was ever heard of before, even in a state legislature, we're defeated at the start."

He had no heart for scenery after that, and we made for the port of Kobe, where we learned that the Republican nominees were Hayes and Wheeler, and that Crawford and Mulcahy were the foremen of a railway construction gang, working on the line between Kobe and Osaka.

It was during our cruise among these islands that I overheard the captain administering comfort in his own peculiar fashion to a party of Japanese who were visiting the ship. They were worried because some American missionaries had settled in their little community, and Christianity was on the increase. "Don't worry about the Christians," said Fyffe consolingly. "We've always had them at home, and we don't trouble."

"But do you have so many?" was the anxious inquiry.

"Do we?" exclaimed Fyffe, "Why, we're simply overrun with them!" and the delegation departed, seemingly reassured.

At the end of our pleasant summer in Japan, we received orders to proceed to Tientsin on the Pei Ho River. It was then, as it is now, the nearest port to Peking that could be reached by men-of-war, and the English, French, Russians, and Americans were each supposed to keep a vessel there. We expected to remain for the winter, for the Pei Ho freezes over when cold weather begins. We had been lying at our anchorage off Tientsin only a short time, when the captain concluded to change his position and drop a little further down river. I suggested that instead of getting up steam, he let me try to "club" her down. In "clubbing", one allows the anchor to drift along, just touching bottom, veering chain when it is necessary to bring the ship up. Our journey down-stream was brief, but full of incident. Our first move fouled the anchor of the English gunboat *Growler*; and we had scarcely got clear of her, when we became entangled with the cable of the French ship, the *Surprise*, and succeeded in pulling out her bitts and part of her rail. Of course there was a lively commotion on board, but our captain immediately became so vociferous about "clubbing" in general, and what he meant to do to me in particular, that the French commander's indignation for his ship almost disappeared in his concern for "ce pauvre M. Clark."

Ice had just begun to form in the river when we got word that Mr. Avery, our Minister, had died in Peking, and Captain Fyffe at once decided that it was his duty to take the body on board the *Monocacy* and leave for Shanghai. He offered his cabin to Mrs. Avery, and as he felt she would need companionship, he proposed that my wife and children should share his quarters with her, while I turned over my stateroom to him. I will merely remark here that Mrs. Clark certainly earned her passage. Mrs. Avery was in a terrible state, and one of her worst obsessions was the idea that her husband's body might be washed overboard at any time. Captain Fyffe thought it might soothe her if she imagined that a guard was always kept beside the remains, so whenever she was heard coming up the ladder for a walk on deck, the nearest sailor had orders to seize a cutlass and march up and down beside the flag-covered coffin. One morning, Mrs. Clark, who had appeared a little in advance of Mrs. Avery, noticing the sailor on guard had a frank pleasant face, asked me who he was. I looked, and seeing that he was the paymaster's assistant answered that he was the "Jack of the Dust."

"What!" she exclaimed, and I instantly saw what she must have thought.

"Why yes," said I, "don't you see? He's a sailor; that's Jack, and he's watching over the remains—the dust. I think it's a very appropriate title."

"What nonsense!" and she marched off with her head in the air to the officer-of-the-deck.

"Mr. Nabor," I heard her inquire, "tell me, who is that sailor by Mr. Avery's coffin?"

"That fellow?" said Nabor, turning to look, "why, his name is Jones, I believe."

"No, no! I mean what's his billet on the ship?"

"Oh! he's Jack of the Dust."

This was confounding. She questioned another officer, who had just come up from below, and having received the same answer, could only conclude there was a conspiracy against her. In fact, I do not know of any good explanation of the name of this rating for the paymaster's assistant.

Whether or not Captain Fyffe's move to Shanghai was approved by the authorities, there was at any rate no chance of getting up the Pei Ho again that winter, so the long anticipated repairs at the Tunkadoo Docks began. During this stay in Shanghai, the first railroad laid in China was completed, and through the courtesy of Mr. Seward, Mrs. Clark and I were among the favored few to ride in the train that inaugurated its opening. It was built to connect Shanghai with Woosung, at the junction of the Shanghai River and the Yangtse, but the Chinese, with their usual dislike for innovations, soon pulled up its rails, and some years passed before another was constructed.

One objection to a long stay in port is that it is apt to be demoralizing to the crew of a man-of-war. It is hard to find enough employment to keep them busy and contented, and an executive officer is constantly on the watch for any disturbing element on board. We had this in the shape of an Irish coal passer named Gannon. While not actually bad, he was idle and worthless, much fonder of haranguing the other men than of doing his own work. I imagine that some of his discourses were meant to be incendiary, but he used to get so tangled up in long words that not only were his hearers thoroughly puzzled at times, but I think he was often quite at sea himself as to his real meaning.

So, one day when Gannon overstayed his liberty, I was not displeased, but feeling I must comply with the government regulation that a reward of not more than ten dollars must be offered for the return of a deserter, I sent a notice to the Shanghai police force that I would pay all of two cents for the apprehension of Gannon. This brought about his instant return, unattended. I refused to recognize him as Gannon, however, unless he came under police escort, and being obliged to concede this point, he stood on the dock and tried to make me admit that this man Gannon of whom we were talking was really worth more than two cents. When he found I was quite steadfast in my idea of values, he asked permission to come aboard and get Gannon's pay and belongings, and with these under his arm, turned to make his final farewell.

"Good-by, me old shipmates!" said he, with a wave of his hand to such of a the crew as were visible. "God bless you all! God bless you, Captain, and you, sir," to the officer-of-the-deck. Then his eye falling on me, where I was standing a little to one side, he added reproachfully. "And God bless you too, Mr. Clark, to a sartin extint."[21]

When our repairs were completed, we made a trip up the Yangtse River. Our first stop was where the Grand Canal and the river unite, and our second at the city of Nanking, which we left the next afternoon, steaming about twenty-five miles above it before we anchored for the night. The captain was anxious to make a very early start in the morning, as he wished to reach Poyang Lake before dark. He had not been feeling very well that day, and told me that he should expect me to get the ship under way. I had heard it said that vessels had swung to the flood as far up as Nanking, but we were two hundred miles from the sea, and the thought that the tide could affect us occurred neither to me nor to our pilot, Mr. Jousberry.

At the first faint sign of daylight we hove short, and as soon as Jousberry thought he could distinguish the banks of the river and keep the channel, we got under way. As the sun rose, I went up on the paddle box to have a look around, and one of the first things I noticed were the walls of quite a sizable city some distance ahead. "Jousberry!" I called, "what city is this we're coming to on the north bank?"

"You must be mistaken," he answered. "There's no city along here."

"Well, there certainly is one," I insisted, "and to me it looks very much like Nanking."

"Impossible," said he, and then following the direction of my finger, gasped, "Great Scott! It is Nanking, and we're going down river! We must have swung!"

I asked, "Is there any place near here, wide enough for us to turn, without stopping and backing? The captain would be sure to notice if we had to back. He'd think we'd struck a snag and would be up on deck in a minute."

Jousberry knew of a good place just below, and by taking the chief engineer Absalom Kirby into our confidence, we got her swung about and pointed up-stream. I then seated myself on the cabin hatchway, ready to head off the captain, should he decide to turn out. Pretty soon I heard him stirring, and unfortunately, Nanking was still in sight. I used every art I could muster to keep his attention on me and away from the scenery. I even urged him to tell his favorite yarn, which I had heard so

[21] This incident was written up for *Harper's Magazine* shortly after my return from China, but as since then it has been told me by two other officers as having happened to them, I think the time has come to prove ownership once more, and I repeat it here. [Author's note]

often I could have repeated it word for word, and when all else failed, I brought up the subject of the farm and his father-in-law. At last the obnoxious city had sunk out of sight astern, and when the captain made another start for the hurricane deck, I did not try to detain him. He soon began to notice remarkable resemblances to places we had passed the day before, and then he got out the chart, and made Jousberry's life wretched by demanding explanations. Jousberry only told the truth once that day, and that was a fatal mistake, for it led him into a perfect bog of conflicting statements. Of course we did not reach Poyang Lake, for we had nearly sixty lost miles to make up. As we were passing its entrance the next day, I approached the captain with the chart under my arm, but he declined to look at it. "Take it away!" he grumbled. "It's a delusion and a snare. I won't believe a thing about this river hereafter except what Jousberry tells me!"

We had expected when we left Shanghai that the limit of our trip would be reached when we anchored off the triple cities of Hankow, Woochang, and Hanyan, so it was an agreeable surprise when we got orders to proceed to Ichang, nearly four hundred miles farther on, and to establish a consulate there. China had just been forced by England to open Ichang as a port, and as we under the "favored nation clause" had equal privileges, our instructions were to get there as rapidly as possible. The English gunboat *Kestrel* also lying off the three cities had similar orders.

Our race up the Yangtse lasted several days, for as the navigation was largely guesswork, the leading ship was likely at any time to mark the position of a shoal or mud flat by piling up on it, whereupon her rival instead of assistance would give her three cheers, and steam on until she in her turn became a warning to mariners. A delay of many hours, just as we were nearing our goal, when we had to carry out our heaviest anchors before the ship could be floated, made us feel that the *Kestrel* had the race in her own hands, but a little later we passed her hard and fast on a particularly vicious sand bar, and so we reached Ichang well in the lead.

While there, we visited the remarkable caves and natural bridges in the vicinity. The former were easily accessible from the towing path that borders the rapids of the Yangtse, which themselves were something to remember. Of course in these days the tourist penetrates everywhere, but at that time these foaming rapids sweeping through their rocky gorges had revealed themselves to few foreign eyes. They made the city of Ichang practically the head of navigation on the Yangtse River.

The summers we passed in Japan were the greatest possible contrast to our life in China. There were practically no social demands, and we had ample leisure to enjoy the natural beauties of the country, and to observe the customs of its attractive people. I think the quality that made the greatest impression on us was their absolute courtesy under every condition. The kindly, gentle manners we saw everywhere must have been more than skin deep, for they were universal and never failing.

We sailed from Yokohama for home on the *City of Peking*, then a new steamer. Her speed would not compare well with that of the ocean greyhounds of the present day, but she reduced the *Colorado's* time of twenty-three days in crossing to seventeen.

Chapter 9

OFF MANY COASTS

A naval officer's periods of shore duty are like the country without a history, the happier for having little to record.[1] My next orders for sea, after my Asiatic cruise, came in August, 1881. They instructed me to proceed to Norfolk, and report on board the old ship of the line, *New Hampshire*,[2] as executive. She was then fitting out for the training service, as a home ship for naval apprentices, and was to join the rest of the training squadron at Newport, Rhode Island. Her captain, Philip Johnson, had not reported, so I was in command when we sailed. The *Powhatan* had been assigned to tow us, and this was the beginning of a very fortunate acquaintance for me with her captain, John G. Walker. Although I had never met him before, his record was well known to me. He had been with Farragut until the taking of Vicksburg, then with

---

[1] The author served at the Boston Navy Yard from 1877 to 1880.

[2] She was indeed an old ship, being one of nine seventy-four-gun ships of the line authorized by Congress on 29 April 1816. Laid down as the *Alabama* at the Portsmouth Navy Yard in 1819, she was ready to be launched in 1825, but was instead put into the nineteenth-century equivalent of mothballs until the Civil War, when she was renamed the *New Hampshire* and commissioned as a store ship for the South Atlantic Blockading Squadron. Following her subsequent service as a flagship of the Apprentice Training Squadron, she was employed as a receiving ship at New London, Connecticut, before being loaned to the New York State Naval Militia in 1893. Renamed the *Granite State* in 1894, she remained in service on the Hudson until 1921.

New Hampshire.

Grant in the batteries, and he had completed his war service under Porter on the Arkansas River and in the North Atlantic. His administrative ability was so conspicuous that railroad managers had tried to induce him to resign from the navy and enter the business world. He had my admiration at once, and the constant friendship he showed me from this time forth inspired me with an attachment that lasted throughout his life.[3]

From our start at Hampton Roads, all went smoothly until the evening of the second day, when, in a dense fog, the *Powhatan* struck on what proved to be the south shore of Block Island. Our momentum carried us past her, our hawser parting as we went, but we managed to let go our anchor quickly enough, so that when we swung round and brought up, we were sufficiently far from the beach to strike it only occasionally, as the sea lifted and then dropped the ship.

The *Powhatan* had grounded so slightly that it was but a matter of minutes before she got off, ran a line to us, and having sent off men to assist our small crew in weighing the anchor we had let go so hastily, had us in tow and was steaming out to sea in seventeen minutes from the time we struck. I was surprised to find that Captain Walker was inclined to make much of the way I had conducted myself during our mutual experience. As even the order to anchor had come from him, I was unable to see that I had done anything except to follow his directions promptly and coolly, but if he chose to think differently, I was pleased enough to have it so, especially when other officers who knew that he was soon to be made Chief of Bureau of Navigation told me how lucky I was to have won his good opinion. He took an early opportunity of showing his friendship, for it was because of his expressed desire that I became captain of the *New Hampshire* in the spring following my promotion to commander, although this ship had always been rated as a captain's command.

When she joined the other ships at Newport, our training squadron had just been reorganized, and was starting with a great flourish of trumpets. It had been formerly maintained under the Bureau of Equipment and Recruiting, but just before this, David B. Porter, the Admiral of the Navy, had been placed at its head, with Commodore Luce in actual

---

[3] Walker graduated first in his class at the Naval Academy in 1856, retired as a rear admiral in 1897, and died in 1907. For information see Daniel H. Hicks, "New Navy and New Empire: The Life and Times of John Grimes Walker," Ph.D. diss., University of California, Berkeley, 1979.

command, flying his flag from the *New Hampshire*, the other ships in the squadron being the steam frigate *Minnesota*, the frigate *Constitution*, the sloops *Portsmouth* and *Saratoga*, and the *Jamestown*, then on her way from the Pacific. All officers in the squadron were to receive sea pay, and their service to count as sea duty. Everything was in magnificent readiness, and "Now," said Lieutenant Sumner Paine, commonly known as "Toby" to his many friends in the service, "the first thing to be done is to catch a boy."[4]

We discovered, however, that one other element was also rather necessary, for while Porter was in control of the system, as far as giving orders was concerned, the Bureau of Equipment was still responsible for the expenditures, and as it looked with an unfavorable eye on the changes that had been made, we soon found we were working on a vacuum.

The situation was such that, Commodore Luce having gone on a cruise across the North Atlantic with the *Portsmouth* and *Saratoga*, I felt it was up to me to have an interview with the Admiral, who was spending the summer at Narragansett Pier. At first he was inclined to simply take it out in cursing the adversaries, but as this, though soothing to us both, did not seem to bring us anywhere, he calmed down and finally suggested that I put down all the facts in a letter to him, and he would go to work on them.

Meantime the opposition in Washington seemed to be spreading. The steam launch with which we made our regular trips to and from Newport needed repairs, and when I put in a request for them, I was informed, by the Bureau of Construction, that we did not need a launch—pulling boats ought to suffice for us—and the *Tallapoosa* would be sent to take the launch away. In a few days she appeared, but as she was a side-wheeler and had no appliances for hoisting so heavy a boat on board, she was compelled to ask our help. Richard Derby, the *New Hampshire*'s executive, got spars and tackles to support the main yard, and soon had the launch suspended from it, ready to lower on the *Tallapoosa*'s deck, when she should come alongside. We signalled that all was in order, and she started towards us. She came with such headway that it was evident that they did not mean to back the engines till the last

---

[4] The formation of an apprentice squadron had long been advocated by Luce as a means of attracting American youth to the navy, a high proportion of whose enlisted force was composed of foreigners. Unfortunately, as the author proceeds to relate, the program received rather less than the full support of the Navy Department and was dissolved following Luce's reassignment as first president of the Naval War College in 1884.

moment, and I felt certain pride in my classmate Kellogg, who was in command, for his nerve in making such a dashing approach. Just as I was about to commend him to some of the young officers standing near, as an example of fine seamanship, he and his executive officer rushed to the end of the bridge and yelled "We can't stop! We're on the center!"

"I'm sorry," I called back, "but I can't lassoo you!"

Meanwhile Derby was shouting orders to let go everything in the way of a brace that could be let go, and to the men to hurry out of the rigging. The *Tallapoosa* surged alongside, ripping out spars, carrying away gear, and swinging our yards about. The suspended launch struck the rounding surface of her paddle box, slid over it, and crashing through her guard, vanished in five fathoms of water. The *Tallapoosa* went on, headed for the beach, but fortunately her engine decided to function in time to prevent her from going ashore. We swept for the unlucky launch, and by night had secured it. The next morning we towed it out into the bay, and anchored it for the *Tallapoosa* to pick up. This time she ran over it, and having sunk it in eleven fathoms, felt that she had done her work thoroughly and departed. The last I saw of our launch, its battered wreck was reposing on the shores of Coaster's Island.

A few days after this, Captain James Gillis of the *Minnesota* returned from a visit to Washington, and announced that "my letter" had started a row in the Navy Department, and that I was going to "catch it." I could not think at first what he meant, for I was not aware of having written anything to Washington likely to create trouble, but then a suspicion came to me and I started posthaste for Narragansett Pier.

"Admiral," said I, "where is that letter I wrote you?" Looking a little guilty, he admitted he had sent it on to the Navy Department. It was good, he said, full of ginger, and just what they needed for their complaint. His endorsement and approbation would make it all right. "All right for you, perhaps, Admiral," I conceded, "you, who are at the head of the Navy; but for me, the bottom commander, trouble is due, and lots of it." He would not allow of this, and said he would stand by me in any case.

In spite of these assurances, I did not look forward with pleasure to the impending visit of the new Secretary of the Navy, William E. Chandler, who being broad-minded enough to realize that a question is apt to have two sides, had resolved to come to Newport to look over our end of the proposition. He came in the *Tallapoosa*, accompanied by several bureau chiefs, and when I went off to pay my respects, it was with a good deal of the feeling of the small boy who has been detected in some "sassiness" towards his elders. I became a little easier when I found I was greeted with neither threatening nor reproachful looks, but was scarcely prepared to have the Secretary come up to me, where I was standing by Kellogg's side, and after saying that he meant to visit my ship, ask me to call with him the next day on the President, who was then staying with Governor Morgan in Newport.

Two days later he made an inspection of the *New Hampshire*, and must have been pleased with what he saw, for he told me he wished I would call again on the President and invite him aboard the ship. When I gave President Arthur the invitation, he seemed a little doubtful whether his many engagements would permit, but after consulting his secretary, said he could come for a limited time.

He appeared punctually with a number of friends, among them the Secretary of State, Frelinghuysen, and Governor Morgan, and long after the hour that had been set for his departure, Governor Morgan whispered to me that the President was enjoying himself more than at any time since he came to Newport. When he finally left, after a visit of three hours which had been thoroughly delightful to us all, those who had had the privilege of meeting him could understand why so much had been said of President Arthur's social qualities.

After this, things went very smoothly for the training station, but I think Admiral Porter had in the meantime rather lost interest. There had been too many irritating restrictions that must have seemed petty to a man who had commanded, in wartime, the largest fleet we had ever assembled. Whatever may have been his reasons, he soon after gave up the position. Commodore Luce had begun to be absorbed, by then, in his pet project, the Naval War College, of which he is sometimes called the "Father", and the officers who had been put on shore pay, and found it difficult to support their families in Newport and meet expenses on board ship at the same time, were generally anxious to be ordered to other stations. So the training squadron, which had started in a blaze of glory, was slowly flickering out. Hearing that Captain Matthews, my instructor of Academy days, was looking for duty in Newport, I asked to be detached, and he was ordered to the ship in my place.

A short interval of shore duty and leave,[5] and I was ordered to Washington for instructions connected with the survey of the North Pacific, which was then being carried on by the *Ranger*. This work was directly under the supervision of the Bureau of Navigation, of which, as

[5] Admiral Clark took a course on torpedoes in 1885.

it will be remembered, Commodore Walker had been made Chief. John W. Philip, afterwards captain of the *Texas* at Santiago, was then in command of the *Ranger*, and I was sent out to San Francisco to relieve him.

The *Ranger* was a beautiful bark-rigged steamer, with square yards to royals, and was pierced for ten guns, but only one of these had been retained for signalling purposes, the decks being kept as clear as possible for sounding machines and other appliances for surveying.[6] I found on her a most efficient staff of assistants, lieutenants, junior lieutenants, and ensigns. These, as their terms of sea duty expired, were replaced by Commodore Walker, who often consulted me in making his selections. I generally recommended that young officers should be sent, telling the Commodore I did not want to spend my time pulling kinks out of old lieutenants who thought they knew, and possibly often did know, better methods than those I proposed. Besides, youth was needed for the work we were engaged in, which, although most interesting, was as hard as it could well be. Older men could not have stood the strain, or felt the enthusiasm required to carry one through a surveying season in the tropics.

Among the officers who served with me on board the *Ranger*, whose ability and energy accomplished so much in astronomical, triangulation, and hydrographic work, or who acquired a high professional reputation in after years, were: C. T. Force, Robert G. Peck, James M. Helm, Arthur W. Dodd, James P. Parker, James H. Glennon, William R. Rush, George H. Strafford, Albert A. Ackerman, Harry Phelps, Albert S. Key, William B. Whittlesey, Ward P. Winchell, Manning K. Eyre and Emil Theiss.[7]

---

[6] The *Ranger* was 177 feet 4 inches in length, 32 feet abeam, displaced 1,020 tons, and carried a crew of 138. Commissioned at the League Island Naval Shipyard, Philadelphia, on 27 November 1876, she was converted into a survey vessel four years later. She was loaned to the Massachusetts Nautical School, where she was renamed *Rockport* (1917) and then *Nantucket* (1918), for use as a training ship from 1909 until 1940. In the latter year she was transferred to the U.S. Maritime Commission for employment as a school ship at the U.S. Merchant Marine Academy.

[7] Lieutenant Peck, who, like Force, was a remarkable observer as well as navigator, changed our methods of sounding to others so effective, that better and much more work was accomplished. Ensign Phelps prepared a table by which the angles between high and low points were at once reduced to the horizontal, and thus entered in the records. Ensign Ackerman was the only one of the *Ranger*'s officers who happened to serve with me on the *Oregon*. He had command of one of her turrets at the Battle of Santiago. Ensign Rush, as a captain, gained distinction in the command of our forces during the first day's fighting at

Ranger.

The hardships to which these young men were exposed never lessened their zeal. They were landed in detached parties in unhealthy localities; often left in open boats in some bay or river, while the ship to save time went off for coal; obliged to climb difficult mountain slopes under the burning rays of a tropical sun; whatever the task demanded of them, they fulfilled it and were eager to attack the next. It was rather remarkable under these circumstances that the health record on board the *Ranger* was a fine one. The only officer to break down was Ensign Glennon, and that was after some particularly arduous triangulation work compelling him to do much severe mountain climbing, ending with the ascent of Mount Turubales. He had typhoid fever, and we were obliged to send him north by steamer.

Occasionally, something ridiculous would occur to relieve the monotony of hard work, as when two of our officers were cutting in some angles along a curving line of beach. One of them was using a red flag to signal, and the other, noticing that this banner had suddenly stopped waving, found on investigation that its color had roused the anger of a sensitive and active bull, who had chased his companion out into the surf, where he was having difficulty in determining the safety line between the sharks, which were swarming in the bay, and the irate animal, pawing sand and bellowing on the beach. It was truly a case of being caught between the devil and the deep sea, but one of the ship's launches solved the vexed question by making an opportune appearance around the point, and rescuing the besieged.

Our working ground was on the west coasts of Mexico and Central America. It had been surveyed before by French and English vessels under De Laplin and Sir Edward Belcher, but as that was in the days when only sailing ships were available, and the portions of coast not deemed important to traders and navigators had been but hurriedly examined, their work, while creditable, left much to be accomplished, and in some cases to be corrected.

For instance, the Gulf of Dulce, which is separated from the Gulf of Nicoya by a stretch of coast backed by lofty mountains and impenetrable forests, figures in De Laplin's sailing directions as an indentation thirty-eight miles long and nearly twenty wide, while on another chart it was represented as a slight curve in the coast. We found its upper portion

---

Vera Cruz. Ensign Glennon, now rear admiral, and member of the commission sent to Russia, was strikingly instrumental in restoring order and efficiency in the Russian navy. [Author's note]

land-locked and well sheltered, but any navigator expecting to find an anchorage there would be sadly disappointed, for its waters, even close to the shore, showed a uniform depth of six hundred feet.

Cape Elena, which marked one of the most exhausting and hazardous efforts of the triangulation party, under Glennon and Winchell, was so far misplaced that a vessel leaving San Juan del Sur would have had to steer nearly forty-five degrees to the westward of the indicated course to avoid running upon it. Indeed, when the *Ranger* left San Juan del Sur at night, we found before going far that our course was blocked by mountains ahead and on both bows.

Cape Elena was at the extremity of a mountainous range projecting into the Pacific, whose northern face, according to the De Laplin and Belcher charts, shows an unbroken and precipitous coast. We found there a magnificent harbor, easy of access and perfectly protected. There were no signs of life upon its beautiful shores, and as the mountains were densely wooded, with tangled undergrowth, and as coasting vessels or fishing boats rarely venture outside the heads in Central America, this harbor was probably first visited by man when Ensign Parker steamed between its high cliffs in one of our launches. The next day he piloted the *Ranger* in, and the survey was begun. At first I called it Port Elena, but later, at my request, and because of this officer's merits, the Department changed the name to Port Parker.

While running lines of surroundings off Cape Colnett, Lower California, we had a chance to observe the curious way in which air currents will sometimes act. We had two parties stationed for triangulation work on the high plateau that terminates the cape. They noted only a moderate northwest breeze blowing across it, and we on the ship experienced the same, when some distance from the shore and to windward, but the instant we got under what should have been the shelter of the precipitous cliffs, the wind became so violent that it was hard to keep one's footing on deck. It evidently accumulated nearly all its force while sweeping down from a height of less than six hundred feet, and expended the most of it on the spot where it landed, so to speak.

It was just a little north of Cape Colnett that the *Ranger* came near ending her career. She barely escaped being wrecked on a lee shore during a terrific gale, in which, despite the fact that we had both anchors down and the engines working at high pressure, she still continued to drag towards the beach. We could not understand at the time why we were not able to obtain greater power from the engines, but discovered afterwards that there was an opening in the steam chest which was allowing the high-pressure cylinder to exhaust upon both sides of the low-pressure piston at once. Just as her stern was almost in the breakers, there came a fortunate lull in the fury of the wind, and by raising our anchors, one by the capstan, and the other by a deck tackle, we managed to steam off shore far enough, so that when the next gust threw us broadside to the beach we were not driven on to it.

This reminds me of another time when luck was with us. We were steaming in towards the Central American shore one night, in a dense fog, and Ensign Rush offered to station himself as lookout on the flying jib boom, a suggestion which I gladly adopted. He had just worked his way past the fore-royal stay, when I saw him wave his arms wildly, and heard a shout of "Stop her, Captain! Stop her! I can hear a baby crying!" When the engine was stopped, we all could hear it. We found, when the fog lifted, that we had been heading for the only village in many a mile of beach, and we were grateful to that baby for being wakeful. The case was so exceptional, however, that I did not feel it necessary to put in the sailing directions for the Gulf of Nicoya, "Stand in, until the baby can be heard."

The *Ranger* was an iron ship, and I found I could reduce the temperature on board considerably, during hours of sunlight, by giving her a coat of white paint. This was done with Commodore Walker's approval, and some time later, when he took command of our first squadron of modern ships, they were painted white, a custom that was followed for years. The story goes that when he was relieved as Chief of Bureau, the Secretary said to him: "Admiral, as you have been running the Navy Department for years, suppose you take the Navy for a while and let me have the Department."

Another story of Walker has been frequently told and yet is so characteristic of him that I repeat it here. A young officer, intent upon securing a coveted billet, hurried into the office of the Chief of Bureau and finding it apparently vacant, called to the occupants of the next room, "Where's Walker? I want to see Walker!" "Here I am," came the unexpected answer, as the Commodore's head rose from behind a desk. "What can I do for you?"

"Oh, Commodore!" stammered the abashed youngster, "I wanted—that is—I didn't mean—excuse me—I'll call again—"

"No, no! don't go away!" said the Commodore urbanely. "Come back, and sit down. Call me John!"

When my cruise on the *Ranger* was completed, I had some years of shore duty, part of it as Lighthouse Inspector on the Great Lakes.[8] This duty brought me into contact with Colonel—afterwards General—William Ludlow, one of the finest examples of a soldier it has ever been my fortune to meet. His heroic conduct in the fierce struggle at Alatoona was equalled—one might say, even bettered—by his splendid work as an engineer at Havana, which still enjoys the benefits of his wise regulations and the sanitary reforms he instituted.[9] It was his brother, Nicoll Ludlow, who as a midshipman had been my companion in London and Paris, and whom I relieved as commander of the *Mohican*, when I was sent to sea again. During the month of May, 1894, while still on the commanders' list, I was placed at the head of the Behring Sea patrol fleet, with orders to enforce the terms governing pelagic sealing, just agreed upon by the arbitrators at Paris.[10]

This squadron, one of the largest assembled since the Civil War, consisted of the *Mohican*, *Concord*, *Yorktown*, *Adams*, *Ranger*, *Alert*, and *Petrel*, men-of-war, the Fish Commission steamer *Albatross* and the revenue cutters *Corwin* and *Bear*. Admiral Ramsey had relieved Admiral Walker in the department, but my former roommate at the Academy, Francis A. Cook, had been made Assistant Chief of the Bureau of Navigation, so my interests were not allowed to suffer. In fact, I was told that a captain who applied to Admiral Ramsey for duty on the Pacific coast was informed that being above me on the list might prove an obstacle to giving him such a billet.

During the greater part of my service in Behring Sea, we enjoyed comparatively good weather as far as storms were concerned, but the fogs were often so dense as to make navigation dangerous. The water ran

[8] The author was lighthouse inspector in Chicago (1887–91) and an ordnance officer at the Mare Island Navy Yard, California (1891–93).

[9] A graduate of the U.S. Military Academy in 1864, Ludlow took his commission in the Corps of Engineers and distinguished himself in the defense of the Union supply depot at Allatoona, Georgia, in October 1864. During the Spanish-American War he became the first member of his class to reach the rank of general. From 1898 until 1900 he served as military governor of Havana. See Eugene V. McAndrews, "William Ludlow: Engineer, Governor, Soldier," Ph.D. diss., Kansas State University, 1973.

[10] Pelagic sealing refers to hunting seals in the water with guns or spears. Inevitably indiscriminate, this practice killed off many breeding females and consequently reduced the seal herd. Regulations governing pelagic sealing were promulgated in 1893, when an American attempt to eliminate the practice altogether by reviving an old Russian claim to exclusive jurisdiction in the Bering Sea was rejected by an international tribunal meeting in Paris. Unfortunately, the regulations were too feeble to have much effect.

deep, right up to the edge of the rocky cliffs, so we were seldom able to ascertain our position by soundings, and the currents which swept past the steep shores of the islands and through the narrow passes between them made the laying of any course uncertain business. The year before, the *Petrel*, which had been lost in the fog to the south of the island chain for days, found when it cleared away that she was close to Boguslav volcano, fifty miles to the north of the pass, through which all unconsciously she had been driven by these currents. Often the echo of the steam whistle from some precipice, or the roar of the surf upon a rocky shore, would be the first danger signal that came to us. The anxieties attending such service were so great that two captains in the fleet broke down under them, obliging me to detach them and order other officers to their commands, but Goodrich, Folger, Longnecker, Emory, and Drake of the navy, and Healy and Munger of the revenue service met every requirement and performed every duty courageously and cheerfully. The whole-hearted way in which they carried out the orders of one so slightly their senior in rank was of course highly gratifying to me, and I have always retained for them the strongest feeling of attachment.

Although by the terms agreed on by the Arbitration Commission, pelagic sealing was supposed to be limited in time, and never permitted within sixty miles of the Pribylof Islands, where the enormous seal rookeries were situated, thousands of female seals were killed and in consequence nearly twenty-five thousand of their pups died of starvation on the rookeries. As the rich quality of the seal's milk enables the young to survive nine days, according to experts, after abandonment by the mother, one can realize what prolonged suffering was entailed by this practice. It seemed to me such an abominable state of affairs that I recommended that the seal herd, which had already been reduced from millions to about six hundred thousand, should be practically destroyed, or at least so reduced as to make pelagic sealing unprofitable. As I looked at it, our Government could not afford to countenance a business which, as I remarked in my protest, would never be tolerated in a stock-raising community. When a bill based on this suggestion was introduced by Congressman Dingley, I was considerably astonished at hearing it proclaimed by some as shocking and wantonly cruel. Whether the outsiders raising this outcry were touched in their sensibilities or their pockets, it would be hard to say, but as far as cruelty was concerned, one would think there could be scarcely a question as to which was preferable, quick death or slow starvation. However, I was on the whole more flattered than hurt to think that an original idea of mine had made such a stir.

Speaking of prolonged sufferings, there was a rooster on board the *Mohican* who really had the sympathy of all who watched his struggles to keep up regular habits during his first summer in Behring Sea. As we got farther north and the nights became shorter, it must have seemed to him as if he had hardly tucked his head under his wing before duty called him to salute the day again. He kept valiantly on, but by the time we started south, he was badly out of condition, and the sailors, who by this time had adopted him as a pet, said that the next season he gave up the contest, and went to roost and turned out by the ship's bells.

I continued on the Pacific coast until March, 1898, the year of the Spanish War. I was commanding the *Monterey* at San Diego,[11] when orders came for me to proceed to San Francisco and take command of the battleship *Oregon*.

[11] The *Monterey* (BM 6), one of the "New Navy" monitors, was commissioned in 1893. The author assumed command of the ship in 1896.

Chapter 10

THE *OREGON*'S RACE

"Six thousand miles[1]
To the Indian Isles
And the Oregon rushed home,
Her wake a swirl
Of jade and pearl,
Her bow a bend of foam."

ARTHUR GUITERMAN, *New York Times.*

The *Oregon*, at the time I received orders to command her, was one of the most up-to-date and powerful battleships our navy possessed.[2] Her presence on the east coast was considered so essential that the government felt the risks of the long voyage, till then untested by a vessel of her class, must be undertaken, even though they included a possibility of meeting with the enemy's fleet.

In starting on this long race around two continents, I could feel I was fortunate in the qualities of both ship and crew. The Union Iron Works of San Francisco, which constructed the *Oregon*, had already built several other vessels for our service, among them the cruiser *Olympia*, but the *Oregon* was their first battleship, and it had been their pride to make her as mechanically perfect as possible. For instance, when the installation of her condenser tubes had been almost completed, it was learned that those on the *Olympia*, which were of the same type, were not giving the best results. The managers of the Union Iron Works at once requested permission of the Navy Department to grant them the time to change the tubes at their own expense, which was done at an extra cost of over six thousand dollars to the firm. So it may well be said that this ship was "built on honor." In addition to the usual proportion of trained and

---

[1] From the Straits of Magellan. [Author's note]
[2] For the history of the *Oregon*, see pp. xv, xvii–xix.

intelligent men-of-war's men and a fine marine guard composing her crew, I found an exceptionally large number of young men drawn from all classes in the States of Oregon, Washington, and California by the prospect of war service. The fashion in which these young fellows, with so little experience to guide them, took up their new duties was remarkable. They met every hardship of the voyage cheerfully, and were always alert and ready for any sort of demand.

As to the *Oregon's* officers, I found them such as I would have expected upon any ship in our navy. Through experience and tradition alike the qualities of the average American naval officer can safely be taken for granted. One can feel as Macaulay did, in speaking of one of the heroes of an older service, that he will perform all that duty demands of him "with the skill and spirit worthy of his noble profession."

The forty-eight hours that I was in command before we sailed from San Francisco were confused and hurried. Stores were being rushed aboard, coaling going on, and officers reporting for duty. Whatever I might feel about the general character of my officers and crew, I was personally acquainted with very few among them, and I can well remember in the crowd of strange faces surrounding me what a satisfaction it was to come across an old orderly who had been with me on the receiving ship *Independence*. He entered the cabin to report at eight o'clock the first night I was on board. I was feeling tired and a little oppressed with the thought of the long and uncertain voyage before me, and when I looked up into this familiar face instead of the strange one I had expected to see, it meant more to me than could easily be imagined.

We sailed from San Francisco[3] on March nineteenth, and our run from there to Callao was uneventful except in the opportunities it gave me to become acquainted with the ship and her personnel. As we approached the tropics, life between decks became almost intolerable, for to their heat was added that generated by the ship's boilers, kept at a full head of steam. When Chief Engineer Milligan informed me that he thought we

---

[3] List of the officers of the *Oregon*: *Captain*, C. E. Clark; *Lieutenant Commander*, J. K. Cogswell; *Lieutenants*, R. F. Nicholson, W. H. Allen, A. A. Ackerman; *Lieutenants junior grade*, E. W. Eberle; *Ensigns*, C. L. Hussey, R. Z. Johnston; *Captain of Marines*, R. Dickins; *Second Lieutenant of Marines*, A. R. Davis; *Naval Cadets*, H. E. Yarnell, L. M. Overstreet, C. R. Miller, A. G. Magill, C. S. Kempff; *Chief Engineer*, R. W. Milligan; *P. A. Engineer*, C. N. Offley; *Asst. Engineers*, J. M. Reeves, F. Lyon; *Engineer Cadets*, H. N. Jenson, W. D. Leahy; *Surgeon*, P. A. Lovering; *Assistant Surgeon*, W. B. Grove; *Paymaster*, S. R. Colhoun; *Chaplain*, P. J. McIntyre; *Paymaster's Clerk*, J. A. Murphy; *Boatswain*, John Costello; *Gunner*, A. S. Williams; *Carpenter*, M. F. Roberts. [Author's list]

should never allow salt water to enter the boilers, I felt it was asking almost too much of the endurance of the crew. It meant not only reducing their drinking supply, but that the quantity served out would often be so warm as to be quite unpalatable. When I explained to the men, however, that salt water in the boilers meant scale, and that scale would reduce our speed, delay us in getting to the seat of war, and might impair our efficiency in battle, the deprivation was borne without a murmur. The very small quantity of ice that was made on board went to the firemen and coal passers, and however much the rest of us may have longed for a little to cool the lukewarm drinking water, I know that it was not only willingly, but cheerfully given up.

Another of the chief engineer's suggestions was the reservation for emergencies of a part of the Cardiff coal taken on at San Francisco. This arrangement entailed extra work for the men, and that of a most exhausting kind, but their desire to preserve these "dusky diamonds" was as keen as if they had been real jewels. The fact that the *Oregon* never stayed or slackened in her race, and was able to lead in the hour of battle, was undoubtedly due to this oneness of feeling in her officers and crew. Everything must be done and everything borne to get the best out of the ship.

With the change of climate as we neared the Straits of Magellan, came also change of weather, and the *Oregon*, which up to this time had sailed comparatively smooth seas, dipped her bows deep in foaming surges. Just after we entered the Straits, a violent gale struck us. The thick, hurrying scud obscured the precipitous rockbound shores, and with the night coming on, it seemed inadvisable to proceed; yet with the ship driven before the gale as she was it was impossible to obtain correct soundings, and making a safe anchorage must therefore be largely a matter of chance. I decided to anchor, however, as the lesser risk. We let go one anchor, and the chain ran out furiously for about one hundred and twenty-five fathoms before it could be checked. At last it caught, and then the other anchor was let go. They held us through the night, though the gale continued to rage. At early daylight we prepared to get under way, and then discovered that our first anchor had been dropped in fifty fathoms, or three hundred feet of water. That forenoon a heavy snowstorm chased us through the narrowest reaches of the Straits, which in some places are scarcely more than a mile in width. With sheer cliffs on either hand and fathomless depths below, there could be no pause or hesitation in this exciting race, and I think there was no man on board that did not feel the thrill of it. Later in the day it cleared, and the sun's

Oregon.

rays, striking brilliance and rainbow lights from the masses of ice and snow, turned the grim landscape into a scene beautiful to remember. In the afternoon we passed the wrecks of two steamers that had left their bones to mark the perils of the passage, and towards evening we sighted Cape Froward, the extreme southern point of the continent. In the night we came to anchor off Sandy Point.

The last time I had seen Sandy Point was thirty-two years before, when I had passed through the Straits in the consort of the *Monadnock,* our first ironclad to round the American continent. Now, on board the second of our armored ships to attempt the passage, I was hurrying in the opposite direction, this time to strengthen our arms on the Atlantic coast.

I went ashore the next morning in order to make arrangements about coal and was surprised to find Sandy Point, which I remembered as a mere handful of scattered houses, so changed. Its population had grown to about four thousand souls, and I walked along streets where formerly there had been only footpaths. There were paths now, but one had to go to the edge of the town to find them. I followed one out into the open country, where in the old days it was dangerous to venture. Now, instead of the wild Patagonians armed with their bolas and attended by their savage wolfish dogs, who used to infest it, I saw flocks of peacefully grazing sheep, guarded by Scotch shepherds and their collies. The agent from whom we purchased our coal was one of these canny Scots, very suspicious that in some way we intended to get the better of him. The coal had to be taken from a hulk in which wool was also stored, and as the wool lay on top, our men had by no means easy work. The agent added to delays in handling by insisting that the hoisting buckets should be frequently weighed. Murphy, one of our boatswain's mates, finally raised a laugh at his expense by calling out, as a loaded bucket reached the deck, "Here! lower again for another weigh! There's a fly on the edge of that bucket!"

We had been warned while at Callao that the Spaniards had a torpedo boat in the Rio de la Plata, and as she had had ample time to get down to the Straits, we took every precaution against a surprise while lying at Sandy Point. Before we left there, the gunboat *Marietta* joined us. She carried six guns, and her captain was Commander Symonds. On the way to Rio she led, making what speed she could, and throwing over barrels, which we used for targets. We showed no lights during this run. As we neared Rio, we left the *Marietta* and ran ahead, reaching there April 30 and promptly cabling our arrival, for we knew that news of the ship was anxiously awaited.

It was at Rio that we first received word that war had been declared. The newspapers were full of rumors of the battle that had been fought at Manila, but I could not rejoice wholeheartedly in our reported victory, for the casualties announced were two hundred, and I knew that my son-in-law was in the fleet.

A cablegram from the Navy Department informed us that the Spanish torpedo boat *Temerario* was reported to have left Montevideo, probably for Rio. This was disturbing information. If the torpedo boat should arrive and had an ordinarily enterprising commander, I felt he would not hesitate to violate the rights of a neutral port, if by so doing he could put one of our four first-class battleships out of action. To justify his attack, he would only have to point to our own conduct at Bahia, another Brazilian port, when one of our ships, the *Wachusett*, captured the Confederate steamer *Florida*. This was a clear violation of international law, but the captain of the *Wachusett* was neither surrendered to the Brazilian authorities, nor punished in any way by us.

Of course, my first move was an attempt to communicate with the American Minister and the Consul General, but knowing this might involve some time, I did not wait before taking the initiative. I got under way at once, with coal lighters alongside, and steamed up the bay, nearly two miles above the man-of-war anchorage. By leaving this anchorage, ordinarily used by men-of-war, to the *Temerario*, I could assume that any move she made up the bay in our direction might be certainly interpreted as hostile, and would give me the right to turn our guns upon her. If we were lying at the anchorage together, any mischief she contemplated might be done before we had a chance to discover her intention. The *Marietta*, too small a pawn in the game of war to form any inducement for an infringement of neutral rights, was to remain at the anchorage. Her commander had instructions to explain matters at once to the Spanish captain, should he arrive, and to state that a constant watch would be kept upon him, the *Marietta's* searchlight being used at night for that purpose.

Before starting up the bay, I had sent an officer ashore to see the Brazilian Minister of Marine and explain our situation. I was a little afraid I might be advised to settle my perplexities by leaving port; but this would not have suited my plans at all, and fortunately I found the authorities most obligingly disposed. They not only concurred in my arrangements, but even suggested ordering one of their own cruisers to watch for the Spaniard, escort him to the remotest part of the bay and see that if he moved at all, it would be merely to leave the harbor. Indeed, before the hurried return of our Minister, Mr. Bryan, from the summer capital at Petropolis, everything was satisfactorily adjusted. Our Government was reaping the reward of having taken measures to secure the friendship and good will of the Brazilians. They were sorely in need of money at the time, and we had offered them one million dollars for the almost worthless *Nictheroy*.[4] She was still undergoing repairs when she was turned over to me and placed under my orders.

Having settled this first difficulty, I found myself confronted by an even more vital question in the next few hours. I think I can give no better idea of the situation than by quoting the dispatches received from the Navy Department from April 30, the time of our arrival, up to May 4, when we sailed. These, of course, were in code and were deciphered by Ensign Johnston, my clerk. There was so much anxiety evidenced in them that I felt they were not calculated to put confidence into the ship's company, so I kept all but portions of them to myself.

That of April 30 instructed me to "await orders."

The one of May 1 said: "Four Spanish cruisers heavy and fast, three torpedo boats, deep-sea class, sailed April 29th from Cape Verde Islands to the west. Destination unknown. Must be left to your discretion entirely to avoid this fleet and to reach the United States or the West Indies. You can go where you desire, or if it be considered as last resort and can rely upon Brazilian protection may remain there under plea of repairs. *Nictheroy* and *Marietta* subject to orders of yourself."

Cablegram of May 2. "Do not sail from Rio Janeiro, Brazil, until further orders."

Same date. "My telegram May 2nd countermanded. Carry out instructions in my telegram May 1st to proceed with *Oregon*, *Marietta* and *Nictheroy*."

May 3rd. "Inform Department of your plans. Spanish fleet in Philippines annihilated by our naval force on the Asiatic station."

The general trend of these telegrams made it plain that the Department felt our position was critical, and that it did not wish at such a

---

[4] An auxiliary cruiser of 6,530 tons, this vessel had been built by the Newport News Shipbuilding and Drydock Company in 1892 and bought by the Brazilian government. The United States purchased her from Brazil on 11 July 1898. Renamed the *Buffalo*, she served successively as a training vessel, transport, tender, and repair ship before being sold in 1927.

distance from the scene of action to take the responsibility of forcing one ship, however great the need for her, to face the chances of so unequal a contest. Therefore it left the decision to me. I appreciated the consideration, but at the same time it was a case where one would have much preferred to be backed by positive orders. In entering upon a course which involved the possible loss of a ship so valuable to the nation, the feeling that you were simply carrying out the wishes of that nation would have been a strong moral support. As I was denied this, I thought the situation over with the utmost care, and came to these conclusions. First and foremost: if this Spanish squadron were headed for the West Indies, as I was inclined to believe, the necessity for the *Oregon's* presence there with our fleet was all the more urgent. If, on the contrary, it was making for Rio with the idea of intercepting the *Oregon*, it could undoubtedly, by maintaining a certain speed, arrive in that vicinity before we could get away, but it did not seem likely to me that the Spaniards would make this attempt to cut off a single ship, especially as there was a possibility of missing her altogether. And if they did come upon us, we would give them a good fight. I made up my mind to take the chance.

I then called all the commissioned officers together and told them of the contents of the cablegrams, except of the permission to remain in Rio for repairs. Their loyal support and enthusiasm was most encouraging. I then laid before them the plan for the conduct of a fight in case we met the Spaniards. It was my intention to make it a running fight, if possible, as we could use six turret guns, and two six-inch guns right astern, and I hoped that by running at our full speed, we might be able to string out the pursuers and cope with them singly, as did the survivor of the *Horatii* when flying from his three weakened enemies. This allusion to the Horatian tactics was referred to by Captain Mahan when he wrote: "Captain Clark drew for support from the fountain heads of history: from the remote and even legendary past."[5]

We sailed from Rio on May 4, and finding a few hours afterwards that we were greatly hampered by the *Marietta* and *Nictheroy*, and knowing that they would be rather a source of anxiety than help in battle, left them off Cape Frio and pushed on.

The morning after our departure, at the suggestion of R. F. Nichol-

[5] The quotation is inexact. Alluding to the benefit to the military profession of studying history, Mahan wrote, "An instructive instance of drawing such support from the very fountainheads of military history, in the remote and even legendary past, is given by Captain Clark [in his plan of engagement]." A. T. Mahan, *Lessons of the War with Spain* (Boston, 1899), p. 134.

son, the navigator, I called the crew aft and read them the dispatches concerning the strength of the Spanish squadron and the uncertainty of its movements. I added that I was sure, should we meet, that we would at least lower Spain's fighting efficiency upon the seas, and that her fleet would not be worth much after the encounter.

The men cheered and rejoiced as though the fleet had been already sighted and a victory assured.

Four days later we ran into the port of Bahia, and I dispatched the following cablegram, which would of course allow the Department control of the situation again.

"Much delayed by the *Marietta* and *Nictheroy*. Left them near Cape Frio, with orders to come here, or to beach if necessity compels it to avoid capture. The *Oregon* could steam fourteen knots for hours and in a running fight could beat off and even cripple Spanish fleet. With present amount of coal on board will be in good fighting trim and could reach West Indies. If more should be taken here I could reach Key West, but in that case belt armor, cellulose belt, and protective deck would be below water line. Whereabouts of Spanish fleet requested."

The Department answered: "Proceed at once to West Indies without further stop Brazil. No authentic news Spanish fleet. Avoid if possible. We believe you will defeat it if met."

On receipt of this dispatch, we left Bahia at once, and two days later, having turned Cape San Roque, the *Oregon* could at last lay a course for home waters.

While off the mouth of the Amazon, the greatest of rivers, we passed the smallest vessel that ever circumnavigated the globe. This was the yawl *Spray*, sailed by one man, Captain Slocum of New Bedford.[6] Before we were out of sight, she hoisted a signal which we did not make out, but he states in the history he afterwards wrote of the voyage that it read, "Let us keep together for mutual protection."

On May 18, about two A.M. we entered Carlisle Roads, Barbadoes, and anchored. The Governor immediately sent word that we must leave

[6] Joshua Slocum, a fifty-one-year-old New England merchant skipper, set out from Boston in the thirty-seven-foot sloop *Spray* on the first solo circumnavigation of the world in April 1895. Homeward-bound at the time of his encounter with the *Oregon*, he was unaware of the outbreak of war with Spain until he saw the battleship flying the signal CBT ("Are there enemy warships near?") above a Spanish flag. When Slocum dropped anchor at Newport, Rhode Island, on 27 June 1898, he had covered 46,000 miles entirely under sail. For his account of the meeting described by Clark, see Captain Joshua Slocum, *Sailing Alone Around the World* (New York, 1911), pp. 264–66.

within twenty-four hours, but added that we could reckon the twenty-four from daylight the next morning, which would give us a little additional time. Later he informed us that as the American consul had sent off a cablegram to the United States announcing our arrival before the order had been given that no dispatches were to be sent, he must in fairnesss allow the Spanish consul to cable the same news to the Governor of Porto Rico. Our short stay in Barbadoes was not of a cheering nature. The first news that greeted us was that our fleet had attacked San Juan and been repelled. From the boats that pulled off within hail—none were allowed to board us because we had come from fever-infected ports— we gathered the pleasing intelligence that the Spanish fleet was waiting for us outside, report having by this time swelled its numbers to eighteen vessels. Three torpedo or scout boats were said to have been positively sighted from elevated points on the island.

We hoped and believed that these rumors were exaggerated, but could not afford to ignore them altogether, for it was possible that Cervera's squadron had been reinforced by gunboats from Cuba; so with the object of making our actions as misleading as possible to those who might be supplying information to the enemy, we announced that we would take on coal as late as two A.M., while actually planning to leave much earlier. Indeed, before ten that evening, the lighters were cast off, and the *Oregon* steaming out of the roadstead. With lights showing, we ran for a few miles towards the passage between Martinique and Santa Lucia, then, extinguishing them, we turned southward and ran back towards Barbadoes. Ater getting well outside, we shaped our course clear of the Virgin Islands, then off the Bahamas, and made for the coast of Florida, the last stage of our long journey.

The latest news that had reached us of our own fleet was that a part of it was concentrated near the Dry Tortugas, and a part at Hampton Roads. By touching at Jupiter Inlet and telegraphing the Department from there, it could send us orders to reinforce either of these squadrons. So it was that on the night of May 24, the rays of Jupiter Light streamed out to the *Oregon* like the fingers of some friendly hand extended to welcome her home. One of our boats, in charge of Ensign Johnston, was hurried ashore with the following telegram to the Secretary of the Navy.

"*Oregon* arrived. Have coal enough to reach Dry Tortugas in 33 hours. Hampton Roads in 52 hours. Boat landed through surf awaits answer."

The reply came: "If ship is in good condition go to Key West. Otherwise to Hampton Roads. The Department congratulates you on your safe arrival, which has been reported to the President."

The *Oregon*, on receipt of this telegram, started for Key West, arriving there May 26.[7] We began coaling at once from lighters we found waiting for us outside the reef. Admiral Sampson's flagship, *New York*, came in for coal the next morning, and it was while making my official call on the Admiral that he told me of the plan for blocking the harbor entrance at Santiago, where Cervera's squadron had just been located, by sinking a steamer in the channel. This idea seemed to me an excellent one, as I think it would have to any one at that time, for the Spanish cruisers were then regarded as much speedier than our battleships, and the only two of our vessels we imagined could bring them to action, the *New York* and *Brooklyn*, would, with their comparatively light armor, have suffered heavily in such an event, if they had not been altogether destroyed. The later annihilation of the Spanish fleet no more disproves the wisdom of this plan as we saw matters then, than the failure of Hobson and his brave companions to effect what they intended disproves their heroism.

On the afternoon of May 27, our crew was increased by the arrival of sixty young men of the Chicago Naval Reserves. They remained with the *Oregon* until she went to New York after the war, taking part in the bombardments at Santiago and later in the decisive battle of July 3, and winning from all our officers and men the highest esteem and friendly regard.[8]

The night following this addition to our crew, we sailed about eleven o'clock, and the next morning fell in with Admiral Watson's fleet.[9] It

[7] While at Key West, or later off Santiago, *Lieutenant* C. M. Stone, *Ensign* L. A. Bostwick, *Naval Cadets* P. B. Dungan, E. J. Sadler, C. C. Kalbfus, H. J. Brinser, C. G. Hatch, C. Shackford and T. C. Dunlap joined the ship and served through the war. One of our naval cadets, Mr. Gill, had become seriously ill on the run from the Pacific and was sent home. Lieutenant H. W. Harrison, who had well performed the duties of both watch and division officer during the voyage, was injured during one of the bombardments at Santiago, and was transferred to the hospital and then home. [Author's note]

[8] These young men later formed a society, called by my name, and by which I was twice handsomely entertained in Chicago. [Author's note]

[9] After the discovery that Cervera had entered port at Santiago drew the American heavy ships there, a squadron of light vessels under Commodore J. C. Watson was left to continue the blockade of Havana. Earlier, uncertainty as to the destination of the Spanish squadron had caused a considerable dispersion of American naval strength, later condemned by Mahan as violating the principle of concentration of force. The public's unfounded apprehension that Cervera might steam into Boston or New York, guns blazing, led to the decision to divide the North Atlantic Squadron in two. The larger portion, under Acting Rear Admiral William T. Sampson, was sent to the Caribbean. The smaller Flying Squadron, under Commodore W. S. Schley, was based at Norfolk, Virginia, where it was ready to steam to the defense of the central and south Atlantic

was Sunday morning, and all hands in the fleet were dressed for inspection. Our decks were still piled with coal, and everybody black with its dust. I was not permitted to report on board the flagship, however, before we had passed the length of the entire line, the crews cheering themselves hoarse as we went by, and the *Indiana's* band playing "The New Bully." Truly, we felt as some one aptly described the Highlanders, "Proud and dirty."

Watson's fleet was practically marking time north of Cuba and near the western entrance of the Bahama Channel, in order to intercept Cervera's squadron, should it leave Santiago and attempt to reach Havana that way. There were two or three monitors in this fleet, and our arrival enabled the battleship *Indiana* to leave for coal. The next morning Admiral Sampson arrived. He was much disturbed by the report that our fleet under Commodore Schley, which was blockading Santiago, had retired to the westward. [10] He at once telegraphed the Department that having the support of the *Oregon* he would start for Santiago at once and blockade for an indefinite time if necessary. So the *Oregon's* worn-out engine-room force must prepare for a dash of seven hundred miles at speed again. All felt that we had come at a supreme moment, however, and gladly made ready to do their utmost.

We were asked what was the best speed we could make without undue strain on our machinery, and answered "fourteen knots." Twice, in the early part of the run, the *Oregon* came racing up almost abeam of the *New York*, and was checked by the signal, "Keep your station better." These checks in full career meant an unnecessary waste of steam and effort on the part of the men, so when another signal came, "Can you maintain speed without too much strain on machinery," I answered, "Yes, if we are not required to keep our station."

This must have occasioned some explanations on the flagship, for it was some minutes before the reply came back. "The Admiral does not wish you to keep in your station."

After that the *Oregon* tore along like a thoroughbred, passing the *New York* or dropping astern, as her firemen and coal heavers flagged, or roused themselves anew.

---

seaboard. Still a third force, the more-or-less token Northern Patrol Squadron, was formed and placed under the command of Commodore J. A. Howell to guard the coast north of the Delaware Capes. Schley's force proceeded south once it was learned that the Spanish squadron had entered the Caribbean.

[10] Fortunately Commodore Schley returned a few hours later and renewed the blockade. [Author's note]

Chapter 11

SANTIAGO

"Through smoke and flame the battle raged,
  And every missile sent
Was planted where it counted most
  And where the gunners meant.
While leading all, the *Oregon*
  Dashed swiftly to the van,
And raked and riddled with her guns
  Each deck where dared a man."

—JOHN FLAGG, *Lyrics of New England.*

Two more days, and doubt and excitement were ended, for in the haze off Santiago our ships were sighted. Their appearance, and later their signals, proved them to be the *Brooklyn*, *Massachusetts*, *Iowa*, *Texas*, *Marblehead*, and *New Orleans*, with several smaller consorts.[1] We took up our station some distance east of the entrance to the harbor and

[1] Names of ships and commanders taking part in battle or bombardments at Santiago:
New York, Captain Chadwick, flagship of Admiral Sampson.
Brooklyn, Captain Cook, flagship of Commodore Schley.
First-class battleships:
  Massachusetts, Captain Higginson.
  Iowa, Captain Evans.
  Indiana, Captain Taylor.
  Oregon, Captain Clark.
Second-class battleship:
  Texas, Captain Philip.
Cruisers:
  New Orleans, Captain Folger.
  Marblehead, Captain McCalla.
  Yankee, Commander Brownson.
Gunboats:
  Gloucester, Lieutenant Commander Wainwright.
  Vixen, Lieutenant Commander Sharp.
[Author's list]

began our part in the blockade which was to last until July third. The night of our arrival, Hobson made the attempt to carry out the plan of blocking the narrow channel. The nature of the enterprise—which seemed full as desperate as that in which Somers, Israel, Dorsey, and Wadsworth lost their lives in Tripoli—was no check upon the eagerness of our officers and men to share in it. Of the many that volunteered for the expedition, only a few could be taken, however. When morning dawned, it was thought at first that Hobson's object had been achieved, for the sunken *Merrimac*, with her smokestack, spars, and upper works showing, seemed to us to be lying directly in the channel. In fact, the *Oregon* and *Texas* were ordered to take positions close enough in shore to prevent the enemy from boarding or moving her. It soon developed, however, that she had drifted too far over to the eastern side of the channel to block it effectively. Speculation as to the fate of Hobson and his heroic crew was relieved by an announcement of their safety from the magnanimous Cervera, who strangely enough had been the one to rescue them.[2]

On June 4, Commodore Schley and the captains were called on board the flagship for a conference. An attack upon the Spanish batteries had been planned for the next day, and the Admiral wished to assign us our stations. Captain Philip suggested that as the date set was Sunday, there be a delay of twenty-four hours, and to this Sampson agreed. As suggestions seemed to be in order, I brought forward one that appeared to me most essential. It was in relation to our defense against attacks by

---

[2] The chivalrous conduct of Rear Admiral Pascual Cervera y Topete (1839–1909) won the admiration of his American adversaries. The fact that he was in one of the launches that rescued Hobson's men was entirely in keeping with his character. He had opposed the dispatch of his fleet to Cuba, warning that, in view of its being materially inferior to the American naval forces, "nothing can be expected . . . except [its] total destruction . . . or its hasty and demoralized return" (H. W. Wilson, *Battleships in Action*, vol. 1 [Boston, 1926], p. 120). The decision for the disastrous sortie of 3 July was also made, over his objections, in Madrid. It is pleasant to relate that his government did not hold Cervera responsible for the defeat he had foreseen. Honorably acquitted by the court-martial convened on his return to Spain, he was promoted to vice admiral in 1902 and appointed naval chief of staff in 1903.

Naval Constructor Richmond P. Hobson, who graduated at the head of the Naval Academy class of 1889, emerged as one of the popular heroes of the Spanish-American War. Resigning from the navy in 1903 as a result of eye damage incurred on duty in the Philippines, he served for many years as a congressman from his native Alabama. In 1933 he was retroactively awarded the Medal of Honor, for which naval officers had not been eligible in 1898. For a light-hearted account of his celebrity, see B. C. Shaw, "The Hobson Craze," U.S. Naval Institute *Proceedings* (February 1976), pp. 54–60.

torpedo boats, at least a couple of which we knew had entered the harbor with the Spanish cruisers. Up to this time, the only watch that had been maintained against what should have been a most effective weapon of the enemy was that kept by our gunboats, which naturally could not get very close to the harbor entrance without being observed and fired upon. My proposal that launches or pulling boats should also be used for this picket duty roused some debate, for our ships, stripped for war service, had only two or three boats apiece, and in addition to this scarcity of numbers, there was the anxiety about their crews to be considered. Should rough weather occur, with a rising sea, there would certainly be great difficulty in picking them up. It was finally decided that the *Massachusetts*, *New York*, and *Oregon* should furnish these picket boats. When Admiral Sampson, as a further precaution, determined to illuminate the entrance with searchlights and the *Massachusetts* and *Oregon*, with the addition of the *Iowa*, were again selected for duty, I felt that honors were coming our way a little too thickly. Every night, within close range of the Spanish batteries, our searchlight making us veritably a shining mark, I used to look at the dark forms of my crew sleeping on deck, for the heat made anything else impossible, and think what havoc in their ranks a well-directed fire would make. With this cause for uneasiness added to the trying picket-boat duty, I thought that the burden might have been shared to advantage with the *Indiana*, *Texas*, and *Brooklyn*.

It may not be out of place here to try to give some idea of the peculiarities of Santiago harbor and the position of its fortifications. There are hills on either side of its narrow entrance, on the one side precipitous, and on the other sloping. The picturesque mass of the Morro crowns the abrupt eastern shore, while on the western slope lay the Socapa batteries. Directly at the entrance the channel makes a sharp turn to the right, seeming to hide itself behind the craggy headland of the Morro. It becomes visible again as it curves to the left to round Socapa Point, then with another bend to the right vanishes behind the high land of Punta Gorda, which to the eye of the observer from outside would almost appear to close the passage. The city of Santiago lies four miles above this tortuous entrance, so it will be seen if we had been obliged to force our way in to fight the Spanish fleet, we would have been exposed to the fire from the Morro and Socapa batteries, then to the mines in the channel, and to the batteries on Punta Gorda, before we were able to reach the squadron which was anchored near the city. The batteries would have given us little concern, since experience had taught us how inefficiently they were served, but the mines were a real menace, for if our leading ship were sunk by one, it would block the way for all the others. I learned afterwards from Admiral Sampson that if circumstances had compelled him to force an entrance, he had intended to have the *Oregon* lead in, so I might have been vitally interested in the position of these mines.

On June 6 our fleet moved forward in two columns to begin the first bombardment. The *New York* and *Brooklyn* led, followed by the battleships and the *New Orleans*, *Marblehead*, and *Yankee*. The columns opened to right and left as they drew within range and brought their broadsides to bear. This bombardment—as well as the others following it—was a very one-sided affair. The Spaniards never fired a shot while we were taking position, and if they replied at all during the attack, it was so seldom as to be scarcely noticeable. As we drew out, they manned their batteries and fired a few scattering shots after us. Even the most conspicuous target did not seem to rouse them to activity, for in a later bombardment the *Oregon* was ordered to steam in, in advance of the line, and silence or destroy a rifle-gun battery on the Punta Gorda, which, as will be remembered, was some distance inside the entrance. After the *Oregon* had taken her position and begun firing, the *Massachusetts* and *Indiana* joined her, and the battery was very quickly disposed of, without damage resulting on any of the three ships.

On June 10, the *Oregon's* marine guard, under Captain Randolph Dickens and Lieutenant Davis, in company with marines from the *Marblehead* had landed on the eastern head of Guantanamo Bay, the first armed force to set foot on Cuban soil.[3] Later in the afternoon, the *Panther* arrived with the marine battalion, and despite several annoying attacks, the position was held during the rest of the war. This guard from the *Oregon* seemed destined to see stormy service, for at least half of them, with the *Newark's* marines, were sent afterwards to form part of the Legation guard at Peking, and in the siege that followed many were killed and hardly one escaped unwounded. Lieutenant Davis fell at Tientsin.

The latter part of June, the entrance of our army into Cuba brought complications in its train. If it had landed beyond the Morro to the eastward and, moving along the crest of the high plateau on which it stands, had made it and the Socapa batteries objects of attack, we could

[3] The *Marblehead* covered this landing, and her commander, Captain Bowman H. McCalla, was afterwards in the expedition to relieve Peking, and in spite of at least three wounds received was always the first in advance and the last in retreat. [Author's note]

have protected one flank during this proceeding, and if it were success-ful, could then have gone into the channel with our small boats and picked up the mines. This would have left the way open for us to enter the harbor and tackle the Spanish fleet. But the army, instead of adopting this coöperative course, had marched inland towards the city of Santiago, where it had fought bravely, but had met with such heavy losses that General Shafter wanted Admiral Sampson to force the harbor entrance and come to his aid. This did not seem good strategy to those who knew that the capture or destruction of Cervera's squadron was the real object of the Cuban campaign, but it was obvious that something would have to be done and done quickly, for the yellow fever season was approaching, and that scourge would have mowed down our forces more relentlessly than any human enemy. So early in the morning of July 3, Admiral Sampson in the *New York* steamed eastward to Siboney for a conference with General Shafter. The *Massachusetts* was away at Guanta-namo, coaling. Owing to the absence of these two vessels, the other ships had slightly changed their usual positions in the semicircle fronting the harbor. The *Brooklyn* was at the end of the line to the westward, then came the battleships *Texas*, *Iowa*, *Oregon* and *Indiana*, in the order named. Also there were the two small gunboats *Gloucester* and *Vixen*, stationed at the eastern and western ends of the circle.[4]

It was Sunday morning, and a beautiful, clear day. I was in my cabin and had just buckled on my sword and taken up my cap to go on deck, for the first call for inspection had sounded, when suddenly the brassy clang of the alarm gongs echoed through the ship, and the orderly burst through the cabin door, exclaiming, "The Spanish fleet, sir! It's coming out!"

I hurried on deck, thinking it must be a false alarm, but as I hastened forward, man after man greeted me with, "You'll see her in a minute, Captain! She's behind the Morro now!"

Just then I saw clearly enough the military top, and then the bow and smokestack of a man-of-war sliding rapidly past the second point in the harbor, and as she disappeared behind the Morro, the leading ship rushed out from the entrance with a speed that seemed inspired by the assurance of victory, firing her guns as she came.

---

[4] The *Gloucester*'s position at the eastern end of the line enabled her to follow and make a brilliant attack upon the enemy's torpedo boats, while the *Vixen*, being just in the track of the Spanish cruisers, could only retreat, but this was done in the most creditable way. [Author's note]

One rapid glance around showed me that under the energetic supervision of Lieutenant Commander Cogswell, everything was being done in preparation for battle. The *Oregon* was thrilling with life. Men were hurrying to their stations at the guns, engines were throbbing, screws beginning to revolve. For the moment I interested myself in the firing of a six-pounder near the bridge, with the idea of spreading the alarm to our other ships. There has been much said about who fired the first shot at Santiago. It is but reasonable to suppose it was either the *Iowa*, or the *Oregon*, for they were the only vessels, which, from their stations, had a clear view of the Santiago channel and consequently of the ship passing Socapa point.

We had a general order from the Admiral, if the enemy should come out to close in on him at once, but I am sure every commander was obeying his natural impulse rather than any order, when the forward movement began. Before the leading Spanish ship, the *Maria Teresa*,[5] was obscured by the smoke of the cannonading which started immediately, I had seen that she was heading to the westward, and as it was almost certain the others would follow her, and it was equally plain they would all be out of the harbor before I could reach its entrance, I too turned west. Suddenly, from behind the curtain of dense smoke, the *Iowa* emerged, close on our starboard side. I gave the order, "hard a-starboard!" for it was evident that we were drawing ahead of her slowly and ought to go clear. Just then, some one near me shouted, "Look out for the *Texas*!" and I turned to see her looming through the smoke clouds on our port bow. For one intense moment it seemed as if three of our ships might be put out of action then and there, leaving only the *Indiana* and the lightly armored *Brooklyn* to cope with the foe. The only thing to be done was to put our helm hard a-port, with the hope that we might clear the *Texas* and that the *Iowa*, seeing that we must either cross her bows or run her down, would sheer sharply to starboard. Captains Philip and Evans, both fine seamen, must have instantly grasped the situation and acted on it, for we did pass between them, but by so narrow a margin that I felt that coming to close quarters with the Spaniards would be infinitely preferable to repeating that experience.

---

[5] Admiral Cervera's flagship, the armored cruiser *Infanta Maria Theresa*, had been launched in 1890. Of 7,000 tons displacement, she was 340 feet in length and had a nominal speed of 20 knots. Her battery consisted of two 10-inch guns mounted in single turrets fore and aft and ten 5.5-inch guns. Her sister ships, the *Almirante Oquendo* and the *Vizcaya*, were a year younger.

A little afterwards the smoke lifted, and somewhat ahead of us, and on our starboard bow, we saw all four Spanish ships, and realized that at last our meeting with the long-looked-for fleet was actually to take place. They showed no signs of the severe punishment they had received at the entrance, and as we did not know then how much their machinery had deteriorated, I noticed with surprise that the *Oregon* was not only keeping pace with them, but was even gaining a little. Indeed, seeing nothing between them and us, for our less speedy companions were considerably in the rear, I said to the navigator, "Well, Nicholson, it seems we have them on our hands after all."

At that moment, some distance outside, and therefore on our port bow, I saw the *Brooklyn*, Commodore Schley's flagship, and commanded by my old friend, F. A. Cook. She was a little ahead of us, and her guns were doing good work. Although we knew that with her light armor and less powerful battery she could not give us the aid one of the battleships would have afforded, yet the feeling of having a comrade in arms near us was much, and I remember saying with some emotion to one of those standing beside me, "My old roommate is in command of that ship."

At almost the same moment, as we afterwards learned, when we tore out of the smoke clouds and were sighted by the little group upon the *Brooklyn*'s bridge, the relief at our approach broke out in exclamations of, "Here comes the *Oregon*! It's the *Oregon*, God bless her!" Ensign Johnston, who was close at my side all that day, reported that the *Brooklyn* had a signal flying, which read "Follow the flag," and I immediately ordered it to be repeated on the *Oregon*, so that the vessels further astern might see it.

About this time we noticed signs of distress on the sternmost Spaniard. This was the *Maria Teresa*, Cervera's flagship. As she had come out of the harbor first and then fallen back to the rear, I have always thought it must have been Cervera's chivalrous idea—he came of one of the old Castilian families to whom such ideas are natural—to cover the retreat of his flying ships and to bear the brunt of the combat. Smoke was seen presently rolling up from the doomed vessel, and making a sharp turn, she headed for the beach. As her colors were still flying, we raked her as we went past—I remember it went to my heart to do it—and pushed on for the next ahead, the *Oquendo*. We closed in on her to a distance of about eight hundred yards, the nearest that vessels approached that day. She could not stand the punishment long. Fires broke out all over her, and she too ran for the shore. Nicholson said, "Captain, that vessel could be destroyed now," but I answered, "No, that's a dead cock in the pit. The others can attend to her. We'll push on for the two ahead."

It took us a little time to come abreast of the *Vizcaya*. We kept up a continuous fire upon her, but it was nearly eleven o'clock before she turned for the beach, in flames. As this last battletorn wreck of what had once been a proud and splendid ship fled to the shore like some sick and wounded thing, seeking a place to die, I could feel none of that exultation that is supposed to come with victory. If I had seen my own decks covered with blood, and my officers and men dying around me, perhaps resentment would have supplied the necessary ingredient, but as it was, the faces of the women and children in far-away Spain, the widows and orphans of this July third, rose before me so vividly that I had to draw comfort from the thought that a decisive victory is after all more merciful than a prolonged struggle, and that every life lost to-day in breaking down the bridge to Spain might mean a hundred saved hereafter.

The *Colon*,[6] the only remaining ship, had drawn several miles ahead, and as she kept on with undiminished speed, I though a shell or two falling near her might give her a hint that it would be well to surrender. So a little after twelve o'clock, when she was still at a distance from us, I consulted Nicholson and Ackerman—both of them ordnance experts—and Eberle, who had been doing fine work in our forward turret, as to whether the great elevation required at so long a range would be too much of a strain upon guns and mounts. We decided to fire once with range set for nine thousand, five hundred yards. The shot fell short and we were preparing to increase the range, when the chief engineer, who had just come up on deck, said, "Captain, I was thankful when I heard that gun. I was meaning to ask you if one could be fired. Our men down below are nearly played out, but if they can only hear the guns, they will brace up again."

At 1.10 P.M. one of our shots fell close alongside the *Colon*, and she headed for the beach, her colors coming down, and with them the last vestige of Spain's power in that New World which had once known her as its ruler.[7]

[6] The 6,840-ton armored cruiser *Cristóbal Colón* was the newest ship in Cervera's squadron, having been launched in 1896. Unfortunately for the Spanish, her 10-inch guns had not been mounted when the squadron sailed, and she went into action carrying nothing larger than 5.5-inch guns.

[7] Besides the four cruisers, Cervera's two destroyers, the *Furor* and the *Pluton*, were also destroyed. Of approximately 2,200 men in the Spanish squadron, 323 were killed, 151 wounded, and most of the remainder captured. American losses amounted to one man killed and another wounded.

Chapter 12

A SAILOR'S LOG

After a victory so absolute, it is usual to begin to count the cost, but to our amazement, our ships, one after another, hoisted the signal "no casualties." The *Brooklyn* was the only exception, and she suffered the loss of but one man. We had a glorious Fourth of July present to offer the nation, for seldom, if ever, in naval history, has there been an instance of such complete destruction of an attacking fleet.

The *Cristobal Colon* was the only enemy vessel that had not been severely injured. Captain Cook of the *Brooklyn* received her surrender. We looked forward to seeing her become an effective addition to our navy, in which the name she bore would have seemed singularly appropriate, but either through accident or treachery, her sea valves had been opened, and in spite of the efforts of her prize crew to save her, she sank where she lay. Her last resting place is one of the most beautiful spots on the Cuban coast. She lies where Mount Tarquino rises abruptly from the shore, to a height of eight thousand feet, green to its summit, and its base bathed in that bright, blue water so wonderfully rendered in W. F. Halsall's spirited canvas,[1] where the *Oregon* is seen firing the last shot in the battle of Santiago.

---

[1] Now in the National Museum at Washington. Taken to San Francisco by the Navy Department for the Exposition, where it was constantly guarded by sailors from the *Oregon*. [Author's note]

One of our officers who had boarded the *Colon* brought me a large silver platter and cover belonging to her wardroom outfit, for as he pointed out, they were both marked with my initials, "C.C."

The *Oregon's* officers and crew could indeed feel, as the signal "Congratulations over the great victory and thanks for your splendid assistance" went up from the *Brooklyn*, that they had deserved well of the navy and the nation. With noble endurance and unwearying devotion they had brought their ship in splendid condition to the scene of the conflict where they had played a foremost part.[2] As I was rowed over in my gig to report on board the *New York*, her crew cheered for the *Oregon* and her captain so heartily and repeatedly, that after rising myself to acknowledge their tribute, I asked my boat's crew to rise, which they did amidst a storm of cheers.

There are a few occasions in a man's life which will remain with him always. That was one, and another, which I can never forget, was the day when, broken in health, I left the *Oregon*. It was a pleasure to find that the boat in which I was to be rowed to the northbound steamer was manned by my officers. That is an honor deeply appreciated by any captain. But I was surprised and hurt, as we left the ship's side, that none of the men were visible. Suddenly, as if moved by one spring, they rose from the decks where they had been lying concealed, and led by old Murphy, the chief boatswain's mate, joined in a ringing shout of "God bless our captain." So the last impression I had of the *Oregon*, as we rowed away, was a forest of waving arms and tossing caps, seen through a mist, although the day was clear and bright.[3]

During my recovery from illness, it was a great happiness to me to read of the enthusiasm with which the *Oregon* was received when she

[2] It was disappointing that these brave and devoted men could not have had the satisfaction that the tribute planned for their ship at the formal opening of the Panama Canal would have afforded them. It was intended that the *Oregon* with as many of her original complement as could be gathered and with the President and Secretary of the Navy on the bridge beside her commanding officer would lead the International fleets through the Canal. [Author's note]

[3] On 7 July 1898, four days after the Battle of Santiago, Captain Clark was appointed chief of staff of the new Eastern Squadron being organized under the command of Commodore J. C. Watson. This force, to consist of the battleships *Iowa* (subsequently replaced by the *Massachusetts*) and *Oregon*, the cruiser *Newark*, three auxiliary cruisers, and three colliers, was to cross the Atlantic and bring the war to the coast of Spain. The prospect of such a visit was instrumental in the Spanish decision to seek peace, and the squadron never sailed. Clark was detached from command of the *Oregon* on 6 August 1898.

came north with the other ships. The fact that I was not bearing a prominent part in these festivities rather added to than detracted from this feeling, for I have never learned to be happy or easy in the spot-light.

And so it was that when my name was joined to those of Sampson and Schley, in the Senate bill which proposed to make the three of us vice admirals, and owing to the jealousies and strife of the famous contest *after* Santiago,[4] it failed to pass, I can truthfully say that it was no matter of regret to me. The prominence and exacting duties of such a position would have been too much of a strain on me at that time, and I feel that better health and longer life have been mine, in remaining a rear admiral and retiring at the age of sixty-two. But what did give me the keenest satisfaction was the knowledge that nearly all the officers senior to me on the navy list, men who had long been my superiors in rank, such as Watson, Higginson, Wadleigh, and Chester, who are still living, and Casey, Barker, Cotton, Sands, and Cook, generously ignoring the fact that I would be placed above them, all expressed the hope that I would be made a vice admiral.

With this same feeling in mind, when President Roosevelt wished to send me as Naval Representative to the coronation of King Edward, I was rather glad to be able to excuse myself on the ground that my income as captain would hardly be adequate to the demands of such a position. The President very kindly suggested that he might be able to secure an extra grade for me. I told him of the objections I had always felt to that

---

[4] Between 1898 and 1901 several proposals were made to revive the rank of vice admiral, which had lapsed with the retirement of Stephen C. Rowan in 1889. The "famous contest" to which the author alludes was the Sampson-Schley controversy, which arose in the aftermath of the Battle of Santiago. Although it did not become public knowledge for some months, Sampson felt that Schley's command of the Flying Squadron during the search for Cervera had been unsatisfactory in the extreme and so informed Secretary of the Navy John D. Long. Long agreed, and when the Senate Naval Affairs Committee moved to consider the promotions of Sampson and Schley to the permanent rank of rear admiral, he recommended that Sampson be advanced more places than Schley on the seniority list. Schley protested so convincingly that eventually the Senate decided to advance both men the same number of places. This had, however, delayed their promotions for some months and tarnished the laurels of Santiago. But the worst was yet to come. In 1901 the Naval Academy adopted as its textbook Edgar Maclay's *History of the United States Navy*, which was highly critical of Schley's actions. Schley demanded that it be withdrawn and requested a court of inquiry to review his conduct throughout the war. After lengthy hearings the court produced a majority report condemning Schley and a minority report exonerating him. In protest of the majority finding, Schley appealed to President Theodore Roosevelt, who brought the affair to a close by ordering all parties to desist from the dispute.

sort of promotion and added that as my small experience of royalty had been limited to a Siwash Indian chief and a king of the Cannibal Islands, I should have little to guide me in court functions. He told me to take a month to think it over, and as at the end of that time I was still of the same opinion, he very generously allowed me to nominate the officer to go in my place. This gave me the pleasure of naming my friend Rear Admiral Watson, whose splendid Civil War record, I had always felt, should have brought him more recognition both during and after the Spanish War. I was with Admiral Watson when he went to thank the President for his appointment. Roosevelt spoke of his strong desire to have had me go, but added that as it appeared a scalping knife or tomahawk might have been brandished at the Court of St. James if I had reverted to my only associations with royalty, it was perhaps better on the whole that another should take my place.

During the years 1899 to 1901 I was second in command at League Island, a navy yard then of minor importance. For a part of this time, however, I was also a member of the General Board, which had just then been formed.[5] This was, and continues to be, the most interesting duty open to a naval officer, since it provides for constant and prompt interchange of ideas between officers serving the navy afloat and those whose experience has best fitted them to watch its interests on shore and to present these ideas in concrete form for the consideration of the Navy Department.

From 1901 to 1904 I was Governor of the Naval Home in Philadelphia,[6] and afterwards had duty in Washington as President of the Examining and Retiring Boards. These last two positions I retained until my own retirement August 10, 1905. I was offered the command of the European Squadron and later that of the Atlantic Fleet.

Our stay in Philadelphia was rendered delightful to us by the many agreeable social relations we formed while there. For Philadelphians, while notoriously reluctant to let down barriers to the stranger, once they have admitted him within their gates, are the most hospitable of

[5] The General Board of the Navy was established under the presidency of Admiral of the Navy George Dewey in 1900. Composed of the chief of the Bureau of Navigation, the president of the Naval War College, the chief of the Office of Naval Intelligence, and eight other senior officers, its purpose was to furnish the secretary of the navy with expert advice on matters of naval policy and operations to coordinate the activities of the War College and the Office of Naval Intelligence. Although without command authority, it represented a major step towards the organization of the modern Navy Department.

[6] It was during this assignment that Clark was promoted to the rank of rear admiral (16 June 1902).

people. It was at this time that I became intimate with Doctor S. Weir Mitchell, a friendship only broken by his death. His lively interest in all things historical pertaining to our country included the voyage of the *Oregon* and her part at Santiago, and he often urged me to put down in black and white what I could remember of it. He was delighted with the diary kept by a marine, one of my cabin orderlies, in the *Oregon*, regarding it as a unique piece of literature. This record came into my hands during a winter I was spending in Greenfield, my wife's old home. Written solely for the perusal of the author's sisters, it had come into the hands of one of their friends, who sent it to me. I showed it to Chief Justice John Adams Aiken of the Superior Court of Massachusetts, who enjoyed it so greatly that he had a private edition printed for circulation among his friends.

I can think of no better way to end this narrative than with Judge Aiken's preface and these "short and simple annals" of "The Voyage of the *Oregon*."

"TO THE READER"

"Almost ten years have passed since the country followed, in scanty telegram from port to port, the *Oregon* speeding down one side of a continent and up the other to Bahia; then came two anxious, silent weeks when apprehension and fear pictured four Spanish cruisers with a pack of torpedo boats sailing out into the west athwart the lone ship's course, the suspense ending only when tidings came of her arrival at Jupiter Inlet; then off Santiago, after a month of waiting, there is the outcoming of Cervera's squadron, when this splendid ship, with steam all the time up, leaps to the front of her sisters of the fleet, like an unleashed hound, and joins the historic company of the *Bon Homme Richard*, the *Constitution*, the *Hartford*, in our naval annals. From the start at the Golden Gate to the beaching of the *Colon* is a succession of events full of thrilling merit and vitality which official bickerings and envyings cannot change or obscure.

"The story has been told from the standpoint of the quarterdeck, the courtroom and the department bureau. Here we have the artless journal of an unlettered sailor, written between decks, without the least notion that it would ever be read apart from his own family circle. The pages of his record give an insight into the mutual regard and confidence existing between the captain and his crew which made the voyage the memorable achievement that it was."

THE VOYAGE OF THE *OREGON*

So we started on the 19th of March and I will try and give you some idea of our trip on this side of the U.S. Capt McCommick got sick and had to be relieved to go on sick leif. Capt Clark was in command of the Monteray at the time and he was a young Capt too. there was no other one around there at that time, so he was detailed to take comand of the Oregon and a prowed man he was too, and we wer a prowed crew along with him. He was glad he got the ship and we wer glad we got him. we knew he was a good Seaman. Any way he called us all aft on the quarter deck and read out his orders and told us that we wer going towards south America. I will now try and give you the trip.

March 19. 1898 Up anchor at 8 A.M. in San Francisco Bay. I had the 8 to 12 watch and we past through the Golden Gate at 9.15 A.M. and left the Fairwell Bouy at 10.5 A.M. and shaped our course for Callao, Peru, it being S. E. ½ E, and at the same time we drop over the Patent Log in the Briny. the Capt gave orders to give 75 turns and that brought her out about 11.5 knots. Every thing is runing smooth and all Hunk.

March 20. Sliding along at 11.8 knots gate. Everything working beautyfull. nothing of interest going on, except the fine Wether.

March 21. Changed course at 10 A.M. to S. E. Will not put down any thing for some time to come as there is nothing unusual going on. But I wonder if we will get there to catch up with the Band Wagon.

April 4. Arived at Calao, Peru, 5.00 A.M., very pleasant trip all the way down the coast, we are doing quick work so far. started to coal ship at 8 A.M. and as soon as we get enough on board we will pull right out for the straights of Magellan and there join the Marietta, our little Gun Boat, which will scout the straights for us in case there is a Spanish Torpedo Boat in one of the Many Coves. She can go in shallow water as she is a light draft boat and at the same time order coal for us.

We have allready made one of the grandest runs on record. Just think of it, a First Class Battle Ship making 4800 miles in just 16 days and used 900 Tons of Coal, That being the longest trip on record for a First Class Battle Ship.

April 5. We are now laying over an old city in Peru. they say when some of the ships hoist there anchor they sometimes rais some of the old houses or part of them with the anchor. This old place is some 109 years old, the Old Callao, I mean. 109 years ago they had an Earthquake and Tidle Wave hear together and did up the city. The public hear speak nothing put Spanish and the Capt thinks there might be som sympathizers amongst Them, so we are keeping the strickest Kind of watch on the ship. We have two steam cutters pattroling the ship all night and men station in the fighting tops as sharp shooters. the steam cutters are armed with two automatic 22 m.m. Rifles, so that would more than be a match for a ordinary Torpedo Boat, and while all the Post on Deck were Double we consider ourselves pretty safe. They are puting coal on board as fast as they can, working night and day to get it all on. we are going to take a big lot this time.

April 6. Pay day today. put on Sea stors today along with the coal, it all gos togather. But what is the diferance, this is War times and we are trying to get in it and I think we will if we get a show. I bought a nice pair of shoes today for 3.50 in U. S. Gold. there is no liberty to any one hear so we have to buy something that is some good to us. Expect to coal ship all night so as to pull out to morrow.

April 7. Got the coal on this morning at 4 A. M. there is about 1750 tons on now, never had so much on before. got 100 tons on deck in sacks. we are knocking some of the coal dust off the sides. She is a very dirty ship now and expect to remain so for a long time to come. There is some talk of a Spanish Gun Boat or a Torpedo Boat in the Straights waiting for us. But I think that will be all right when the Marietta gets there to patrole the place for us. We expect to go out to night some time. 7 p. m. left Port. The Capt dont know wether to go round the Horn or not. But if we go, as the Dutchman says By the Horn around, we will get a shaking up. But every body seems to think we can take care of our selves where ever we go. Capt Clark is all right, we dont think he is afraid of the whole Spanish Navy. the wether is very fogy. Expect it to lift when we get a little ways.

April 9. Alls Well, everything doing fine.

April 10. Just came on watch; have all four boilers on now and we are peging along at a 13.7 and a 14 knot gate. you dont know you are at sea in this ship if you would stop between Decks. guess there is not much doing to day, so I will steal forward for a while the old gent sleeps a little. I forgot to speak of having a little practis with the 6 pounders. They threw over Boxes and barrels and as we would get away from them we would fire on them for Torpedo Boats. we did some good shooting. All the Marines Man the seccondary Battry. The Capt got the chief engineer to fix the 8 inch turets to turn in Board 9 more degrees so as to shoot over the stern of the ship. So that would bring to bear on one point 2, 13 inch Guns 4, 8 inch Guns 2, 6 inch Guns and six 6 Pounders aft, and the same forward. We could shoot for a Broad side 4, 13 inch 4, 8 inch 2, 6 inch and about 12, 6 Pounders on either side.

Of corse this is Sunday and we all ought to be good. But we will be as good as we can By having a Gen feild day and clean up a little, as this is the first chance we have had to do any scrubing since we left San Francisco, Cal. I think we will meet the Marietta in the Straights of Magellan. we have found some grate Bars for her under the coal dust. We all think Capt Clark is going to be a ring tail snorter for fighting. I dont think it will be easy to whip him, he seems to be so quick to catch on to every little thing, he is all over the ship at once and he talks to every body, stops any one to ask them any thing he wants to know about the ship. he is very quick to take the advantage of every little thing.

April 11. Very heavy wether. Wind Blowing Great Guns and a head sea. But we are Bucking it and making 11.6 knots. the Capt dont think we will run up against any thing in the shape of a Torpedo Boat in the Straights. We had some more practis today with the 6 Pounders and did some good work. I think we could make it very interesting for a Torpedo Boat. I dont see how they could get at us, unless it was in the night and then there would have to be something the matter with our search lights and all hands on Board would have to have the "Buck Feaver."

April 12. We lost a little today on account of the forward 13 inch Turet, somthing got Jamed. all going well once more, and still bucking a head sea and making 11.7 knots right along. 4 P.M. Heavy wind has turned into a gale, but she is like a duck on a Mill Pond and still making 10 knots, Gale or no Gale. she has not roled over 10 degrees since we left Port Orchard, Wash.

April 15. Whooping her up for all she is worth, want to make all she can. Wether is fine but quite Cold. Making all the way from 14 to 15 knots.

April 16. Everything is still doing well, and still going a mill tail. Passed Smiths Straights the first part of this morning, early, and in the fog that has Just come on we are still going it. the fog raised for a while and showed us the Destination Island, and then we wer shure we had only 30 miles to go to get in the Straights. Just at Dark we droped our mud hook in just 45 fathoms of water in the entrence of the Straights of Magellan. 9.45 P.M. had the 8 to 12 watch and She more than blew. I though the ship would drift. But she held on like grim Deth to a dead nigger. The wind Blowed so hard I expected to be lifted off my feet.

April 17. Making all posable speed to Sandy Point, making about 15 knots ever since we started this morning. 12 O clock Midday, there is some of the most beautyfull and grandest sights I have ever had the pleasure to look upon. I am shure if I could only write on the subject I could make it very interesting. I never seen such beautifull wild nature in all my travels; there is mountain after mountain of Glacier and they seem to have all the colors of the rainbow, it was a little cold too and the whole Mountain sparkled like diamonds. 6 P.M. drop anchor in the Harber of Sandy Point, Chili. Had the public bin able to see us, They would not stop runing for the next week to come, for we cleared ship for action and had the guns all loaded up and ready for business and to Blaze away at any thing that looked as thoe it wanted to fight. Capt Clark belives in for warned for armed, and takes no chances. had the two Steam Cutters patroling the ship as usual.

She made one of the grandest runs on record for 11 hours making an average of 15½ knots; it knocks the Worlds record sky high. Just think of a first Class Battle Ship making 15½ knots for 11 straight hours on a straight away run, and we all think she could beat that time. But we had over the bow 2 anchors with the flukes of both in the water 3 feet. I am sure that held her Back 2 tenths of a knot. And the Marietta is not hear. the Capt dont know what has become of her.

April 18. Well the Marietta is hear this morning, she came in at 12.15 this morning. She was in the straights when we past her, she was laying off in one of the coves waiting for us, the man on look-out sighted us as we pased her, and told his capt and he said let her go, we will up anchor and overhall her in a short time. it hapened that the lookout was on board of the Oregon and he told his Capt that the Marietta could never catch the Oregon. Well any way she came in a little after mid-night.

The first thing this morning we started to coal up. I havent found out how many tons we are going to take hear. But the price is $25 a ton. I think we will take about 800 tons. all the men on the Marietta say they had a very rough trip. We are in a great rush to get out of hear. Capt Clark asked Capt Simons if he had any towing Bits. Looks as thoe we were going to snake him along with us. I am detailed to go into the fighting top to night as capt of one Pounder and look out, we have a double watch on now all the time and it makes the Duty very hard thies war times.

April 19. Still coaling up, was working all night to night, expect to be through to night sometime. Puting on sea stors along with the coal. Meat, Can goods, coal dust, all mixed up togather. What is the defirance, it all goes thies times. The Marietta had some trouble in geting coal to day. She only got 40 tons since 1 A.M. this morning, so Capt Clark ordered him to go along side of the Coal Hulk and take all he wanted, for Capt sais we must have the coal and therefor must take it as we are going out of hear to morrow. 3.30 P.M. there was an Argentine Gun Boat came in Port and I would not be surprised to see a scrap hear before we left. Chili and Argentine are in hot disput over this place, it seems they both clame it to there Boundry line. Chili sent a company of Soldiers hear the 18th and they expect a Transport with som Soldiers from Argentine to night som time, so I for one would like to see a good scrap of som kind for an appetizer for us, Just to take the rough edge off you know. we are standing by our Guns all the time and sleep by them by night. While the Jackies coal ship all hands are doing there part and there is no fudging going on. of corse there is all kinds of War talk in the air.

April 20. At 12.30 A.M. still coaling up. Every thing working smooth and nothing to stop, it is a beautyfull night and the Southern Cross looms up with more beauty than I ever seen befor. But the ships bum Boat is all right too, she loomed up with a big ketle of hot Steaming cocoa, Just the thing a man wants when he has the mid watch. the wether is very cold down hear. a few of the men is going ashore to morrow. I dont think I will be able to go as I will have the afternoon watch, any way I dont care much as I am use to the ship now. I could stay hear for a year. I wish we wer around to Key West so as to be with the Band wagon when she starts. Mr. Giles, Midshipman, is a very sick man, he was taken ill in the Cabin this morning. I went for the Doctor for him at 1.45 A.M. Doc said he had a hemorrhage of the lungs caused by concussion. 3 A.M. he is asleep and doing fine now. I woulden like to see him die, he is a fine fellow. 3.45 A.M. coal all on board. 4.30 P.M. the Capt is on the warpath, he is mader than a wet hen for he tryed to get out of hear by 2 P.M. to day, But could not on the account of the Marietta having some trouble with her coal, so we both go tomorrow morning at daybreak.

April 21. Called all hands at 5.30 A.M. and up anchor at 6 A. M. I called the old man at 5.40 A. M. Signaled over to pullout and we are tailing on behind untill we get out of the Straights, going about 10 knots; at 6 Bells met a steamer Bound for Klondyke, we drop a whale boat and sent our Boarding officer to find out the news if there was any But was disapointed. She had no news, she was 15 days from Rio Janeiro. 7.30 P. M. all is going well. The Marietta is astern now and likely to remain so untill we get in the next Port. we past another steamer about 3 P. M. and when I go on watch to night at 8 I will try and find out something about her. Came off at 12 midnight and she signaled to us no news of War. We have to go slow on account of the Marietta. had some targate practis today with all the Guns. We travel at night with all lights out now adays so as not to let any thing slip up on us, and at the same time slip up on them.

April 22. Wind is very high, lost a life Boat this morning at 5.20 A. M. from the after Davits, good thing the wind is head on, the Sea is runing high. 8 P.M. Sea and wind has gon down considerable. Making about 10½ knots. Ellis is sick poor man, I am standing his watch to night. 11.45 P.M. going about the same and all is well.

April 23. I think we will have a dash of Gen Quarters, Just to shake the Boys up. the old man is anxious to have targate Practis, he believes this ship whips the shoes off any thing that floats in the line of Battle ships, of corse Baring a Torpedo if one should hapen to hit, and I think the old man is right too, for this crew feels scrapy now. I think we would fight fer Keeps. Had Gen Quarters in the morning and Church in the afternoon.

April 24. All is well, at 12 Oclock noon to day we wer in Lat. 44° 23m and Lon 57° 48m. had some fire drill to day mixed with a little collision drill.

April 25. 4 A. M. Just came on watch and I am going on deck to get a cup of cocoa to wake me up abit. the old man is in the Chart house snoozing, so I guess it is safe to go. Every thing has settled down to the same old thing except when we have some Targate Practis By throwing boxes over board.

April 26. 8 A. M. All is well, same thing, Making 10½ sometimes 11 knots. Had clear ship for action today.

April 27. Every body begins to feal the trip now, geting tiresome now. since they have taken all of our ditty Boxes and benches and all extra mess chests and stored them away, we have no place to sit down except on deck and let our feet hang over. then the men forward cant get enough water to keep themselves clean. I am more lucky than most of them for I have a chance to steal a Bucketful one every night. our cook is no good, he makes sour Bread and would make good schrapnel for clearing the decks, and of corse your humble servant has to chew Hard Tack. had more Targate practis to day.

April 28. good stiff Breeze to day. Expect to have more targate practis to day with ful charges of amanition; no practis, wind too high.

April 29. good day to day, guess we will have it to day, no we dont have it. the old man has changed his mind and we will try and make Port to morrow.

April 30. Started to pul out this morning at 5.30 A.M., useing forsed draught, making 14.5 knots, going to try and make it by 4 P.M., have a head wind and light head sea. Droped anchor at 3 P.M. in the beautyfull harber of Rio de Janeiro, and befor the Mud hook struck the botom we had the news that war was declared on the 21st of April 1898, the very day we puled out of Sandy Point. as soon as every thing was put to order we Broke out the Band to give us the Star Spangled Baner, and the Crew diden do a thing But yell and whoop her up, so they had to play it over 4 times. The Marietta got in at 7 P.M. The Forts at this place were not going to let her in. But when they see her Signal they let her pass O.K. started to coal up at 8.25 P.M. and we get out of hear as soon as we can. I hear the Spanish has got one of our Merchant ships, the Shanandore, loaded with English goods. I wonder how that is going to com out. Every one on this ship is crasie to get at the Spanish.

May 1. Just come on watch. Beautyfull morning and still coaling ship. Hear is where you can get lots of sour frute and Bananas by the ship load for a little mony. But we are not aloud to Buy any thing that isent sour on account of Yellow Feaver at this place. The Brazilian soldiers stop up all night to be up erly in the morning; they started to give us Revelee about 3 Oclock this morning, dident get through until 4 A.M. it sounds very pretty early in the morning when you are all ready awake, and such a beautifull morning as this is you can hear the echo of the drums up in the hils far away. You would all most wish you could stop hear all the time and be a Brazilian for good. But I coulden leave my Dear land for all the pretty sights Ive seen togather.

May 2. American Minerster Just com on board and told us the news of the Battle of Manila, the Yanks did up every thing there. coal is coming on very slow and the old man is geting ancious to get out.

May 3. going out to-morrow morning at 6 A.M. The crew is very enthusiastic over the war. got out this morning all right But going slow. I think we are fooling around hear. Have Nictheroy as a transport boat. She has 2000 tons of coal on Board for us and they say she is an 18 knoter.

May 4. I guess the war is on for keeps now. We have com back to Rio or near it to wate for a Spanish Torpedo Boat that has bin laying around hear for the last 3 days and at the same time to take the Nichteroy.

May 5. lost some time waiting for the Nictheroy But she came along at dark. the Marietta will look out for her and we will pull out for Key West I think.

May 6. Every thing doing well and making 10 and 11 knots right off the reel now. at 8 P.M. the old man called all the Ward Room officers in the Cabin and read the tellegrams to them from Washington Which wer his sealed Orders and one of them reads like this: four armered Cruisers left Cape de Verde at some date and 2 Torpedo Boats, Destination unknown, and the old man is told to beware. The old man had a consul of War to night, so if we have to scrap, we will have to cut a lively gate for them. they say the Spanish is some Kind of a fighter him self. But we all think we can show him a trick with a hole in it. that was a great fight of the Manilla bay.

May 7. Every thing doing well, except this morning at 4.50 A.M. Gen Quarters sounded and there was a lively old time for a while. Every body thought we wer in for it then and there. I cannot describe the fealing of enthusiasm about the Decks. you see we had our orders to send in a Gen alarm when ever any thing looked like a Manowar got in sight. there was a little rain squall and some old sailing ship was in it, and just as she cleared away our lookout sighted the ship and sent in the alarm; it was the Capts orders to send in the alarm even if he was not there as he would get there all right. at 9 A.M. the old man called all hands to muster on the Quarter deck and told us the news he had received at Rio: there was 4 first class cruisers and three Torpedo Boats going to meet around hear some where and do us up. we all expect they will if they can, But the pruf of the Puding is the eating of it and we will have something to say about that. And after telling us about the fleet that was going to whip the socks off us he made a little speach to us; he said of corse it was his duty to the Goverment to get the ship around on the other side and stear clear of the fleet if posable. But in case he did meet the fleet he was sure Spain's fighting efficiency on the sea would be demineshed. So we all gave him three rousen Cheers and the old man Blushed, but he is a dandy Just the same.

May 8. got to Bahia, Bra. at 8.30 P.M. after making a good run and having Targate practis with full charges of Powder, don some fine shooting with the Big Guns. I dont think it will be a bit too healthy for the Spanish to bump up against us, for we have a good eye. We put in hear as an excuse to put on War paint saying our engines wer Brok down and at the same time to get more coal if we can.

May 9. Put on War paint to day and we are out for it now. we have the ship cleared for action now for keeps. got some coal and fresh water, filed up with every thing we wanted. at 8 P.M. the old man got a telegram and at 10 P.M. we wer on our corse for the West Indias.

May 10. going along smooth and nothing doing.

May 11. still expect to meet that fleet and if we do meet them there is going to be a "Hot time in the old town to night."

May 12. Every thing the same, some of us think we past through the fleet last night, there wer several lights all around and acted Mighty quer.

May 13. Nothing doing and will wate untill we get in Port.

May 18. got into Barbadoes at 4 A.M. this morning and found lots of war talk going on; we are puting on coal Just now, expect to go out of hear to morrow morning erly. 8 P.M. up anchor once more after geting 250 tons of coal on and ready for buisness. Guess the Spanish dont want any of this craft, it seems we will get there without firering a shot.

May 24. arived at Jupiter light house after making a flank movement to the northard and not a ship to be be seen.

May 25. up anchor once more for Key West, got there on the 26th; of corse the Capt dident know how things stud so he had to go slow, About 4.30 A.M. the man on the life Bouy gave the alarm, saying there was a small dark objict coming this way; the Officer of the Deck roused up the Capt and the next thing we knew Gen Quarters sounded. What should it be But the tug with our Pilot on board for us, the "Hudson" was the name of the tug.

May 27. still puting on coal, expect to go down to Cuba with the New York.

June 1. I herd the first shot in this war to day, Santiago de Cuba and with the flying squadron.

June 2. we had a wild goose chase.

June 3. nothing doing but laying off hear and watching what looks like to me a big hole in the grond. same thing the 4th and 5th.

June 6. Stand from under, we Bombard the forts and water Baterys to day for 4 hours but dont know how much damage we don.

June 7. staying out hear and doing nothing.

June 8. same thing.

June 9. "   "

June 10. we went down to Guantanamo Bay to put some coal on and landed 40 Marines in the Morning. we wer the first to put foot on Cuban soil in this war. The 9th the Marblehead and Dolphin Bombarded the place and made them look like Munkys; they ran away and left every thing behind them.

June 11. came back to Santiago on the 10th. and laying off hear as befor.

June 12. Same old thing. Expecting Troops every day.

June 13. Dito.

June 14. the New Orleans was ordered to run in close to the shore and do som Bombarding By her self Just to break the Monotony and to let us believe we wer at war. we don a good Job all right, she silenced the east Battry and the west one too, and made them show up a water Battry which we did not know any thing about. havent herd how many got kild or wounded on the other side. But I know they never hert any one on this side. Got some news from Guantanamo to day. Co. Huntington and his Marines of 800 Had a Brush with the Spanish, it is reported that 6 marines wer kild and Doctor Gibbs was shot through the head by accident. there is at Guantanamo Bay the Texas, Marblehead and Porter and 800 Marines; they expect to have the cable work soon and the Harbor well under Hand. I forgot to say the Vesuvius landed 3 shots of dinomite in the Harbor on the night of the 13th at Santiago and did great damage to the Shore Batterys; the latest report is that the Cubans are flocking in to Huntingtons camp.

June 15. coaling ship and still retain our position on the Blockade.

June 16. At 3:30 A. M. this morning all hands was called and the coffie was passed around with som hardtack and cand Beef at 4 A. M. Turn to, some 15 to 20 Minutes later Qen Quarters sounded. Then we went at it to try and see if we could not knock thoes Batterys off the earth. Bombarded until 7.15 A. M. Nobody knows how much damage was don, except we silinced all the Batterys they had and made them show up a nother one inside of the harbor of which there seems to be lots of them. I will say right hear that if we take this place its going to be a hot old Job, and som of us will think we run up against a Hornets nest when we get in side. they have been talking of forsing the Chanell and Capt Clark signaled over to the flag ship and asked permishion to take the leed, and I am sure we will stay with him as long as the ship floats for we love him. The Vesuvius fired three more shots last night at about 12. dont know what damage was don But I know we are all tired of this fooling. if they would only send some soldiers down here from the regular army, say 6 Regiments of Infantry and 3 of Cavalry, I think, with what we could put up, that forse would more than be a match for them and take the place with all ease. The latest Bulitin of the day is that the Forses at Guantanamo have bin Joined by some Cubans and had a Brush with the Spanish, and the report is that 40 wer kild on the Spanish side and 17 taken prisoners of war, one Spanish Lut. 2 Corp and 14 Privates. On our side 3 Cubans Kild and 2 wounded, 3 Marines wounded and 17 overcome by the heat. But all recovered. Routed the Spanish and distroyed the water suply and Block House. The Dolphin held there posision from the water frount and the Texas sunk 2 small Gun boats.

June 17. come down to Guantanamo Bay this morning, put some 300 tons of coal on and throde some shells over in an old Fort and then puled out right away for Santiago.

June 20. Bully for the Soldiers, they are hear at last, "I thought they would com tomorrow," some of the papers say there is 20.000 of them, that is enough to eat the plase up for lunch. Well I hope we will soon crack this nut that is so hard to crack. I hear there is 15000 Spanish soldiers over hear.

June 22. the soldiers are landing all O. K. and doing well, and only a few horses and 2 men lost so far, so the Flag Ship says.

June 26. Started in this morning to see if we coulden knock down that Spanish old Morro or else knock something cruckit around it. Well we pelted away for an hour or more and the flag ship signaled over to the Iowa to close in and pump at the Smith Key Battry. The Iowa signaled Back that her forward Turet was out of order, so it fel to us, we went in to 700 yards of the shore Battry and did knock down the Spanish flag with an 8 inch shell and knocked over one of there Big Guns. I believe if the flag ship had not called us off Capt Clark would have went in along side of old Morro and give him a tutching up.

June 28. I am geting tired of trying to keep cases on this thing. there is nothing doing but laying around hear like a lot of sharks watching for a fish.

July 4. The fish has come out to see us. On the 3rd the Spanish fleet came out of the Harbor to fight and get a way if posable. (I would have put this down on the 3rd But I dident have time and was too tired that night so put it off for today.) Well the Fleet came out and went to Davy Joneses locker. It was Just 9.25 A. M., first call had sounded on our ship for Quarters and we all have our best dudds on; we wer going to listen to the Articles of War this morning and to have chirch right affter, But we never did. all of a suden the Ordly on watch made a dive for the Cabin head first, and told the old man the Fleet was coming out of the Harbor. the old man jumpt up a standing. as soon as some of the men seen the ships there, they went to there Quarters with out any further dealy. I was standing on the Quarter Deck waiting for the last call to go. I heard the news and looking around the affter Terets seen the first one. I thought she looked Biger than a Mountain. But then I thought affterwards we could cut her down to her natchral size. of corse it takes longer to tell about it than it taken us to get ready, for we wer allways ready, and all we had to do was to sound the Bells and stand By our Guns, they wer allways loaded so all we had to do was to turn on the fors draught and pull the triger.

By 9.27 the Oregon fired the first shot of the Battle of July 3rd, 1898 at the first ship that came out of the Harbor. I dont remember the ships as they come out, But we went in to meet them and passed them som good shots as they cep coming. about 7 or 9 minuts after they got started good, one of our 6 inch guns blew up one of the Torpedo Boats, struck her squar amidships, she sunk like a rock with all on board. and right hear is where I had to stop for a moment to admire one of there Guners. I do think he was one of the bravest men I ever had the pleasure to look upon. That man must have known he was going to a shure Deth, he stud on Deck and cep firing at us all the time, and the last time I seen him he was Just going up in the air. As the ships came out of the harbor they sircled to the right, or Westward, and Capt Clark knew they were trying to escape. they did not think the old Oregon was such a runer as she was a fighter, so we Just tailed on with them and giving them shot for shot. In about 20 minuts the first ship went on the Beach, plumb knocked out, and 15 minutes later the secon one went on the Beach, a short ways from the first. Then came the tug of war for we had to run to catch the Vizcaya and the Colon, but we catched them both. The Vizcaya was about 4000 yards ahead and the Colon was about 3 miles ahead, and the poor men in the fireroom was working like horses, and to cheer them up we passed the word down the ventlators how things was going on, and they passed the word back if we would cut them down they would get us to where we could do it. So we got in rainge of the Vizcaya and we sent her ashore with the secondary Battry and 6 inch guns, and then we settled down for a good chase for the Colon. I thought she was going to run a way from us. But she had to make a curv and we headed for a point that she had to come out at. We all think there is no man in the Navy like Capt Clark, he is a Brave man, he stud on the Forward 13 inch turet though the thickest of this fight and directed his ship to the final results.

Coming back to Santiago we waited untill we got to where the first ship went on the Beach and there fired the national salut. We have 3 Spanish prisoners on board and they thought we wer at it a gain, and it was all the sick Bay man could do as to quiet them. I hear there is over 1800 Prisoners and 650 kild and 800 wounded on the third. the three men on board tells the sickbayman that we run through there fleet coming around hear, for the next day they found a Pork Barrel ful of holes and had marked on the head U. S. S. Oregon. We all seem to think we could take care of our selves Just the same. it is Just 6.50 P. M. now and the men all say there is no flag flying in the Morro. But I can see Just as good as any and I can not see any either, But then I think we are out too far.

July 5. At about 11.45 the danger Signal was flashed by the lookout from the Massachusetts, she being the one to show her serchlight at the entrance of the Harbor for the night, the Spanish was trying to sink one of there old ships in the Chanel so as not to let us in. But Just 3 or 4 shots from the Massachusetts Big 13 inch Guns help them to do the Job, for she sunk befor they got to the Chanal. there is Spanish menowar and Torpedo boats strung all along the Beach for 60 miles.

July 10. We are laying off now in Guantanamo Bay filing out to go to Porto Rico or on the Coast of Spain.

This is all in regards to the trip of the Oregon.

R. CROSS.

ADDENDA

"If there's a fight
By day or night
We're ready for it now."

From Nesbit's Oregon poem in the Baltimore "American."

THE speed so unexpectedly shown by the *Oregon* at the crisis of the battle, due primarily to the efforts of her officers and men, already referred to, was because she was never without full steam on all boilers while off Santiago. There was a statement, accepted for a time at the Navy Department, that she was about to shift from forward to after boilers and so only happened to have full steam when the Spanish fleet rushed out. But this was answered effectually at the Schley Court of Inquiry when the commander of the *Brooklyn* was recalled.

Knowing how deeply officers, seamen, firemen and marines on board the *Oregon* regretted that the Department failed to recommend that a medal be struck to commemorate the service of their ship, I addressed the Secretary of the Navy, March 29, 1900.

"Therefore in justice to officers and men who exerted themselves so much and endured such hardships during the long and arduous voyage from the Pacific, that their ship might be present and efficient in the hour of need, whose willingness to encounter single-handed the enemy's fleet if it should cross her track was so evident, and whose enthusiasm in battle was so inspiring, I feel that I should emphasize the following facts: That the *Oregon* speedily gained a position nearest the enemy, that she held that position during the crisis of the battle, that she attacked in succession all four of the enemy's ships, and that she passed none until

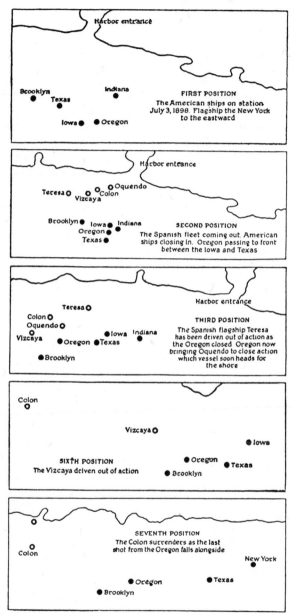

FIRST POSITION
The American ships on station
July 3, 1898. Flagship the New York
to the eastward

SECOND POSITION
The Spanish fleet coming out. American
ships closing in. Oregon passing to front
between the Iowa and Texas

THIRD POSITION
The Spanish flagship Teresa
has been driven out of action as
the Oregon closed. Oregon now
bringing Oquendo to close action
which vessel soon heads for
the shore

SIXTH POSITION
The Vizcaya driven out of action

SEVENTH POSITION
The Colon surrenders as the last
shot from the Oregon falls alongside

Positions of American and Spanish ships at the Battle of Santiago, as shown by
the Board of Navigators, one officer from each ship engaged.

they turned for the beach, three on fire and the fourth with her colors coming down."

The following is from my letter to the Department after the battle.

"I cannot speak in too high terms of the bearing and conduct on board this ship. When they found the *Oregon* had pushed to the front and was hurrying to a succession of conflicts with the enemy's vessels if they could be overtaken and would engage, the enthusiasm was intense.

"As these vessels were so much more heavily armored than the *Brooklyn* they might have concentrated upon and overpowered her and consequently I am persuaded that but for the way the officers and men of the *Oregon* steamed and steered the ship and fought and supplied her batteries, the *Colon* and perhaps the *Vizcaya*, would have escaped. Therefore I feel that they rendered meritorious service to the country."

INDEX

Note: The rank of an individual is the one he held when first mentioned in the text and not necessarily the highest rank he achieved. Ranks are all U.S. Navy unless otherwise indicated.

ABOUT THE EDITOR

JACK SWEETMAN is a member of the History Department of the U.S. Naval Academy. Born in Orlando, Florida, he graduated from Stetson University in 1961 and later served as a company commander in the U.S. Army. He was a Ford Fellow at Emory University, where he received his Ph.D. in 1973. Formerly associate editor of the Naval Institute *Proceedings*, he is the author of *The Landing at Veracruz: 1914* and *The U.S. Naval Academy: An Illustrated History*, translator of *Battleship Bismarck: A Survivor's Story*, by Baron Burkard von Müllenheim-Rechberg, coeditor of *Changing Interpretations and New Sources in Naval History*, and series editor of the Classics of Naval Literature.